PROGRESS IN RELIGION
TO THE CHRISTIAN ERA

T. R. GLOVER

PROGRESS IN RELIGION
TO THE CHRISTIAN ERA

BY

T. R. GLOVER

FELLOW OF ST. JOHN'S COLLEGE, CAMBRIDGE,
AND PUBLIC ORATOR IN THE UNIVERSITY

*Author of "The Pilgrim," "The Nature and Purpose of a
Christian Society," "Jesus in the Experience of
Men," "The Jesus of History," etc.*

NEW YORK

GEORGE H. DORAN COMPANY

PROGRESS IN RELIGION TO THE CHRISTIAN ERA. II

PRINTED IN THE UNITED STATES OF AMERICA

CONTENTS

PROGRESS IN RELIGION
TO THE CHRISTIAN ERA

PROGRESS IN RELIGION
TO THE CHRISTIAN ERA

I

INTRODUCTION

FASCINATING as the course of research has been among
the religious ideas of primitive peoples—and those who
caught the gleam of the *Golden Bough* a quarter of a
century since will not readily forget its appeal—the history of Religion includes many races who are not at all
primitive. The time comes now and then when it is less
urgent to ask *how* religion began than *why* it continues
and what changes it has undergone. In some quarters,
one guesses, the view has prevailed that, if the origins
are lowly, the developed product is discredited—that if
religion began in the grossest superstition or in close connection with it, and was for long almost indistinguishable
from magic, so much the worse for religion. There has
been an air of polemic about the work of certain re-
searchers, which at least suggests this line of reflection.
But another line seems equally possible. If, in spite of
these unhappy early associations, religion has maintained
itself in the respect of the peoples of the highest cultures
—if with every advance in thought, in powers of seeing
and feeling, in social culture and in morals, religion has
kept pace—then it may at least be argued that religion
is not a regrettable survival from a bad past, a weakness
of the feebler spirits of the race—an accident at best—
but something inseparable from the rational life of man,

something as inherent in human nature and as essential to it as art or morality or any other expression and means of human life. This is arguable, at least. In any case, if the study of origins is a legitimate subject for the human mind, surely the study of what is developed from those origins needs no defence. All our educationists emphasise the value of child-study: can we suggest that grown people are *not* a proper study of mankind?

In any case, there are religions of the higher culture —and, without beating about the bush, I am more interested in them myself; I have studied them, and I propose to continue to study them. So, with no more apology, I turn to my subject—Progress in Religion.

In Cambridge—it is our reproach—we are perhaps a little more matter-of-fact than Oxford people, a little more content to confine ourselves to verifying our references and to recording what we find. I will not defend our habit of mind; it is so obviously useful and so essentially scientific. But in this book my object is something different. I am not aiming at making a complete epitome of the history of religion from Moses to Mrs. Eddy. I am rather pursuing what one of the keenest guides of my undergraduate youth somewhat truculently called "the spirit of History emancipated from the bonds of fact." I hope not to part company with fact, but I do not want to be in bondage to it; it is the wood and its habits that I wish to understand, not to count the trees. This will involve a tentative use of theory as well as of fact. My endeavour is to get hold of the factors that make for progress in men's religious ideas—to understand why mankind as a whole is always apt to be revising its religion and cannot let it alone. I also want to master the factors that make for retardation in this progress. I turn naturally to the peoples of the ancient Mediterranean world—the peoples who, since I first learnt to read, have been my chief study, to whom I am not at all ashamed to have given my life so far—and I propose to draw from them the main part of what I have to say on progress in religion.

The comparative study of religion began a long time ago. Xenophanes, as we shall see, noted the divergencies of men's conceptions of the gods. Herodotus marked coincidences and shrewdly suspected certain religious teachers, whose names he would not mention, of plagiarising their inspiration from Egypt. Justin and Tertullian in the second century of our era remarked similarities between the rites of the Christian Church and the heathens. "This, too," says Justin, "in the rites of Mithras, the evil demons have delivered to be done—in imitation. That bread and a cup of water are set forth in the initiation ceremonies with certain formulæ—you know or may learn." [1] "The devil," says Tertullian, "baptises. He promises remission of sins from his font. If I yet remember, Mithras seals his soldiers on the brow"; [2] and so forth. The current explanation has generally been borrowing. The devil and his dæmons got early word of what Christian rites would be—and borrowed. Or else, say some modern scholars, the Christians, remembering their old ways in religion, borrowed on their side. The explanation of Justin and Tertullian seems a little old and odd; the fashion to-day is to find analogies between Christian practice and the mystery religions, and a little to discredit the Christian in consequence.

The weakness of this line of comparative study seems to me to be that it does not reckon with development. Likeness in rite and ceremony, in phrase and even in ideas, there may be; and it may be of singularly little consequence. The questions to be asked are of the move-

[1] Justin, *Apoc.* i. 98C.   [2] Tertullian, *De præser. hæret.* 40.

ment, the direction, the guiding spirit, the purpose, the aspiration. Two sacraments may be closely alike—to the distant student—at a particular point of time; and their influence on human history unspeakably different. We have always to bear in mind that there is a stage beyond, and that what matters in the study of a religion is what bears most upon the stage not yet reached. The key is in the last stage, the highest development, as Aristotle said. Our task is not to predict the last stage, but to examine certain stages, and to discover, if we can, the disturbing forces, the factors that have from time to time made the future, that have driven men forward in spite of themselves.

Let us begin by a broad contrast of what have been and what are the commonly accepted conceptions of religion. At the dawn of History, and for very long after, men conceived of religion as a matter of practices—certain things were done, and done in certain ways; the way mattered, and the action mattered, not the spirit, nor the belief that went with it. To-day, on the contrary, we conceive of religion as being above all things belief— as faith; and ritual and ceremony, however desirable, however necessary some hold them, are admittedly only of value as expressions of real belief, of faith. Religion has changed, then, from being predominantly an external thing to being the most intensely inward and intimate of all things, a law, an intuition within. It *was* a traditional thing—inherited, unexamined, independent of reason, unconnected with moral judgment or moral conduct; but it *is* individual conviction, and even where tradition is given the utmost value, it is as a result of criticism and thought, and these are individual; religion without reason is inconceivable to us, and we hold its relation to morality to be vital. It *was* racial or local; it *is,* and long has been, even in pre-Christian times and non-Jewish circles, universal, independent of race or place. It *was* a system of polytheism with all the inherent disorder that polytheism involves; its gods were at best doubtfully personal, or if personal, arbitrary, non-moral, and irrational. To-day, Religion is primarily monotheistic, or, at the worst, monistic; and where it really lives, its God is personal, and justice and goodness are the first of His characteristics.

These contrasts are patent, and certain consequences follow. We obviously give a higher value to-day to personality; to the individual; and religion gains or suffers correspondingly. The strength of the old religions lay in the fact that they were national, and that is the weakness of Hinduism to-day. One might, on the other hand, say that the strength of the modern type of religion is that it is *not* national, it is at once more and less than national. It is above nationality; and in every case of a really living nation and a really vital religion, masses of the nation reject, or misunderstand, or neglect religion; those who are convinced are religious with an intensity unknown in the old days, while the rest make less and less pretence of religion. We cannot have it both ways. The savage emphasised the tribe and had a social religion; the Greek discovered the individual, and we have to put up with the consequences.

Certain things, however, stand out from the contrasts which we have drawn. The emphasis on personality affects all our thought of God and man; while a progressive attention to morality goes with the discovery of the individual, and involves changes as fundamental in religion. To these two points we shall have to return again and again.

At this stage certain observations have to be made on the general subject of the study of religious movements, historical, primitive, and pre-historical.

First of all, as Andrew Lang emphasised, man is not to be caught in a primitive state; his intellectual beginnings lie very far behind the stage of culture in which we find the lowest known races.[3] We are in a worse plight by far than the geologists in their worst difficulties. The ichthyosaurus had his day, and lay down and died; and nobody took the slightest interest in him till Miss Anning dug up the first discovered of his tribe at Lyme Regis a hundred years ago. Nobody was concerned through the centuries to explain that he was still an ichthyosaurus, *semper eadem* as it were, or that he never had been an ichthyosaurus at all. If another beast or bird died on top of him, or under him, and their bones got mixed, they were not so very hard to sort out; and I suppose that what applies to the beasts is true broadly of the rocks, in spite of faults and the sea and the volcanoes. It is very different with the anthropologist's evidence. His fossils are graves and offering-pits and sculptures—for inscriptions are as bad as books; and he has to explain his fossils by their living representatives, which are worse again than books or inscriptions. Religion, in particular, in its earlier history and for long after, is to be studied in survivals—in myths and usages and beliefs. But words change their meaning without giving those who use them any notice—change them to fit new outlooks on the world, and in turn affect the beliefs expressed in the words. Rites and usages are corrected to fit a theory of a day—that is to say, they are restored, and we know well how often restoration means complete change. Silent adjustments, small misconceptions, shame, apology—all confuse the evidence. As Professor Lewis Campbell wittily asked, how far do the practices of Scots on Hallowe'en or Hogmanay illustrate or explain Scottish religion? They obviously had some

3 A. Lang, *Making of Religion*, p. 39.

origin; but it is History that will give the clue to it, and
History, as we shall soon find, is a much more intelligent
witness than Archæology—arrives later on the scene and
thinks; and that always confuses the evidence.

Words do not very greatly help us; and of words the
most treacherous are definitions, and the abstract nouns
associated with them. I am constantly impressed with
the havoc that our facile definitions, our preconceptions,
and our abstract nouns make of our thinking; and one
large part of every student's work is to achieve independence of the definitions and technical terms of his teacher.
A classification does not necessarily advance knowledge;
I find in King George's reign that what I *knew* in Queen
Victoria's reign I *know* no longer—that I have no glim-
mering of things I once knew to satisfaction. In every
field of study it is the same—we do not add to our facts
by framing theories, even when our theories are definitions. I shall have to speak a little later on of Magic,
and I have already burnt my fingers over it and fallen
out with my friends. And the definition of Religion is
hardly easier. I am not at all convinced that primitive
man was stricter about his definitions than his descendants are. I am quite sure that he did not draw all the
inferences he might have, and should have, from what he
knew. At the same time, it is not safe to assume that
primitive man was as simple and unreflective a creature
as is sometimes half-suggested. In Pre-History—before
what we can call History began—how soon did man begin to think, to imagine, to be an individual? From
that date confusion began. His words meant one thing
to himself, another to his stupider son, and something
quite different again to his bright son. His spiritual experience, the emotions he felt, the laws he observed, may
well have been simpler than the inner history of his descendants, just as the colour vision of the savage fails to

distinguish shades and even colours in vivid contrast for civilised man. But he was no fool; and his drawings and his skill in hunting, with all the observation and the reflection which these imply, suggest that we should rate him rather by his progressive descendants than by the retarded or the reactionary. It is extremely hard to be sure what primitive man meant and how much he expressed of what he meant, what were the extra-values of his thoughts, and so forth. In such inquiries neither our evidence nor our definitions take us very far.

What has been suggested as to Pre-History extends to History. It is extremely difficult, even where we are dealing with a race that keeps records and statistics, to get at the history of a religious movement in its early stages and in its formative period; still harder to recapture the impulses, the instincts and intuitions that lie behind it. When we deal with the causes, it is generally the conditions that we mean; and the same conditions produce no effect whatever on minds which seem to us quite as good as those in which the movement began.

Contemporaries constantly miss what matters most, and their words reflect their failure. When they do notice movement, they are surprisingly apt to misunderstand it—to put down as irreligion what is in truth the awakening of reason, the stirring of moral feeling.

Two instances, both illustrative of our general subject, may be taken. If we compare England in 1520, 1620, and 1720, we find extraordinary changes. In 1720, Mr. Lecky estimates, the Catholics were one in fifty of the population. In 1620, whatever the figures, everything was ripe for civil war on a religious issue underlying a political issue. In 1520, to all appearances, England was solidly Catholic. The late Dr. James Gairdner's book on *Lollardy and the Reformation* is a monument of the perplexity that the study of mere records may produce. To his reader it seems that there was nothing to effect the vast change which we observe; or else that Dr. Gairdner missed exactly what was most important to discover. For the change was swift, drastic, dramatic; and an explosion rarely occurs where there are no explosives. England must have been charged with forces which escaped the record-keepers and the record-searchers. Or, again, what were the antecedents of the monotheism of the Hebrew prophets? Here history, it would appear, has been re-written, more than once, by the ancients themselves, but when the best endeavour has been made to reach the real state of things in Israel before the rise of the great prophets, we find a people admittedly *not* monotheistic either by instinct or reflection. Yet the prophetic movement did capture Israel, and it had some antecedents—unless here, as in Dr. Gairdner's England, History makes the leap that Nature refuses. And that is hard to believe.

Or again, to take two outstanding theological terms, how difficult it would be to write the history of Sin and Redemption in human thought! How vital these conceptions are for the history of religion!—and how difficult to trace their development without big gaps and great guesses! Here, above all, the history of a single word would give us all the problems we could solve. The term "holy," if we could trace it through all its successive suggestions, would be a tell-tale word, as it moved from the physical and all but irrational onward through the moral to the spiritual. Probably most of our tell-tale words would be ethical terms, for even "truth" is as essentially ethical as intellectual.

In the third place, we must observe that Progress in Religion is apt to coincide with progress in social life, in arts and crafts, in political life, and in philosophy. We talk of men "thinking in compartments," and there are those who so think; but mankind never really rests content with that habit. The mind once quickened ranges in a new way over every aspect of life. Religious awakening means political regeneration, as we see in seventeenth-century England. Political stimulus makes for individual self-consciousness, and that involves religion. Crafts develop into arts; and artists see things intensely, and rightly or wrongly think swiftly—seldom quite wrongly; and whatever meaning they give to the word "religion," their contribution to the range of the human spirit requires of religion that it too enlarge its borders. "Whatever widens the imagination," wrote Lecky, "enabling it to realise the actual experience of other men, is a powerful agent of ethical advance." [4]

Life is the great iconoclast, the great emancipator. Life has a tendency to outgrow Religion in complexity, and the question in every generation is whether Religion will wake up to the new problems and overtake life. Mankind, as it grows adult, will not have old religions; old forms it may keep but it re-interprets them. Where re-interpretation fails and the old forms are not shaken off, a race or people atrophies; for man is progressive or he is lost; and the question often arises, What will liberate a race from its religion? In Israel and in Greece that question rose, and answers drastic enough (as we shall see) were offered by Plato and Jeremiah. Contemporaries, no doubt, thought them the enemies of religion; and moderns, whose definitions require them to distinguish between religion and knowledge, may be driven to comments as superficial. Yet these two men had no idea but that they were working with religion, reaching the heart of it; and ever since their day those who have deeply cared for religion and felt its power have recognised the deep debt they owe to such men.

[4] *History of Morals*, vol. i.

We have not to forget, however, cases that look exceptional; and here Rome is the outstanding example. Roman religion, one is tempted to say, never kept pace with the Roman mind. This is partly true, and Rome paid terribly for it. But it is not all the truth, for the Roman looked elsewhere than to the dim gods of his ancestors for real religion—to Greece, to Phrygia, and to Egypt.

Plato and Jeremiah bring us to our fourth observation—the immense rôle of the individual in the Progress of Religion. One feature, as we saw, in this Progress is the heightened significance of the individual; and that discovery is made by the individual. All progress in craft and art is the individual's doing; the guild and the caste are against him at first, perhaps for ever. Justice is rarely done to the pioneer on any side of life, either while he lives or after. The significance of the Jews and of the Greeks in the history of Religion is after all due to the intensity of individuality in their prophets and thinkers. In India—and it is true in measure elsewhere—it is in the sects that the living forces of religion are felt, that the great movements begin; and the sects are produced by the individual minds, and are far more dependent on them than the main body is or need be. The real life of Islam is Sufi-ism. The real life of Hinduism is in the Bhakti sects; they revolt, they influence the great mass of opinion slowly, and the dead hand at last gets hold of them, and they too grow petrified, but a contribution has been made. It is much the same elsewhere. The rebel starts the new idea and forces it on the community. One could hardly expect a great organisation to leap with swift intuition at a new truth, any more than a committee to write English. The great Classics in every language are written by individuals; even the Authorised Version of the English Bible has Tyndale behind it.

The feeling that slowly or swiftly brings the new certainty is the individual's endowment. The great organisation stands for authority, for a decent consideration of what our fathers found of truth; if it demands more, there are rebels; and Progress in Religion again and again has depended on the rebels making good their point, and on the old organisation appropriating it when made. Great statesmen and great journalists think in millions, and their generalisations very often screen life from them. The prophet and the poet have fewer formulæ, fewer phrases, few dogmas; they are less in bondage to routine and conventions and interests; they come from the desert, the slum, the slave market, and the house of pain, where solitude and beauty, hunger, oppression and sheer misery, set them free from conventions and goad them into discovery of the real and the spiritual. If they are canonised afterwards, it is, as the brilliant French biographer of St. Francis says, "the bitterest irony in history."

Summing up what we have so far gathered, we shall agree to handle our evidence carefully, to expect gaps in our knowledge of origins, to look for progress in religion where the activities of man's mind crowd thickest and most distractingly, and to keep our eyes upon solitary figures, to watch for the "voice crying in the wilderness," the poet in exile, the unpopular teacher in agony and bloody sweat. And as we gather our evidence, and co-ordinate it, and begin to understand it, we shall ask questions about one religion and another, to learn their comparative value. Our standard will be the standard of Progress. What we learn will modify our conceptions of Progress, no doubt, and will give it more content. One question will suggest another, and they will all be related. All our questions will, in one form or another, bear on the fundamental issue of the relations of Religion and Truth. But for clearness we will put separate aspects of that issue separately, and here are some of the questions we shall ask.

We shall ask pre-eminently about any religion a number of questions as to its philosophy. That perhaps is not the prevalent fashion of to-day, but men have always intellectualised their religion—inevitably, for man is incurably intellectual. The progress in religion has been made at every stage by the thinkers more than by the mystics, and incomparably more by both than by the adherents of the cults. Man is always working at the unseen, to get it reduced to intelligible law and order, to make it more moral, more spiritual, more rational—to fit it more to his mind, to adjust his thought in turn to the unseen, to get a working unity in his experience and his conceptions. There never is such a thing as simple faith; it is always intellectual; and the simplest faith is that for which thought has cleared the issues and got them into order and perspective.

We shall ask, then, what a religion makes of man. Does it believe in him enough? This is the individual again. Is it abreast of the best instincts of man, his deepest intuitions? (Some religions, as we shall see, are conspicuously behind these.) Is it developing these instincts still further? Does it urge man to look beyond the grave, whither certain instincts point? Is man, "a dream of a shadow," as Pindar said, or a "heavenly plant," as Plato preferred? Man's instincts involve morality too. How wide, then, is the religion's range in morality? What does it make of sin, of evil generally? What does it say of pain and suffering? All these questions imply the individual from the start; we are taking our cue from the higher developments of Religion, and we can hardly help doing so. But sin and morality imply also the community, and one function of religion is to induce the individual to sacrifice his own interests, his fancies and feelings—yes! and his own rights, to his neighbours and to the community. Does the religion, then, whichever we are considering, comprise the community, and how wide is that community? Are women reckoned in, and slaves, and foreigners?

We shall ask, what a religion makes of God, whether it speaks of Him in the singular or the plural, the neuter or the abstract. And here we shall find that progress more and more depends on the personality of God—that this militates against polytheism and safeguards the personality of man and all the morality bound up with the society of men. Personality and morality will be somewhere involved in all the questions we ask. St. Paul, in a very remarkable passage, with great insight traces all the corruption and misery of the world to false views of God. God's personality and man's personality are going to stand or fall together. Does the religion claim enough of God for man; does it claim the utmost, including immortality?

We shall ask—for our conception of society and of religion is dynamic rather than static—how far each religion is adapted to meeting changes in society, knowledge and thought. Another philosophical question; for the answer depends on how far the tenets of the religion are avowedly related to experience, how close it is intended to keep to truth. Does it prefer Truth—or something else, authority or tradition, emotion, archaism, an easy mind, or ecstasy? And our question implies yet another on its attitude to freedom. Does it stand for "more beyond" or for a closed book—for a Holy Spirit, or for a Koran or Shastras? Is it, in fact, in day-by-day experience, moving forward to higher intuitions and their verification? Is it attentive or inattentive to art, to poetry, to science, to politics, to ideas generally and the ceaselessly moving life of man? Or is it afraid of them? Once again, we shall have to ask what it makes of God. Is God away behind somewhere, or in front? Is He in touch with what men are doing?

Following up this question, we shall ask at some point, is the religion universal? Does it carry any conception it has of the unity of nature and the unity of mankind to the corollary of propagandism? This is no mean test of a religion; it involves the sense of truth, the sense of the relevance of truth to mankind, and mankind's turn for truth—the unity of mankind, and monotheism itself and the Personality of God.

Some such series of questions seems inevitable, and when we have put them and have begun to get our answers into a sort of order, what follows? For my part I find a certain progress in the religions, certain stages, which, however uncertain their edges, are themselves distinct and clear. This is not out of the way. However many "missing links" we may eventually discover, upwards or downwards from the Piltdown and Neanderthal people, Homer and the Chimpanzee have nothing to do with each other. It is obvious at a glance that, a religion (in one sense) being a system of thought, it may very well be imperfectly thought-out; and in fact we may often find in the same mind religious ideas which do not cohere, which do not belong to one another and never will. Nor is it only on the lower spiritual level that we find this. St. Paul was able to hold incomparable ideas; at least he held, or thought he held, ideas which we realise to have been incomparable; but perhaps the explanation may lie in a distinction between ideas he held and ideas of which, as he says, he was apprehended. I find, then, three great stages in religious thought, and I find further that, distinct as they are, certain historical religious systems have shown and do show traces of more than one, sometimes of all three. I distinguish three great types of Magic, Morality and Personal Relation.

In Magic we touch a term very difficult to define. M. Reinach says simply that "every primitive ritual is in its origin magical"; [5] but then his definition of religion is perhaps even simpler—religion is "a collection of scruples which impede the free exercise of our faculties." [6] I do not think things are quite so simple. Scholars differ a good deal as their definition of Magic. It has been called a "disease of religion," but this is not clear; it seems to imply that religion precedes magic, and that magic is a depravation of it. Sometimes religion does seem to lapse into magic—and there magic will indeed be a depravation of religion. Historically, in a broader sense of the word, there is ground for finding in magic an ancestor of science, of political and social morality, and certainly of medicine. All these, and religion too, are again and again found in association with what we must call magic—cannot call anything else. But there is a difference, and some thinkers find it in the attitude of the man who uses the means. If his main idea is to impose his will on god or spirit or demon, then his action is considered to lean to magic. If his idea is to influence god or spirit or demon, and, failing this endeavour, then to submit—that is held to lean to religion.

I am not going to risk a definition of magic myself, but I am bound to try to indicate what I mean by a magical type of religion. The dominant mark of magic I take to be outclassed thinking, arrested intuition, unexamined and unexaminable. Here I am glad to have the support of Sir J. G. Frazer, who regards magic as simply due to a misapplication of the laws of the association of ideas. Mr. Marrett says this is too intellectualistic, and that magic must be studied on its emotional side. [7] No

5 *Revue des Études Grec.*, 1906, p. 344.
6 *Orpheus*, p. 4.
7 R. R. Marrett, *Threshold*, p. 29.

doubt unchecked, unexamined, emotion has a great deal to do with magic as with all sorts of arrested developments. Arrest seems to me the mark of magic; it is commonly sterile, it means no progress; it is an antithesis to progress. On the other hand self-criticism is a mark of religion and one of the fruitfullest of its characteristics. Magic rests at last on fancy and is inspired by fear —by fear that paralyses thought and is never transcended. Magic leaves men pre-eminently *afraid* of the gods—too afraid of them to try to understand them. As Professor Gwatkin wrote: "As long as magic is stronger than science, the gods must be supposed variable and weak of will." [8] Magic, again, does not allow enough dignity and value to the human mind, does not credit it with reason, unless on reason's very lowest plane; it condemns man to the performance of dodges; and it bans the exercise of thought. It is non-moral and non-intellectual—an impossible combination for the religion of any people progressive in ethics or thought.

I am perhaps using—like others—the word magic in a sense of my own; but my purpose is not to define magic but to explain what I mean when I say that Religion has had a magical stage, that there have been and are religions of a magical type. Whether modern anthropologists approve or not, I am at least erring with Plato, who, in the second book of the *Republic,* draws the distinction which I am trying to make. Indeed, I believe I got it from Plato, and his strong words in that book bring me naturally to the second type of religion which I have named.

Plato insists that religion is not the indulgence in rites and sacrifices, with an element of jollification in them, but no discernible moral purpose or moral effect, no relation to conduct or to principle. "Adorn the soul," he says,

8 *Gifford Lectures,* vol. i. p. 260.

"in her proper jewels—temperance, justice, courage and nobility and truth.   In these arrayed, the soul is ready to go on her journey to the world below, when her time comes."   It will be seen in an instant that this is a religion of another type altogether; it has no relation to feast or hecatomb, to libation or sacrament.   The adornment of the *soul* is the thing, not the performance of any rite or the securing of any charm; there is nothing physical or external about this type of religion.   The ethical virtues get all the emphasis—and they all have a strong intellectual element; especially, we may say, Truth, the very last thing that has even the slightest relation with magic, however we define it.   Much the same attitude was maintained by the greater prophets of Israel toward the religion of sacrifice—it had no relation to righteousness and therefore could be of no interest to Jehovah. In emphasising the reference to a personal god, they struck a very different note from Plato's: but with him they represent that type of religion of which the essence is morality.   The stories will, in the pages that follow, afford the most striking example of this type—a fact that reminds us of its chief weakness.   To religions of this group a personal god is not necessary, or may be irrelevant; but they find it hard to carry mankind with them to this point.

The religions of the third type are the most interesting, and for Western thinkers St. Paul is the outstanding example.   He devoted himself to religion of the second type and gave himself in earnest to the achievement of morality; but as his insight deepened, he realised that he was engaged upon an impossible task; he made a great change and became content "not to have his own righteousness," to accept rather than earn, and to live a life dependent upon Grace.   Though he is the outstanding instance of this type, and became normative for Chris-

tianity, the type is not only found in Christian thought.
As I understand it, all the schools of thought in India
which emphasise *Bhakti* belong in degree to this class.
The *anhangs* of Tuka Ram, the Maratha poet of the
seventeenth century—I only know them in English but
the verse renderings of some of them, if surreptitiously
printed with Cowper's versions of Mme. Guyon, might
pass without remark. The "Cat-Theology" of the Ten-
galai followers of Rāmānuja in contrast with the "Mon-
key-Theology" of their rivals seems to be of the same
type.[9] The cat herself carries her kitten; the baby mon-
key has to hold on underneath its mother as she leaps
about; which is the picture of the soul's relation with
God? Those who decide for the cat stand for something
very like divine grace. Distinctions spring up when we
ask what it is hoped that divine grace will effect; and
we realise that Tuka Ram and Mme. Guyon have very
different hopes. Mme. Guyon looks for salvation from
sin, Tuka from re-birth. I surmise that the Shinshu sect
in Japanese Buddhism shows some affinity with this type
of religion. One part of our task will be to observe how,
both in the Hebrew and the Greek world, men kept moving to the conception of real relations between God and
man, even at the cost of losing something in morality and
of dropping back into magic.

But to sum up, and to reach a conclusion. My thesis
is that a progress is to be observed in men's conceptions
of Religion. We shall look to find it in the development
of their sense of the value of the individual man, both
as an agent and as a passive member of society, in virtue
of his personality; and in connection with this, we shall
find a progress in men's ideas of conduct both as regards
the individual and society; their conduct will depend on
their estimate of personality, and that, as already sug-

9 Cf. Nicol Macnicol, *Indian Theism.*

gested, on their sense of personality in their God. All his relations with men will be interpreted in the light of his personality and its bearing upon the personalities of men. The impulse to conceive in this way of the relations of God and man, we shall find, came partly along the lines of men's experience of common life and their slow discovery of the value and beauty of moral law, partly along the lines of reflection upon God. We shall find a steady drive to a morality that is ever higher, and a drive, as steady, toward monotheism, while religion ever claims more and more of life. We shall find that the soul refuses to be satisfied on any level but the very highest, and that, as a German thinker has said, "man is for nothing so grateful as for the advancement of his spiritual life." We shall find that man has a firm belief that nothing but the truth will help him, and an undying faith that he will find truth or that it will be revealed to him; and, in the end, that he and God stand face to face for eternity and can adjust their relations on no basis less than ultimate and perfect righteousness.

II

EARLY MAN AND HIS ENVIRONMENT

To understand a man, an epoch, or a period, some familiarity with antecedents is always inevitable. Our present task will be impossible without some general view of man's progress in religious thought in the long period of his history, which in the West ends with the poems of Homer and the beginning of what we can definitely call Greek literature. A general view of man's progress—not a history of human thought—in a score of pages is an undertaking formidable enough. It will be something like a résumé of a fifteen-hour journey in a half column of Bradshaw, with this drawback that, while Kettering, Leeds and Carlisle do convey very definite ideas to the mind, our stages will be more like the stations in the Delta of the Ganges, halting-places in the open with only this to recommend them, that for the moment they are out of the water. A progress is discernible; its history, especially its earliest history, is too often conjectural. The main thing is plain enough—it is the story of long and steady application of intelligence, observation and reason to Religion, and its slow but remarkable transformation in the process.

Here and there there must be allusions to "primitive man," of whom I have this to say at once. The fact that some descendants of primitive men have achieved civilisation and clear thinking while others have remained savage or become savage, and are content with the minimum of thought, suggests that primitive man was not a fixed type, and that the name should perhaps not be used,

without caution, as a constant term. We cannot put all
the differences down to Geography; the Turk has lived
for centuries among the same scenes that Homer and
his heroes knew, and among civilised neighbours, and is
still a barbarian; and it is not all due to his religion, for
the Persian also is Moslem. Why race differs from race
is a secret not yet wrung from Nature. Primitive races
do some things very much in the same way; and the evolution of tools and weapons can, down to a certain point,
be made out by laying together the remains of different
peoples who may be very widely removed from each
other; they fill one another's gaps, till at last a common
progression in parallel can be made out.[1] Parallels, in
like manner, with limitations already considered, are to
be traced in the religious ideas of men; and perhaps their
development followed similar courses. Perhaps; but
some things are done in very different ways by different
races; and in this sphere—perhaps even for ages before
the dawn of history—the individual counts more than we
are apt to allow. How early did man begin to notice his
environment and to explain it? How soon did he begin
to be subject to trance, to hysterics, to low spirits? "Blessings on the man who invented sleep!" says Sancho
Panza; and who invented the strange habits of the mind
that follow hunger and disease, or result from the use
of fruits and fluids that have fermented?

We shall have to look at some of those strange things
in Nature, in which man is apt to surmise that there are
feelings and a mind like his own—strange things which
surprise him with their ordered ways and their apparent
preference for law—strange things which appear to refuse the very notion of law. We shall then have to consider, in outline only, man's habit of explaining to himself what he has observed, of interpreting it, of getting

[1] Cf. Pitt Rivers, *Evolution of Culture*, pp. 102, 142, and plate xii.

it intelligible and orderly. We shall have to leave a number of ragged edges; "primitive man" had the same difficulty; but, as we study him and his ways, we find a confirmation of Carlyle's sayings: "Is not all work of man in this world a *making of Order*? . . . We are all born enemies of Disorder." An unwritten chapter of *Heroes and Hero Worship* would be about these primitive men who "got acquainted with realities" and were "sons of Order." We shall not be able to write it, but we shall come on the tracks of some very genuine heroes. In the third place, we shall have to glance at man's ways of arranging his relations with the strange things he finds alive about him and credits with powers beyond his own. This will bring us to the factors making for progress and to those which tell against it; and then we must try to sum up what results we have reached. If Aristotle pled guilty to treating Ethics "in outline and not with precise detail," another may ask forgiveness, if under greater limitations he leaves some things unwritten, and credits his fellow-students with memory and imagination.

No one can tell where man's first observation began of what we roughly call the superhuman. Nature is full of strange and terrible things; quite apart from tempests and earthquakes, her common ways are mysterious enough. The breeze, the cloud, the rain are unaccountably wayward. Summer and Winter are more orderly in their habits—not that mere orderliness makes a thing intelligible. Leaf and fruit come about their business but make little noise as to their methods and minds. The moon's four weeks come round, and round again, with some sameness; the sun's proceedings take longer to make out, but are not quite beyond understanding, though why these great lights behave as they do, and what their relations to each other, and what (if any) to the stars, who can guess? Who could guess the explanation of eclipses? Turning to earth again, there are rivers for a man to puzzle over, and the sea. There are the birds and the animals—very like people, with languages of their own and tribal habits and rules, clever, cunning creatures; and there was no one to say dogmatically that they had no connection with men, or were a different order. And here I may be told that I am going too fast; are not the very stones and rocks and trees living things, too, with feelings and fancies and perhaps uncanny ways of their own?

Man lived in an untracked jungle of life and mystery. And even where he was surest of himself, surprises were thickest. *Was* he sure of himself? What was he? Body, soul and spirit, we have been taught to say. But that is the teaching of civilisation. Which was *he*? "The wrath of Achilles," says Homer, "sent many goodly souls of heroes to Hades, and gave *themselves* as a prey to the dogs and to all the birds." And Homer comes very late in man's story—early enough in History, but far down the ages. Is a man's soul himself? Is it? Can he be quite certain of its doings? When he sleeps? or faints? or is wounded and the blood flows? Is the blood the life? The soul and the life, are they two, or one, or several things? There are many such questions. And when a child comes into the world, how has that come about? There are tribes who reckon the child's life to begin with the quickening and cast about for some spirit-cause, that fluttered into the mother when she felt the first stirring. The many rituals for "purification" of women after childbirth point back to notions more primitive than we sometimes guess. After all, we are not so far ahead; there are many things about life which we have not guessed; and with all our cleverness we have not quite succeeded in manufacturing it. We can destroy it and transmit it, but not make it or explain it.

But, waiving all these profounder questions, how was one to explain dreams? Are the things you see in dreams real? When you dream of a living friend, does he come to your side, in reality? He? Which *he* comes? one asks again; and I have perhaps modernised too much by dragging in our abstract phrase, "in reality." When you dream of the dead? "Ah me!" cries Achilles, waking from his dream of the dead Patroclus, "then there is, even in the halls of Hades, soul and form, yet not . . ." (*Iliad*, xxiii. 103). Here my knowledge of Greek breaks down, though I thought I knew the words.[2] How terribly modern our language is! how elusive in truth are Homer's terms, $\psi\upsilon\chi\dot{\eta}$, $\epsilon\overset{"}{\iota}\delta\omega\lambda o\nu$, $\varphi\rho\acute{\epsilon}\nu\epsilon\varsigma$! and how far he is from anything we could conceivably call "primitive man"!

Then there is loss of consciousness to explain. What has gone, to leave the body thus dead and not dead? Has the soul played a trick on *you* and slipped away? And trance is stranger still. Stranger those changes of personality—the modern phrase again, with its semi-scientific air, cloaking sheer ignorance still, and confusing the primitive record; let us be done with it and start again. What was a man to make of it when his wife or brother fell in trance and a strange voice spoke from the familiar lips—spoke, I almost said, with a strange spirit—was a spirit the explanation?—spoke (to be plain) with an unfamiliar tone of anger or lustfulness, with a hint of frenzy and madness—chanted rhythmically of things unseen by those who stood by, of presences and influences? Modern words again, these, undisguisedly abstract nouns; but what *were* the things, *those* things, which spoke through the lips of the unconscious figure, the changed nature? What did hysteria mean? or mad-

---

2 "Semblance and life though thought is theirs no more" (Conington); "A spirit and an image, without life" (Purves); "Second self, an image of the body, no intelligence, *nous* or emotions" (T. D. Seymour); "A spirit and phantom of the dead, albeit the life be not any wise therein" (Lang, Leaf and Myers).

ness? or any of the states we now call psychopathic?
And when the mood, the affection, or whatever we moderns call it, leapt from the one possessed to another and
another, and swept over a community, what did it mean?
The modern psychologist, when he sees such things, calls
them "primitive traits"; [3] he speaks in a jargon that we
call "scientific"—not altogether wrongly, for it at least
sets us on a new track and so far makes for knowledge.
He speaks of nervous instability as a fundamental trait
of the primitive man; of his remarkable imitativeness,
his lack of inhibition, and the extreme plasticity that results.   But the primitive man himself—certainly some
of his descendants, who are not yet scientific—had a
quicker way of explaining it.   A spirit, a god, a daemon,
something like that, did it all.   For primitive man, as
the same psychologist tells us, is strong in perception, but
weak in the logical interpretation of what he perceives.
He has no large amount of accurate tradition by which
to check his perceptions, and he fills in his gaps by imagination; and what he imagines, he sees, and he believes
what he sees—as any common-sense person does; and
the chain of evidence is complete—and wrong; but it
holds with terrible strength, holds for centuries.   Now
add mesmerism and all the varieties of suggestion that
work on the "suggestible," particularly when reason
checks things so slowly; and grasp, if you can, how much
in every initiation, in every mystery, in every sacrament,
is "suggested," and we shall realise that primitive man
had a good many things to explain; and here again the
quick way was to imagine the intervention of a spirit.
And then add prophecy and second-sight and mind-read-
ing and thought-transference, remembering the cases in
which prophecies do come true, and the cases in which the
very making of them gets them fulfilled; and again you

3 Davenport, *Primitive Traits in Religious Revivals,* p. 18.

touch a world of wonder and things promptly classed as superhuman.

In modern times we have a good deal of evidence of the association of these strange activities and passivities of the mind with religion, particularly with new movements—with revivals in the United States, with the development of pilgrimage centres in France. The Greek poets made much of the strange experiences of the Bacchanals,[4] which I used not to believe, but which I now see to be confirmed or confirmable by modern observation, to be not out of the way but normal for the region of experience concerned. The Hebrews recorded of their Nebiim acts and states, which the traveller to-day can see in the Dervishes of the modern Semites in a religion descended from that of the Hebrews.[5] It is not an extravagant use of hypothesis to suppose that primitive man saw and did the same sort of thing as his descendant, white, black and brown.

A great step forward was taken when man really began to systematise his ideas of his ultrahuman or spiritual environment. (Once again the adjectives are too modern or not modern enough.) It appears that to the earliest thinkers of our race all things were isolated particulars; they had so little notion of order or connection, of a regular course of nature, that miraculous and non-miraculous was not one of their distinctions.[6] Superhuman and supernatural are therefore not words that we can well apply when we are dealing with their thoughts. But however apt they were to entangle beast and human and what *we* are driven to call divine or spiritual, the mind of man makes for order and coherence; and we can trace stages in the progress of men's ideas.

---

4 More upon this in Chap. IV.
5 Cf. Chap. V. p. 125, and the reference there given to D. B. Macdonald, *Aspects of Islam.*
6 E. Caird, *Evolution of Religion,* i. 306, 307.

For fifty years the term Animism has been used to describe the earliest of these stages, but Mr. Marrett has
of late suggested that there was one still earlier, which
he calls (not very gracefully) Animatism—a stage when
a rock, a boulder, a meteorite, any oddly-shaped stone,
might be credited with vague but dreadful attributes of
power;[7] before the spiritual was, in homely phrase,
sorted out, and the rock or meteorite from being animate
became merely the home of something animate. Then
follows the animistic stage, when all things, or nearly
all, are credited with soul or something like it, something
vague but potent, and divisible; for the hair of the animal, the nail of the man, the rag a man has worn, the
water he has washed in, the remnant of his dinner,[8] even
his shadow,[9] carry something of his soul with them. In
many parts, even of Europe, there survive superstitions
which derive directly and not so distantly from such
beliefs. The whole world is infested with spirits, erratic,
incalculable and terrible; and among them are the souls
of the dead. A man's soul may, as we have seen, play
tricks upon him even while he lives; how much more
upon his kin when he is gone? And the mystery of death
takes away the familiarity and the friendship. *He* was a
friend; but what guarantee is there in that, that his *soul*
will be a friend?

Animism is by no means dead yet; there are tribes
and races the whole of whose outlook on the unseen—
soul, god, nature—is best classed under this convenient
name. But progress can be seen in the movement of
men's minds in several directions; though this is not to

[7] R. R. Marrett, *Threshold*, p. 18; cf. Sir Bampfylde Fuller, *Studies of Indian life and Sentiment*, p. 99, on the ammonite fossil as a god in India.
[8] Cf. F. E. Maning, *Old New Zealand*, p. 96.
[9] Cf. J. C. Lawson, *Ancient Greek Religion and Modern Greek Folklore*, p. 265. Mr. Lawson's life was saved by the rough benevolence of a stranger, who dragged him back and adjured him to go to the other side of a trench, that his shadow might not fall across the foundations and be built in among them.

deny that the paths of thought cross one another a good deal and sometimes run together for long distances.

We can recognise the development of great spirits or daemons, who acquire or have assigned to them control over great departments of life—itself a step towards order. Who or what these spirits are, and the degree to which they assume personality, are questions the answers to which depend on many different factors. There are daemons in charge of vegetation—or associated with it—many of them; and their stories vary. And now we have struck a great factor in our survey of Progress in Religion—the myth; but it must wait a little. For the moment, we must note that behind the great Demeter of Eleusis so human and so full of sorrow and graciousness—behind the less attractive Cybele in Phrygia—behind Isis—and all the differentiated gods and goddesses of fertility—lie daemons, mere spirits, of whom, to begin, little can be predicated. When my motor-bus crossed the frontier into Travancore, a little way beyond the custom-house, it pulled up at a temple of some sort, and a priest begged of us. "The temple," said an old Brahmin who had been befriending me, "is being restored by public subscription." "And what," said I, "is the name of the goddess?" "She has no name; she is known as the goddess at Mukandal." She belongs to a very large family, none of whom have names, but many of whom fill a large sphere without a name. Those scholars who hold by "collective emotion" are apt to find in it the origin of some of these vague powers and (one is tempted to say) to look on them as the real old aristocracy of all our pantheons. Palestine in early days knew many of them, and called them vaguely *Baals,* lords. They lack character and personality, and when they begin to acquire myths, it is a sign that they are passing out of this class.

They have not—it is hard to see how they could have—
any very clear relation to morality.

If the paths were not so interlaced, one might say that
from here the road divides.   In some lands these old
vague great powers remain predominant; in others they
are dimly felt to be in the background behind younger
and brighter figures.   But from here the paths seem to
divide.   Some of these powers are associated with animals—*are* animals, in some queer way, and never quite
lose traces of their origins.   Sometimes, as with the
Greeks, according to some scholars, the god emerges
splendid and human, and the beast or bird sinks into a
creature merely sacred to him, and remains so in popular
belief.   Sometimes it looks as if the god started to become
human, changed his mind, and halted halfway, and Anu-
bis keeps the jackal's head and Ganesh, or Ganpati, his
elephant head and trunk, while the rest of them is human—dreadfully human, as one sees in every picture of
Ganesh in his heaven.   The Greeks, as a rule, had a very
characteristic distaste for this sort of mixed god, though
traces of it are found in Arcadia.[10]   Where the type became established, the one escape, when the worshippers
reached a higher, a more moral and more reflective stage
of culture, lay in some form of mysticism.[11]   The mystic
theosophy that pervaded the later paganism of the Roman Empire is constantly looking to Egypt.   Only by
allegory, and that sometimes desperate, could this sort
of religion be brought into effective connection with morality.   Of totems, like Herodotus, "I do not speak,"
though not for his reason; for I do *not* know.

The other path was followed by those who, more or
less confidently and completely, humanised their gods—
or found them grow human as they thought about them.

10 Farnell, *Greece and Babylon*, 79.
11 Farnell, *Inaugural*, 16.

Whether the daemon definitely became anthropomorphic, or whether the god proper came some other way, I do not know. Professor Toy says categorically that "it cannot be said that a daemon has ever developed into a god.[12] Plutarch was quite as definite to the contrary; but it is possible that they are using words in different senses and not contradicting each other. Wundt explains the emergence of the anthropomorphic god as the result of the fusion of the "hero" and the daemon, the "hero" being a new creation of the mental life of a later age, when human personality enters into the very forefront of mythological thought and the value set on personal characteristics is enhanced.[13] The "hero" is associated, he says, with the ancestor, who now recedes. There is some suggestion of evidence for this in Mediterranean lands. Homer's brilliant Anthropomorphism belongs to the next chapter, but while we think of his great Zeus, cloud-compeller, lord of gods and men, we should not forget that there was another story. The Cretans were always liars, another poet tells us, and he finds their champion lie in their statement that Zeus was burned in their island. Tertullian, in his turn, made a great use of this in supporting the thesis he borrowed from Euhemeros, that all the pagan gods had been men once—and what a pity, he adds, they chose such bad men to deify![14] But we must not digress to Tertullian and his theories about the Olympian gods, which are not Miss Harrison's, though we may note that he stands in the great succession of revolt against them in honour of morality.

To return to the "hero" for a moment before we quite leave him. It is interesting to ask when the theory began to reign that he was of mixed origin, the son of a god by a mortal woman. We know it in Homer; but how

12 C. H. Toy, *Introduction to History of Religions*, § 694.
13 Wundt, *Folk Psychology*, p. 282.
14 Tertullian, *Apol.* 11: *Quot tamen potiores viros apud inferos reliquistis?*

much older is it? The early Semites believed there were marriages of human and daemon, and, Plutarch tells us, so did the Egyptians.[15] Indeed, the curiously common explanation of twins as one the child of a man and other of a spirit [16]—taken with all the legends of snakes, in dream and otherwise, in the pedigrees of special heroes, and with the peculiarly naïve notions of some surviving savages as to conception—points to the primitive idea of the daemonic origin of all life. But here perhaps we are digressing again, a little way. My defence must be that excessive relevance is no key to the primitive mind.

Gods, however, do not all arise in the same way. "The higher gods of the Rig Veda," says Professor Macdonnell,[17] are almost entirely personifications of natural phenomena, such as Sun, Dawn, Fire, Wind. Excepting a few deities surviving from an older period, the gods are, for the most part, more or less clearly connected with their physical foundations. The personifications, being there but slightly developed, lack definiteness of outline and individuality of character." These are gods, I understand, and not the daemons of Miss Harrison and Mukandal. We may note in passing that scholars who speak with authority are very unanimous in holding that no influence from the *Vedas* can be traced in the growth of the Greek pantheon.[18]

With the arrival of gods with names we reach the outskirts of the higher cultures. The forward steps are now clearer—they are not always easy; perhaps they never have been easy. Miss Harrison is against us here; she will not have us "assume offhand that the shift from nature-god to human-nature-god is necessarily an advance." Yet all the progressive peoples either make it,

[15] *Life of Numa*, 4.
[16] Cf. Rendel Harris, *The Cult of the Heavenly Twins*, chap. i.
[17] *Sanskrit Literature*, p. 69.
[18] Cf. C. H. Toy, *Intr. Hist. Relig.*, § 539; "When the true gods appear, the totemic and individual half-gods disappear."

or, if conditions are too hard for them, they try to make up for it, by borrowing, by allegory, by interpretation; and the old nature-gods have to change their character to keep pace with growing intelligence.   Unless we are prepared to say that thought is an evil, we shall not "assume offhand" that even so charming a writer is necessarily right on this point.

When men begin to deal with gods instead of vague, impersonal, intangible and really unthinkable daemons, thought has a chance to assert its right to control the whole of man's life.   Blind fear is, in the last resort, the attitude of man toward the daemons; the shift to gods means a shift to thought.   With all man's avowed and surmised ignorance about gods, there is the feeling that a god can be known.   Modern men feel that a law of nature can be known, but the old daemon was not a law of nature, and his control of nature was uncertain and incalculable.   But, with all the surprises of personality, personal gods had something in common with man, and they were intelligible so far.   And intelligible things all belong to the same order.   So the gods, with all their differences, can be grouped and co-ordinated and related in some rational way with the world; and this process gave rise to a good deal of Mythology.

Mythology in itself is a triumph of the human mind. Myths have been divided into three main classes—those which explain traditional practices and rituals and the holiness of certain places; and here we must remember that in every case the myth comes from the usage and not the usage from the myth; secondly, those which attempt to reduce the vast congeries of local and tribal cults, beliefs and myths, to order; thirdly, myths that embody the beginnings of larger religious speculation.[19] This grouping is frankly logical rather than historical.

19 Robertson Smith, *Early Religion of Semitics,* p. 18.

If it is our object to reach the earliest knowable stage of religion it will appear that the ritual or practice (if we can recover it) will be our best evidence; but for the study of Progress in Religion, mythology is incomparably more important—particularly if we can trace its growth. In ancient religions myth took something like the central place that dogma has in the religions we know. It was less thought out, less related to man's general experience, and less authoritative; sometimes alternative myths would be offered to explain the same ritual; and the worshipper might accept any of them, or none, or all, provided the ritual was duly performed. The primitive god required the rite; he was not interested in his worshipper's speculations. To the modern student the myth is of value, for it will generally be a sincere attempt to explain something, and it will contain implicitly a faithful picture of the god as man conceived him, and sometimes of the first-beginnings of scientific thought. For there were all kinds of myths in time—myths to explain the origin of the world, of sun and stars, of man, of differing races and their social customs and their genealogies. When once we reach civilised man, we find no new myths of cosmogony; the task of explanation passes over to the philosophers. Myth has the advantages of being more or less fixed [20] and yet subject to development—and the disadvantages.[21] With time the myths are told better and better; there is more literary skill and appeal about them; crudities and what offended the feelings and morals of a later day were toned down; and as men gained a clearer understanding of the laws of nature and higher and more intellectual conceptions of deity, these gains were reflected in the tone of the myths. None the less, for those who

---

[20] Cinderella sticks to glass slippers; Orestes goes barefoot and his footprint is recognised from its likeness to the family footprint; see Verrall, *Choephoroi*, p. lv. Similarly with stories of the gods.
[21] See C. H. Toy, *Intr. Hist. Relig.*, chap. viii. §§ 819 ff.

did not share these deeper views, who preferred a tale as it was told to them, the rude features of the old tale remain, and are inherited long after they have ceased to be anything but a drawback to thought and progress—an heirloom of reaction and even of pollution. One class of myth we must not forget—the myths of the world beyond; for, while perhaps not the oldest of myths, they were eventually associated in men's thoughts with speculations upon sin and righteousness and judgment, of the utmost consequence to human progress.

With order as an instinct, and myth as a convenient tool, man began to group and arrange his gods, a process a good deal easier than his next task—as we shall see when we reach Homer, perhaps sooner. For his methods were simple; story is added to story, for many stories may be told in many places of the same god; in them god is equated with god, and there emerges a god with a number of names, some to fall into the background and to be of only local interest, some to coalesce into a single expression. Phoebus Apollo is one person and one name—not two; but Smintheus is a little out of the way, though still Apollo.

It was when morals began to take more and more predominance in the thoughts of men that the trouble began to be serious about the gods and their characters. The accumulation of myths had gone on without much reference to their moral implication. Man was more concerned to unify Phoebus Apollo than to moralise him; but when this later and more serious task had to be undertaken, there were all the myths to be dealt with—some were toned down already, some half-moralised, and some remained utterly unmanageable. They lived on and on, and re-emerged again and again, and always for mischief. The most desperate attempts were made to allegorise them; but in the end there was no remedy for them, the

gods they dealt with had to be thrown over. Intellect
and moral sense made Anthropomorphism inevitable; it
was a next step forward, the more significant because the
next step had as inevitably to be taken. It made for
clearer thought and thus was an impossible resting-place.
It implied the application of moral standards as man
knows them to the gods; and the moralisation of the
pantheon was the great battleground of ancient thought.

There was only one end to the struggle. The old myths
and the old gods stood together, and both had to go.
There was nothing possible but monotheism of some kind
or other; men were forced into it, sometimes by the instinct for unification, sometimes by the passion for
morality. And monotheism is unlike other forms of belief; it is intolerant, earnest to fierceness.[22] Plato, the
Hebrew prophets, the Christian, the Moslem—they are
all fierce. They are fighting a battle for God and for
mankind, and they see that there is nothing so fatal, so
damning for men, as false thought about God. Love of
men, love of morality, love of truth, and eventually love
of God, give a force and a passion to all their work, an
edge to their thought and speech, and edge sometimes to
their temper. Why is man always re-modelling his conceptions of God? What drives him to it?

Before we embark on any answers to this great question, something must be attempted as to man's ways of
relating himself to the spirits or gods whom he conceives
to surround him. Our attempts will for the present
chiefly take the form of questions. First of all, how
many different ranges of ideas are covered in man's
various endeavours to make some accommodation, some
working arrangement, with the spirits, daemons or gods,
with which he has to do? Obviously every type of idea
that he has formed of these beings will be reflected in his

22 Cf. E. Caird, *Evolution of Religion*, ii. 17.

cult, and a good many that other people have formed will also be included, for the sake of safety. Even ideas which intellectually he despises will influence him when a sudden call means instant action. Some of his doings we shall only be able to class with Magic; some have their origin in moral ideas; and last of all (as Paul saw) comes the spiritual as a factor in worship. Minnehaha,[23] the wife of Hiawatha, in Longfellow's poem, goes through elaborate ceremonies in the planting of Mondamin to assure a good crop of maize. A similar motive and a similar ritual lie among the origins of the Mysteries of Eleusis. Magic or religion? We cannot go back to that question; even if it could ever be answered categorically one way or the other, it is not supremely relevant to our inquiry; origins are not of first importance for us. We shall see in the story of Israel how moral ideas became associated with ritual, till the idea of sacrifice dominated all others, with a constant succession of developed meanings.

A further series of questions, and these of importance, will turn upon who does the sacrifice and performs the ceremony and on behalf of whom? And here, wherever we can, we ought to date the conceptions which we find to prevail. Is the sacrifice a tribal act? Does the chief, king or priest (the titles and functions overlap) who performs it, do it on behalf of the tribe, the community or city, or on his own account? Robertson Smith in his great book, *The Early Religion of the Semites,* suggested that sacrifice antedates historically the rise of private property.[24] This means that certain values found later on in Jewish and other sacrifice do not concern us when we are dealing with origins. The sacrifice done on be-

---

23 Her name, a Dakotah has told me, does not mean "Laughing Water," but "Waterfall"; the difference is made by the first H, which is really a guttural.
24 *Early Religion of Semites,* p. 385.

half of a primitive tribe will probably not be the outcome
of moral, and still less of spiritual, motives. It will be
a practical transaction, an affair of Magic, or of that un-
differentiated Magic-*cum*-Religion, which we find before
they become distinct spheres. As long as the tribe or
community, collectively (whatever the agent, king or
priest) manages its relations with the spirits or gods, the
answer to our next question will be fairly easy. Of what
character will the ritual be? It will be what the Greeks
called *drômena,* doings, things done in a prescribed and
traditional way, where the detail of procedure is all-im-
portant and the spirit of the proceedings is negligible.
When the individual begins to sacrifice for himself or
for his family, changes follow. He comes in with his
individual ideas, fears and hopes; and even if he prays
for the community, he is acting on his own account, he
has his own motives, and he plays for his own hand.
Both types of religion, tribal and individual, exist together; there is no very obvious incompatibility; the individual's action can hardly hurt the community. Once
again we note, as so often, the appearance of the individual with his emphasis, conscious or unconscious, upon
himself, as one of the great factors in the transformation
of religion.

Two chief types of sacrifice are recognised by modern
investigators—not incompatible, but distinct and springing from different conceptions—the communion type and
the piacular type; and I think the former is the older.
Here, first the tribe—later, no doubt, as we shall see, the
individual—seeks some sort of union or communication
with the spirit or god; the tribe is perhaps, as Robertson
Smith suggested, seeking to humour its spiritual pro-
tector, or even to reconcile him; they give him the blood
of the victim if they are Semites, or burn certain parts
of the body if they are Greeks, and in either case they

eat the rest, and they share wine. "The fundamental idea," says Robertson Smith,[25] "of ancient sacrifice is sacramental communion, and all atoning rites are ultimately to be regarded as owing their efficacy to a communication of divine life to the worshippers and to the establishment or confirmation of a living bond between them and their god." It depends, as he shows, on a very ancient belief in "the full kinship of animals with men" (p. 365; cf. also p. 124). Bound up with it was the feeling that the life of the sacrificed animal reinforces both divine and human life.[26] God and man drew near together in a renewal of life and friendship. This merry sacrificial feast is the centre of ancient religion; and it rests on the belief that with the help of the gods life can easily be made all right, that the gods are easy to deal with, content with themselves and not exacting with their worshippers.[27] In the Roman Empire this type of religion rose to new life, and men made a practice of linking their lives and souls to gods, who generally had no connection whatever with their tribes or races, in ceremonies the meaning of which they could not explain and did not think worth while to try to explain; they rested on the tradition that this was the way, and on the assurance of their feelings that they had achieved what they sought—on nothing more objective.

The other type has a gloomier aspect. Here the worshipper offered a gift to induce the god to be friendly, to get him to do something, or to go away. The gift was a bribe, a form of wheedling, a bargain. The view of life implied was a severe one—life was not easy at all; the gods were awkward, even irritable, and needed to be placated; questions were asked. Had the tribe offended? had the man sinned? To the other type of sacrifice there

25 *Early Religion of Semites*, p. 439.
26 Jevons, *Hist. Religion*, p. 352.
27 Cf. Robertson Smith, *op. cit.* 257, 258.

properly was attached no sense of sin; to this type it emphatically belongs. Here, though the tribe may be concerned, we can see that the individual will be in the ascendent. On one side this type of religion can be associated with very crude magic; on the other it is bound up with elemental notions of morality. The Greeks leant to the communion view, the sacramental conception of sacrifice. The Hebrews gradually turned to think of sacrifice as sin-offering. The development of the priest seems to belong logically more closely to this type.

Both types are old, and both lived long; the same community could maintain both. If it were suggested that the older of the two types is constantly associated with reaction in religion, some religiously-minded people might resent it, but perhaps without being able to give any clear account yet of what happens between the soul and God. This at least can be said, that the piacular type emphasised an attention to morality which is not carried by the other, and doing so, it lent itself to the development of those conceptions of Sin and of Conscience which have above all things been powerful in the advancement and progress of religion. If the Stoics invented the word Conscience, they assuredly did not invent the thing, as Aeschylus and Plato bear witness. Darker things than conscience go with the piacular type—terror and the horrors it brings with it—human sacrifice, too, which the theories of the ancients led them to suppose older than animal sacrifice, and to which fear, prompted by those theories (now held by many to be false), drove them back in hours of national strain and darkness.

For our own purposes let us note, before we pass on, how, in this matter of sacrifice too, the discovery of the individual and the growing emphasis upon him, the attribution of very personal feelings to the god or gods, and the gradual shifting of interest to moral issues, all har-

monise with what we discover elsewhere in the field of
religion.

It remains to make a brief survey of the factors which
historically have advanced and retarded the progress of
religion. Some have been touched upon necessarily in
dealing with other matters. Here, for the sake of that
instinct for order which primitive man transmitted to us,
we must try to group what we are discovering; and I
think it can be done briefly.

One thing stands out for the student of religion—
that, in spite of our casual modern way of discriminating
between sacred and secular, the story of religion is bound
up with things that we might offhand say had nothing to
do with it. And there we may begin. Primitive man
was not always thinking about the gods, even if we do
concede that he was never irreligious, as many of his
modern descendants are. His chief battle, as Carlyle
said, was against hunger—a long-drawn war indeed of
many engagements and many mishaps; and in the prosecution of it he too sought a place in the sun, he fought
for fresh woods and fertile acres where he might expand.
Where we can recapture at all even the bare outlines of
his history, it is a long record of migrations and wars,
invasions, enslavements and destructions. Look at the
savage wars of the Iroquois and Hurons, which the
French chronicled in Canada, in which to their loss they
meddled on the wrong side. The Iroquois, from what
is now New York State, raided the Hurons in Quebec
Province, as we call it, and with English guns and powder
swept them out and exterminated them—drove the remnant of the tribe over to the Lake that bears their name
and pursued them there. But they did not kill them all;
they had a way of incorporating lads in their own five
tribes; and the captive Huron boy grew up to be an Iroquois warrior and to carry on the war against his own.

Much the same, though without guns and French historians, must have been the story of antiquity. One tribe drove another out of its forests and lands, captured its daughters, incorporated its sons as slaves or warriors—and suffered the same from a third. Clans perished, men relapsed into brute life, and sank into savages; or they fled for refuge to other lands—mere units with wife or child. In any case there was endless crossing of stocks and of ideas. All the syncretism of ancient religion is not the work of the Roman Empire. Hundreds of years before Homer, Smintheus-es and Phœbus-es began to be amalgamated with Apollos. The captive bride taught her children not quite what their grandmother had taught their father; and the children, born in exile, grew up with little interest in the shrines and holy places from which their fathers had been driven. But the holy places became a concern to the conquerors; lions perhaps grew bolder in the devastated lands, and the newcomers concluded that it was because they knew not the manner of the god of the land, and got priests of the old stock and served the old Lord of the land and with him the gods they had brought.[28] There were changes in men's ideas of the gods—old sanctions weakened, new fears prevalent, confusions of rites and ceremonies, old priesthoods fused with new, alien families kept as sacrificers and confusing familiar and unfamiliar teaching. Sometimes one set of conceptions will survive amalgamation with rites that belong to another; sometimes the rites prevail; and unconscious compromise must have been universal.

All this belongs to Pre-History; and when History (from which, not unnaturally, our definite illustrations are taken) begins to dawn, it shows us much the same processes at work in different ways. Tribes are growing into nations, cantons into little towns, and changing ideas

28 2 Kings, xvii, 24-41.

mark every stage of such growths. Wars are on a larger scale, but their effects are much the same—disintegration and recombination; and the institution of slavery perpetuates the mixture of races. Men begin to trade and to travel—to learn new crafts and arts. Metallurgy progresses by leaps and bounds, and makes new men of its craftsmen, new states, and new theories of government, as the chief sinks into the ranks of armed demesmen, no longer alone possessor of bronze shield and sword. And democracy knows other gods from the old clans; or, if they are the same gods, it knows them differently. Instead of the broken tribe flying to new lands, we have the ordered colony crossing the sea; but it too finds new gods and brings old ones; it too finds the old gods not quite the same in the new home and adds something to the new gods. The Assyrian comes down like a wolf on the fold; or the Lydian slowly conquers the Greek sea-coast and meddles with Delphi; or the Afghan sweeps all over India; and in every case religion shows the results. India knows "more than fifty accepted external forms of Hinduism." [29]

Out of all this storm and stress, confusion of war and tribe and tradition, one person emerges—more secure of existence as every organised form of thought and government collapses—the Individual. He has to fly for his life—*his* life, not the tribe's now; he marries a girl of another clan, with such rites as they can manage, and they breed their children inevitably to be little individuals; and then he shifts, with his foreign wife and his half-breed children, to a colony newly settling; he picks up a new trade, perforce, in the new place, and it suits him; he works in improvements, and his boys take ship and sell his wares all round the Mediterranean and bring back wealth and more foreign women and new ideas. Without

[29] Meredith Townsend, *Europe and Asia*, p. 254.

realising what they are doing, that family makes a revolution in thought. They were cosmopolitan before Socrates, and the world knew hundreds of them. Afterwards they drew a veil, in many communities, over the mixtures of their origin, but the mixtures told. There were larger ideas of human kinship; the Greek grew to be Panhellenic and then went to Egypt and Babylon and Spain, and reached some conception of a humanity larger than Hellendom. And it is all reflected in speculation— unity grows to be a larger and larger circle; gods are fused more than ever, interpreted in new tongues and domiciled in new pantheons. In the Greek world a greater unity than any pantheon begins to be conceived. Nor is this all. Law emerges more and more in the cities, and Justice takes a larger place in men's thoughts; then the gods must come under the reign of law, for the cosmos cannot have a ragged fringe; and if law is to rule the gods, we must show the heavens more just. All the while the alphabet is working its miracles; those handy letters, the traders' useful device, serve other ends; books spring up, and books mean modernity. Science and Philosophy seize their chance, and things are said in books that make Olympus look strange and old; it will need overhauling, and it gets it.

But all is not progress. The sick child sweeps the philosopher's family back into superstition; the foreign priest or prophet knows a new miracle to cure that sickness, or the home priest remembers something done amiss. So the old things must be kept. The marriage life of the community is pure, its ideals for husbands and wives are high; but the goddess belongs to an old order, she is conservative, and her temple is a focus for every evil instinct, where impurity is solemnly kept and maintained as religion with priests and priestesses saying, singing and doing things in honour of the gods from which the

children of a decent house will be screened by their
mother and father.[30]   Or a great disaster impends upon
the state; and we know the cry: "Hang morals! I want
to win the war"; and we have seen the moral deliquium
it brings.   In Carthage once it involved a human sacrifice
of 300 lads—*not* slain by the enemy, but by the priests
to induce the gods to save the state.   The moral sense
grows indeed, but still there is the haunting fear that your
fathers' old religion may be true—that the gods may be
unclean, bestial, filthy and cruel, and must be worshipped
in their own way.   You with your moral outlook may be
all wrong; who are you to claim that the gods are morally
ahead of men? they may be far behind—and then where
are we with our moral notions?   Best *not* be too good
to invoke the gods to help us on their own terms.   And
the priesthood say so; and if you hint that they are never
the intellectual pioneers of the community and that they
have reasons for crying: "Great is Diana of the Ephesians!" the child is sick, the enemy is at the gates; give
the gods what they like—blood, filth, folly—and be moral
after the war.[31]

Idolatries die everywhere, but they die hard; superstition lives long, and ceremony outlives even belief in
the gods to whom it is addressed.   But mankind is committed to morality and personality; and Truth prevails.

30 This is true of Corinth, Comana and Madura alike.
31 Strabo, *c.* 297, says everybody thinks women are leaders in superstition,
and quotes Menander's evidence on the point.

III

HOMER

Iт was the belief of the Greeks that their religion owed a great deal to Homer and Hesiod. "They lived, I think," says Herodotus, "four hundred years before me, not more. It was they who made a Theogony for the Greeks, and gave the gods their added names [1] (ἐπωνυμίας), divided among them their honours and тneir arts, and described their appearances" (ii. 53). Modern archæologists have warned us that this is rather the belief of an educated Greek of the fifth century B.C. than a certain and final verdict of History. The nineteenth century laid bare from the soil of Greece and Asia Minor, and the early years of this century in Crete, a mass of evidence which we are probably right in assuming to have been unknown to Herodotus and his contemporaries—evidence the value of which, as happens so often when we are dealing with matters of religion, we may not ourselves estimate aright without a great deal of care.

But our subject is not the archæology of pre-historic Greece, and we are not concerned to set out with any detail what the earliest Greeks—or their predecessors, their forerunners, or even their fathers—believed. Our question is one more interesting, and it concerns the Greeks themselves. How did they come to get away from that group of old beliefs, old rituals, superstitions and preconceptions, which seem to be indicated by the remains that the archæologists discover? Here, as whenever we touch the Greeks, it is with a certain sense of relief.

The readers of Herodotus had little doubt as to what

1 Patronymic and local names.

or who the Greeks were. We know who and what Eng-
lishmen are. "The Greek race," says Herodotus (viii.
144) "is of one blood and one speech; it has temples of
the gods in common, common sacrifices, and ways of like
kind." Blood, speech, religion and culture—these, shared,
make a people, or a race, or a nation, one; he says nothing about politics. The definition of a modern thinker
would be more difficult, for he knows a distinction between a race and a nation; he recalls very well nations
of very different racial origins, where religious differences are very great, or look very great; and yet he
knows, and we all know, more or less what we mean
by English. The ancients knew what they meant when
they said Greek; they had no doubt at all as to the difference between Greek and barbarian in spite of political
or other perplexity as to where the Macedonians were
to be ranked in the scale.

We do not know very well who or what sort of people
had the religious ideas indicated by the Archæological
data. They were not Greeks, and yet, in a sense, they
may have been; as Hengist and Horsa, who led our ancestors to Britain, were English, but not the eventual
English whom we know. The truth is, a race is not so
stable a thing as for ethnological convenience we sometimes could wish it to be; it is a thing constantly in flux,
for ever developing. We may set the Veddahs and the
Arunta aside; we know nothing of their history, nor do
they themselves. In the civilised world, in Burma to-day,
in India yesterday, in Asia Minor, Greece and England,
we know that race is always changing somehow. The
Greeks emerge; and it may be true—truer at least than
the critics of Herodotus sometimes allow—that Homer
and Hesiod shaped their religion. For Homer and Hesiod did a great deal more to make the Greek race than
Hengist and Horsa to make the English.

Homer, then, is exactly the sort of witness we want, if we may cross-examine him a little. He stands between something that was not quite Greece and something that pre-eminently was Greece. We can believe that he inherited his language, and found a diction and a metre something like what we read in his poems. He borrowed his legends, very probably, and used a theme or themes familiar to his hearers; perhaps he borrowed actual lays of a master or masters. He found a civilisation actually existing, or lingering in the memories of tribes. He was familiar with that *quidquid agunt homines* which is the neglected background of ordinary people and the raw material of great poets. All this he found. We are reminded of what Heine said of Shakespeare: "He borrowed all the plots of his plays; all he did was to give them the spirit (Geist) that made them live (beseelte)." Homer did something as miraculous, or even more so, with what he found. He took what he wanted, he used it, and Greek life and Greek thought began. That eternal flux of things which we call human history became rapid and momentous.

It is sometimes assumed that Homer gives us the current views of his day upon the gods. But it has to be realised that a man of genius, who gets his thoughts well before the world, neither represents things as they are nor leaves things as they are. The latter we shall all concede; the fallacy is in the former. Things never are as they are; as Heraclitus says, you never step into the same river twice—no, nor once. The human mind never took a photograph of a situation; it is not rapid enough, nor stupid enough. There never was in religion, there never is, a standard state of things. Homer does not give us, could not give us, a picture of religion as it was in his day, nor can any other great poet or thinker or even artist do it. It has to be remembered, too, that

Homer was not a lecturer on Natural Religion, not even a Manu or a Moses. His theme was not religion, either in the sense where cult predominates or where philosophy is the main thing. He was making songs, poems, to sing or to recite, and not quite like Demodocos in his *Odyssey*. He told of men and of human life—of their attitude to gods and to the unseen as it bore on life or made life, of gods as they came into the life of his heroes. Surely he could have given—so little was he concerned directly with gods or cults or beliefs—what we call an objective treatment to these things; but it could not be done.

A poet's art rests on selection, and many things go to make his habits of selection—the limitations of his subject and of his audience, their interests and beliefs and fears, but above all his own mind, his own outlook on life and humanity. Thus at the very dawn of Greek history, as we know it, we find the most characteristic Greek thing known to us—a great mind handling and developing human life. We have to ask, then, what Homer makes of religion; and this involves two types of question. What did he find? and what interested him?

What he found, we can more or less surmise from the poems themselves, taken in conjunction with the data of Archæology and the recorded practices of later Greeks. The Archæologists may be giving us wrong data, or wrong interpretations of them; and the later Greeks may have got their practices from neighbours and not from ancestors. I do not press these suggestions, though it is as well to remember them. Let us then assume that our teachers in Primitive Religion—ambiguous as the phrase is, let it go unchallenged for the moment—are right in all they tell us about those forerunners of the Greeks, about the fears, the fancies, and the instincts that make the religion of early man and backward man—especially the latter—about their cults, and observances, their taboos, totems, fetishes, their daemons and witches, their god-possession and devil-possession, their ecstasy and prophecy, their sacred stones and sacred trees, and all the survivals of savagery and magic. It would be bold to say that they are right in every particular, but let us assume it. What does Homer make of it all? I am reminded of what Renan wrote when he read Amiel's Journal:—"M. Amiel asks what does M. Renan make of sin—*eh! bien!* I think I leave it out!" (*Je crois que je le supprime*).[2]

We must recall again that Homer was not writing as an Archæologist—that he was not called by his subject to deal with the antiquarian aspects of Religion—that he was looking to a constituency of laymen. It is held by some critics, who have at least a right to speak, that superstition and magic must have been more rife than we should conclude from Homer's poems, but that the Greek (or whoever he was ethnically just then) was not apt to be daemon-ridden.[3] Conjectures are made as the cults and beliefs of the invaders who appear to have reached the Aegean world from the North, and of those whom they found and conquered on their arrival. Later Greeks certainly show a good many traits in their religion which it is agreed to call primitive. The great poet, however, chose a subject which did not involve him in these discussions, which took him out of the twilight into the open air, which meant for him not guesswork as to the unknown but interpretation of what he knew, what he had suffered, what he had been—in a word,

Et quorum pars magna fui.

His poem is autobiographical, as all great interpretation is.

---

2 Introduction to Amiel's Journal, Eng. trn., p. 11.
3 Cf. T. D. Seymour, *Life in the Homeric Age*, 392 ff. Farnell, *Greece and Babylon*, 158, 178.

Here I may seem to be digressing to Homeric criticism, but one is surely allowed to cross-examine a witness, to know whether one is questioning an individual or a chorus. It is hard to believe that in the Homeric poems we have not to do with a personality and a very great one. There are difficulties still, which suggest later hands. Others may have added their quota to the work, differing here and there it may be in their treatment of a character or an episode, but the great original dominated his school, he selected its interests, and he gave it its tone. The more one studies poetry, the more one feels the presence of a great nature behind great poetry,[4] and the great natures gravitate to the great factors in life—inevitably. Homer wrote—or sang—or whatever be the right word—of the gods; and it is irresistible that Homer thought about the gods. If my point, already attempted, is right, even if he meant to portray the gods exactly as ordinary people conceived of them,[5] he could not do it; he was not an ordinary person. Euripides is the only poet of genius, known at all to me, who can be credited with the plan of drawing the gods exactly as ordinary men imagined them, and he did it for a purpose; his pictures are individual and characteristic of himself to the last degree—the protest and the irony cannot be escaped. But with Homer we do not think of protest or irony; his purpose is other. We might even say he has no purpose but the artist's—to present men οἵους δεῖ ποιεῖν,[6] as they ought to be drawn, and gods no less.

He is not conscious of making a challenge, we gather, nor does he expect to be challenged. Here as elsewhere he keeps his own amazing serenity. So much the better

---

4 Cf. Longinus, 9, 2, ὕψος μεγαλοφροσύνης ἀπήχημα.
5 As commentators suggest; e.g., How and Wells on Herodotus ii. 53.
6 Sophocles on his own practice; so Aristotle, Poetics, 25, 11, 1460 b. Cf. J. W. Mackail, Lectures on Greek Poetry, p. 157, whose interpretation of the famous phrase, more interesting than that of the editors, serves my meaning best.

a witness he will be for us. But none the less he will be
re-creating what he interprets, adding something and developing it.

Homer shows so many of the great Greek characteristics that there is much to be said for the view that the
Hellen had come to his own already in that day. Homer
has already the strong preference for clearness that
marks the best minds of Greece—the instinct for the
fact and, above all, for the relevant fact; he has the
turn for order in his ideas that all thinkers cultivate, and
in a high degree the Greek loyalty to form and freedom
as equal and indivisible factors in all art and all sound
thinking. In a word, he has, without talking about it,
the gift of criticism—a natural turn for "examining
life" (in Plato's phrase [7]). All these faculties come instinctively and unconsciously into play, when he thinks
of the gods; and with them another gift of the artist
makes itself felt. He has that passion for personality,
that is the mark of great creative natures. Aristotle [8]
remarked upon his way of letting men and women and
others develop their own characters in his story. What
he loves in men, he cannot deny to gods; his gods are
inevitably personal and individual.

Miss Jane Harrison brings a fierce indictment against
the gods of Homer—"the Olympians," as she names
them with scorn. The Olympian god sheds his plant or
animal form, she tells us; he refuses to be an earth-
daemon, or an air-daemon, or even a year-daemon; his
"crowning disability and curse" is that he claims to be
immortal, which fixes a great gulf between him and mankind; he has personality, individuality; and he claims
reality, "the rock on which successive generations of gods
have shattered." [9] To all these charges—apart from the

---

7 *Apology*, 38 A.   There is a great deal more to be said for Matthew Arnold's
definition of literature as a criticism of life than some people allow.
8 *Poetics*, 24, 7, 146 a.   9 J. E. Harrison, *Themis*, pp. 447-477.

comments interspersed upon them—Homer must plead guilty. He has done all these things—he has re-created his gods, rid them of their older and odder forms, and given them the qualities denounced. His gods are no longer the cosy, "delightful," homely, Brer Rabbit affairs of the twilight, which primitive man imagined and Miss Harrison prefers.

Two comments may be made at this point, and then we may pass to a little more examination of what Homer has done. As Professor Webb has pointed out,[10] the tendency, which has led to the development of the "Olympian," is a necessary and abiding factor in religion.[11] And further, when such a transformation is originated, or at least used and developed,[12] by a mind and nature as rich as Homer's—when it is associated with so great a forward movement in national consciousness, in life and culture, as we find accompanying the spread and ascendency of Homeric ideas—it will require some proof that the transformation is not itself a necessary and helpful stage of progress.

The gods of Homer are a community of persons, of characters as markedly individual as the Greek heroes themselves.[13] Whatever their origins—and the descriptive epithets that pursue them through the poems, those epithets which Herodotus seems to credit Homer with inventing, are commonly taken, as we have seen, to be relics of older and less glorious days,[14] and indications

10 C. C. J. Webb, *Group Theories*, 172.
11 Cf. also J. Girard, *Le Sentiment Religieux en Grèce d'Homère à Eschyle*, p. 42.
12 Readers will recall the indignant attempts of some Shakespearean scholars to discredit Coleridge's criticism of Shakespeare's subtlety in giving Romeo a first love before Juliet, on the ground that the lady was in the original story. The real point is that Shakespeare kept her. Whatever may have been done in "Olympianising" before Homer, he used certain ideas and discarded others, and we must ask why.
13 Edward Caird, *Evolution of Religion*, i. 277, suggests that the marked outlines are due to the poet's effort to realise and to picture; popular religion could never have been so definite.
14 It is hinted, for instance, that *boôpis* Hera was not merely "ox-eyed" originally, but had a whole cow's head. *Glaukôpis* Athena was originally the goddess with the eyes, or face, or aspects of an owl; and she was represented

that the eventual god with his group of epithets, local
and other, is a conflation of a number of divinities—
whether the god was from the first a single god of a
tribe or a place, or whether he is amalgamated out of a
variety of predecessors, he is individual, a person perfectly self-conscious, and as thoroughly independent of
his "sources" as an American of his ancestors. The gods
are not in Homer, what the Stoics later on tried to make
them, personifications—one of grain, another of wine,
a third of some process or other,[15]—not at all, nor are
they even exactly gods of this and of that. Hades, it is
true, is god of the world below, Poseidon is god of the
sea,[16] but much as Joseph Bonaparte was King of Spain
and Jerome Bonaparte King of Westphalia—because in
the allotment of a conquered universe those kingdoms fell
to them by lot or were given to them by a supreme
brother. Still less are they gods of places, though they
have friendly feelings for certain places as they have for
certain people. It is suggested that they have gained
somewhat by being, like the heroes, themselves away from
home, dissevered for purposes of war from their ordinary business and, to a large extent, from their cults
and myths as well. Like the heroes in the Greek camp,
they are brought to a common level, a common denominator, to new relations. They may have their favourite
heroes, but they are all relevant to all the combatants,
Greek and Trojan.

Here we have touched one of the main contributions
of Homer to Greek religion. Whether he had predecessors who pointed the way we cannot guess. Possibly he
had; "all art," it has been said, "is collaboration." Observation of the modern world and the records of the

---

in art as an owl with human arms or human head, before she became the
anthropomorphic goddess with the bird for her attribute.
  15 *Conflict of Religions*, p. 95; Cicero, *de Nat. Deor.* ii. 60-70.
  16 *Iliad*, xv. 187 ff. He "knew less" than Zeus.

ancient tell us how polytheists instinctively accept the
gods of others and blend them—equate them with their
own. But here at this early stage of Greek history, before even the term Hellenes was widely accepted as the
name of all Greeks, Homer creates or develops—or so
emphasises and vivifies as to all purposes to create—a
Panhellenic religion. There was, and there remained,
a parochial element in Greek religion—queer old gods
and goddesses, and local heroes, survived in corners down
to the period of the Roman Empire; perhaps they were
there before Homer's day. But they did not contribute
to the growth of the Greek consciousness. Why should
an Argive regard the gods of Corinth,[17] or an Attic
peasant of one deme the family gods of the noble family
of another deme? Even the gods concerned would not
expect it. A city wanted city gods as against gods of the
clan or gods of the canton; and Greece gained something
from her Panhellenic gods. Common religion was, as
we saw, one of the strands of nationality according to
Herodotus; and this was, in large measure, the contribution of Homer. So much could a great poet achieve—
thinking his way instinctively into human life, into religion, and giving beauty to his interpretation of what
he found. His gods never made one nation of all the
Greeks, but every thinking Greek was influenced, in his
outlook on the Greek world, in his relations with his
Greek neighbours, by the Panhellenic Olympus.

There was progress, too, in another quarter.[18] Far
away on the horizon are strange figures, divine and monstrous—the Hundred-handed "whom the gods call Briar-
eus but all men call him Aegaeon" [19]—Titans now in
Tartarus [20]—things or beings that fought against Zeus

[17] Xenophon thought the Argive should have regarded Corinthian altars,
Hell, iv, 2, 3.
[18] See Girard, *Le Sentiment Religieux*, bk. i, ch. ii.
[19] *Iliad*, i. 402.
[20] *Iliad*, viii. 479.

and fell. The father of Zeus was a Titan and was de-
throned by his sons. Zeus and his dynasty represent
something higher and better, something more human, one
says instinctively—mind and reason rather than sheer
brute force. Passion may influence a god, like the hate
of Poseidon for Odysseus, but it is intelligible anger, it
has a reason which any rational being can grasp,[21] Poseidon is a being with a mind, with a domain of his own,
on which he does not mean to have his brother Zeus
trespassing and he says so. Take, then, the pageant of
Poseidon, and remembering how strong are his feelings,
how clear and vivid his mind, ask what it means. At
Aegae, "in the sea depths, his famous house is builded of
beaming gold imperishable; there came he, and yoked beneath the car his bronzen-footed horses, swift to fly, with
long manes of gold; and he arrayed himself in gold, and
grasped a golden well-wrought whip and stepped upon
the car, and drove across the waves; and the sea-beasts
came from their chambers everywhere, and gambolled
beneath him, knowing well their king, and the rejoicing
sea parted before him; swiftly the horses flew, and the
bronzen axle was not wet beneath." He came to the
ships of the Achaeans with a purpose, "sorely wroth
with Zeus." [22] This is the typical Homeric god—the sort
of picture that the *Iliad*, taken as a whole, leaves on the
mind. Ultimately impossible, yes, but in the meantime
splendid. As Dr. Edward Caird put it, the anthropomorphism humanises the nature powers and substitutes
a relation to man for a relation to nature, and so mediates
a transition to subjective religion.

Hints of the goal are given elsewhere by Homer. At
the very beginning of the *Iliad*, in a most vivid scene,

[21] *Odyssey*, i. 68. My point is perhaps all the stronger, if Mr. J. A. K.
Thomson is right in saying that the blinding of Polyphemus is not the primary
motive (*Studies in the Odyssey*, p. 12).
[22] *Iliad*, xiii. 22-30 (Purves).

Athene plucks Achilles by the hair to check him as he thinks to draw his sword on Agamemnon. In the *Odyssey* she speaks to the mind of Odysseus suggesting a thought rather than uttering a command. But more striking is a passage where the poet says, "As when the mind of a man runs up and down, a traveller over much of earth, and he thinks in his deep heart, 'Would I were here or there' in his keen desire; as swift as that did the lady Hera fly." [23] The swiftness of thought haunts Homer; and here for once he makes his goddess as spiritual in one aspect of her being as thought itself.

Over all, and very nearly supreme, is Zeus. "Make trial," he says to the gods, "if ye will, that all may know; let down a golden chain from heaven to earth, and all ye gods and goddesses take hold, but ye will not draw down Zeus, the most high Counsellor, from heaven to the ground, no, not with much endeavour. But were I to draw, and put to my strength, I could updraw you all, and earth and sea to boot, and bind the chain about a horn of Olympus, and leave all hanging." [24] He is the Thunderer, he sends cloud and storm, rain and snow, and sets the rainbow in the heavens. Olympus trembles at his nod. He rules the issues of war, and dispenses joys and ills to men (*Iliad,* XXIV. 527); he is the guardian of strangers and suppliants. Neither God nor mortal, says Hermes, can elude his notice or thwart his plans (*Od.* v. 104).[25] So Homer conceives of One who rules the world and has a place for man in his thoughts.

But Zeus is not always omnipotent nor always omniscient. Hera beguiles him, in a famous episode; sleep ensnares him; his attention wanders (*Iliad,* xiii. 7), and Poseidon takes advantage of it. Zeus goes to feast with

23 *Iliad,* xv. 80.
24 *Iliad,* viii. 18-26.
25 Cf. passages set out by T. D. Seymour, *Life in the Homeric Age,* p. 421.

the blameless Aethiopians, apparently unaware of the storm of trouble to break on the Greek camp before he returns (*Iliad*, i. 424). Zeus himself has to shed tears for Sarpedon, but he cannot save him from death, nor Hector either, though he pities him. He commits adultery, but he warns Aegisthus not to do it (*Od.* i. 37). He shows anger and enjoys the bickering of his court.

In short, there are inconsistencies in Homer, as we might expect. Some of them may, as scholars have said, be due to differences of date and hand in the final form of the poems. Some are obviously due to the difficulty of expressing the unseen and the spiritual in the language available. Homer as a rule tells of nothing but what can be seen, or at least pictured under conditions of sense; and he has the drawback of every great thinker, especially of poets—that swiftness of mind which seizes a thought and transforms it to vision there and then, regardless for the moment of other thoughts; which impulsively makes a new conception its own and leaves a mass of ideas to be corrected or transformed later on, if at all. If he were a modern dreamer, if he were not an ancient poet, supposed to be simple and naïve, he would not be expected to achieve consistency in his picture of the divine in relation to man and the universe, perhaps hardly even to aim at it. After all, he does give a fair representation, with the means at his disposal (who could demand more of a poet?), of the difficulty and confusion of the world, of its subjection to moral law and to ideal forces, and of the gaps that men find with agony in the moral order itself. Those ideal forces, the spiritual element in things—perhaps because he has to represent them along the lines of tradition, perhaps because his own mind sees and feels all things in pictures— he represents in the shape of other beings like men.[26]

26 Using suggestions of Dr. E. Caird, *Evolution of Religion*, i. 288-291.

The gods are not men, but to bring gods and men together he has to get them on one plane, visibly, actually, and Athene, unseen by the others, takes Achilles by the yellow hair and checks his fury (*Iliad*, i. 197). Homer is not using metaphor of purpose, nor playing (as Virgil sometimes does, or seems to do, and Spenser often) with a hapless compound, an allegory half spiritual principle, half material symbol, concocted for an ethical purpose to the ruin of reality and art. He sees what he tells, he does not moralise it—it is moral of itself; but, as Dr. Caird says,[27] he exercises an instinctive selection, which is as enlightening as a scientific man's deliberative selection of illustrations to throw light on a law of nature.

To say what a great poet intends to teach is to speak rather naïvely. Wordsworth, in his famous *Letter to a Friend of Robert Burns,* deals with Tam o' Shanter— "I pity him," he says, "who cannot perceive that, in all this, though there was no moral purpose, there is a moral effect." Poets do not, till they decline into the auto-biographical stage, tell us their purposes. Homer, so far as we know, never reached that stage, and we have to divine what he "meant" and what he thought. His picture of the world of gods is full of inconsistencies and impossibilities; and so far it fairly represents the order and disorder of the world in which he lived and we live. He has no theory of the universe, complete, satisfactory, and water-tight. The authors of such theories rarely live or gain acceptance. Homer gives us views, impressions, intuitions; some part of what he gives is, no doubt, traditional, some of it is his own; a minute analysis of this is beyond us, but happily it is not necessary.

Over all, perhaps over Zeus, we are told, Homer finds Fate (*Moira* and *Aisa*).[28] Perhaps he did, but intermit-

27 E. Caird, *Evolution of Religion*, i. 288.
28 On all this, T. D. Seymour, *Life in the Homeric Age*, p. 419.

tently, and with no such interpretation as a modern determinist gives to it. But his expressions vary. Sometimes Fate is superior to the gods of Olympus, sometimes it seems subject to them. Sometimes it is associated vaguely with Zeus, and is actually transcended ὑπὲρ Διὸς αἶσαν, Iliad, xvii. 321) ; sometimes with a vague *daimon* or god (*Odyssey,* xi. 61, 292). No prayer is addressed to Fate; how could it be? A man has his *moira,* and there it is; there is an end of it. Zeus himself laments the *moira* of his son Sarpedon, who was fated to be slain by Patroclus (*Iliad,* xvi. 434, 435), and he wavers as to rescuing him; but Hera reminds him that Sarpedon was "long doomed by *aisa*" πάλαι πεπρωμένον αἴσῃ, 441), and warns him that other gods will wish to save their sons, and Zeus submits. Zeus, speaking of Aegisthus, protests how vainly men blame the gods for evils which they bring upon themselves (*Od.* i. 32). Sometimes it looks as if the will of Zeus were itself Fate; there is the "thought of mighty Zeus," which is destiny (cf. *Iliad,* xvii. 409 and xvii. 329). When Achilles and Agamemnon quarrel, and their wrath sends many goodly souls of heroes to Hades, "the counsel of Zeus was fulfilled," we are told; and we learn a little later that Zeus was away among the Aethiopians at the time of the quarrel, and only later at the prayer of Thetis planned death for the Achaeans. But if Homer is inconsistent with himself when he speaks of Fate, who yet has spoken of Fate and escaped inconsistency?

The weakest point of Olympus is its morality. Many of the scandals are due to the syncretism which welded, as we have seen, many gods into one god, and gave many legends to one Zeus. The Zeus of one place has a hero son by one woman, the Zeus of another shrine by another; but there is only one Zeus, so the women and the sons and the scandals multiply, and Homer, in a mali-

cious mood, or more probably an interpolator, seizes a
chance to recite a string of such episodes at once (*Iliad,*
xiv. 314-327). Other gods had their local legends, and
they also paid the same price for the splendid individual
personality that the poet gave them. But this is not the
only source of these legends of light love; for it ran
long in the Greek mind that one of the real advantages
of power was its freedom to follow impulse.[29] When
the gods became anthropomorphic, they were given human desires and human passions—an advance indeed
upon plant or animal life, and upon the dim bogey existence, but not a final stage. They had reached a point
where moral judgments were inevitable. No one could
profitably apply moral criticism to a seamist,[30] a river, or
a tree. When the gods became persons, they came under
a higher law, at first fitfully recognised. Mankind has
long found it hard to believe that absolute power does
not absolve from moral responsibility. Islam and the
history of Sultans and Roman Emperors bear witness
to that weakness of thought. But thought prevails, and
morality is inherent in a thought-out view of personality;
the gods had to become moral. In Homer they are behind the best of the heroes in those qualities which men
recognise as highest; and the point could not escape notice. "Even in Homer," writes Professor John Watson,
"there are elements which show that the Greek religion
must ultimately accomplish its own euthanasia. There
was in it from the first a latent contradiction which could
not fail to manifest itself openly later on."[31] It is a
mark of progress to have reached an impossible halting-
place, to be compelled to move onward.

When we turn to Homer's heroes to learn their mind

29 It was not till Euripides that protest was made against myths of the
loves of the gods; Aeschylus, Pindar and Sophocles accept them.
30 If Thetis comes up from the sea like a mist (*Iliad,* i. 359) she came as
a person, with a personal motive.
31 *Christianity and Idealism,* p. 29.

as to the gods, all is so simple and natural as to occasion
at first little remark.   The priest Chryses prays as simply
and directly to Apollo as if he were talking to a human
being.   "If ever I have laid roof upon thy fair temple,
if ever I have burned to thee fat thighs of bulls and goats,
fulfil my prayer." [32]   This is the regular line of appeal
to the gods, and they expect it (cf. *Iliad*, ix. 953 ff.; xv.
368 ff.).   And Apollo does fulfil the prayer.   If Chryses
had ever been initiated, if he had known rapture, illumination, identification with his god, we should never guess
it from his prayer and his attitude.   After all, identification with Homer's Apollo, or Homer's Athene, is not an
aspiration that would readily occur to any one.   They
are definite persons—concrete, one might say—not vague
spirits, not influences.   There is no atmosphere of mystery about them—in any sense of the word mystery.
Homer knows of rites proper to the gods concerned, of
sacrifices to accompany the cremation of the dead, of
offerings to take Odysseus safely into the realm of Hades
and out of it again—but he does not know of sacraments
strictly so called; or, if he does know, he disregards them.
While he knows of priests like Chryses, most of the heroes manage their own religion without priests.   It may
be that in the *Iliad* the heroes are all away from home,
far from familiar or even recognised shrines, but in the
Odyssey most of the people are at home or near home
and are as little concerned with such things; and among
the tales the heroes tell, among the long fictions of Odysseus and the long reminiscences of Nestor, nothing occurs
that suggests the intenser forms of religion which later
Greece knew—no trance, no ecstasy, no rapture.   Nor
are there very clear traces of those earlier rituals, found
among primitive peoples, found too in a modified form

---

[32] *Iliad,* i. 39; cf. *Iliad,* xxiv. 33, Apollo to the gods on the subject of Hector's sacrifices.

among later Greeks, rituals of sowing, reaping, and vintage—mysterious "doings" to make the seed grow or the vine bear. Once again, if in the *Iliad* the Homeric people are abroad and away from home, in the *Odyssey* they are not.

Arguments from silence vary in value a great deal with the subject concerned and with the opportunities of speech; here silence does not seem accidental. Either Homer did not know of such matters, or he was not interested in them. Guesses as to the tribal cults of the various peoples in his poems—Achaeans, Northerners, the Mediterranean race [33]—have some interest, but guesses as a rule do not greatly add to knowledge. It is likely that some mysteries, some agricultural "doings," were to be found in the world round Homer; but whether he sang to please his hearers and we are to conclude their tastes from his silences, or whether he sang to please himself—as poets seem more apt to do—what he does say and what he does not say are both significant. There is endless debate on Shakespeare's mind, and no one can say that his constituents or patrons (as one may prefer to describe them) were not interested in religious controversy; are we to say then that it was only because the law was against such discussion in the theatre, that he kept off religious questions? Or did his mind move more naturally in other directions? One mark of genius is that it feels very little the hamperings of tradition, accepts them, and goes its own way none the less and finds the freedom that is supposed to be denied it.

On the other hand, we have to consider the Lay of Demodocos and how all the gods came to see Ares snared in the arms of Aphrodite, and how one commented lightly to another—and the stories of the beguiling of Zeus by Hera, of the wounding of Ares and of Aphrodite by

33 Cf. W. Leaf, *Homer and History*, 258-262.

heroes in battle, of the limping of Hephaistos and the laughter of the gods. Are they from the same hand as the rest of the poems? Interpolations are admitted; are these interpolations? Are they from the same school? Were these gods worshipped? Is there a "Milesian" irreverence about the tales and about the tone, that implies either that these gods had lost the faith of the people or had not yet gained it—that "Olympianism" was dying or had not yet got its foothold? The answer is that these questions are in the vein of Plato and Protestantism; they imply an intenser belief in God than we find in such periods of religion as we are considering. There is little to choose between Plato and John Knox in the fierceness with which they do battle for God and His character. But if we turn to India—at any rate before European culture became a factor in its thought— the legends of Krishna were accepted more or less as they stood by men whose religion was intensely personal and even spiritual. The moral issue was not considered, or it was waived, it was not relevant, and broadly it did not occur to the mind as bearing on the reality, or the godhead, of the god. It is when a community wakes up to progress in religion that such an issue becomes vital and of first importance; and then the first defence, as we see in Plato, in Plutarch, and in Hinduism, is Allegory. But for Homer there is not Allegory, despite his Stoic and Neo-Platonist commentators. For Hesiod there is.[34]

In the background, waiting for a congenial renaissance, are the gods of earth and grain, of mystery, intoxication and psychopathic phenomena. They are to re-emerge, but it remains that the first great Greek—in the deepest and most Hellenic sense in which anybody could be called Greek—was not interested in such gods;

34 Cf. page 81.

and that is as significant as any polemic. *Ἐν γὲ φάει καὶ
ὄλεσσον*—says one of the heroes: "Kill me, yes! but in
the light." [35] Homer stands in the daylight—a mind with
the characteristics of open air and sunshine; and, as we
gather from the Fourth Gospel, a mind of that type is
dynamic, vital in its tacit criticism, in its telling effect.

There is for the Homeric hero a relation between his
gods and morality. Zeus does not himself punish Aegisthus for adultery and murder, but he warns him that he
will not go unpunished (*Od.* i. 37). "The blessed Gods
love not wicked deeds" (*Od.* xiv. 83). Zeus sends storms
and floods in anger upon men who give "crooked judgments" (*σκολιὰς θέμιστας*) in the assembly (*Iliad*, xvi.
387). "Of the Ten Commandments of the Israelites,"
writes Professor Seymour, "the Achaeans in strictness
had but two—'Thou shalt not take the name of a God
in vain,' and 'Honour thy father and mother.'" With
respect to Zeus, a third commandment may be formu-
lated as "Thou shalt have respect unto the stranger and
the suppliant to pity them" (*Od.* v. 447; ix. 270; xiv.
404).

The two dominant conceptions which rule conduct are
Custom and *Aidos*. Custom we can still, even in such
an age as this, understand, if we do not give it the old
respect. It made a large part of life throughout Greek
history, as the complaint that tyrants change old customs [36] tells us. Custom is the protective thing in religion. The element that makes for progress is *Aidos*—
a hard word to translate alike in every passage—but a
conception intelligible to every simple and clear nature;
it includes reverence for others, for the aged, the suppliant [37] and the dead—self-respect and the sense of duty

35 *Iliad*, xvii. 647.
36 Herodotus, iii. 80.
37 Cf. the great passage about Prayers, "Daughters of Zeus" (*Iliad*, ix. 497-
512), and the coming of Priam to Achilles (*Iliad*, xxiv.).

—honour. These are the sides of life where education
is continuous, where by the unobtrusive play of sympathy and human feeling the outlook broadens and the
insight deepens, and new gleams come of something beyond custom and tradition.   Horizons grow wider, as one
learns to know and to respect one's enemy—the man one
hates—the foreigner, the Trojan.   Priam's helpless age
—his grief for his son—the laughter of Hector and Andromache, as the baby turns his head away from the nod-
ding plumes—the tales of old Eumaeus—the sight of the
helpless dead; do they bear on religion? How can they
but bear on it? "It is not holy to boast over men slain"
(*Od.* xxiv. 412).   The gods, it is true, show little trace
of *Aidos.*   Zeus twits Hera with her readiness to eat
Priam raw and Priam's children with him (*Iliad,* iv. 35).
And yet the gods too can be appeased by sacrifice and
supplication, if a man have sinned (*Iliad,* ix. 497 f.).
Athene enjoys the cunning and the lies of Odysseus (*Od.*
xiii. 287.).   She deceives Hector at the crisis of his fate
—"Athene hath betrayed me!" (*Iliad,* xxii. 296); indeed the gods habitually deceive men.   But "hateful to
me as the gates of Hades," cries Achilles, "is he who
hides one thing in his heart and speaks another" (*Iliad,*
iv. 312).   There lies the promise of progress.

Homer moved everything forward when he gave to
the gods their bright personality, and made every one of
them so intensely individual, so human; when he brought
religion into daylight, out into the field of battle, into the
council chamber, away from cave and shrine and twilight.   He moved everything forward when he turned
his imagination on to the life of heroes, when he conceived and worked out Achilles in his heart and in his
brain, when he woke to the finer shades of honour and
feeling, and wove them into the characters of the men
whom he gave us to love and to admire.   His decalogue

is a short one, but it can be summed up in words he never
spoke or hinted. He loved men and their life—their
fierce, keen, bright, tender spirits; he was a "human
Catholic" indeed, and such men are never far from the
Kingdom of Heaven. He never told us to love men; he
knew of no Kingdom of Heaven; his other world is very
dim, very empty of life and personality; but he did believe in men.

What does a great poet achieve? Let us borrow words,
and, altering a tense and a pronoun or two, say:

> He gives us eyes, he gives us ears,
> And humble cares, and delicate fears,
> A heart, the fountain of sweet tears;
>   And love, and thought, and joy.

And these gifts are dynamic. Homer gave them to his
fellow countrymen. He made them Hellenic, taught
them how to see and what to look for. "Love and
thought and joy" may be an abstract way of describing
the effect of his work; but it is true. He made the Greeks,
and he taught them to think and to feel. The pictures
he gave them of gods would not endure—because he gave
them something else, the spirit that makes men ask more
of themselves, more of the universe, more of God. His
heroes are, morally and spiritually, ahead of their own
gods. Custom is reluctant to accept new views of the
gods; Poetry forced new ideals upon the Greeks. Homer,
by making his gods so human, brought them into the
sphere where they must be amenable to the new ideals.
The gods did not reach those ideals; they slowly died
away into insignificance; the ideals lived, and the Greeks
moved forward to a higher view of God. But Homer
also delayed their progress. He had indeed, as Herodotus suggests, given form and look and function to the
gods; he gave them personality; he fixed their legends

and made them immortal by the beauty of his thought and the beauty of his word. He gave currency to a conception of the gods, which warred with the quickening of the Greek mind. The spirit of the poet set things moving; his words, his pictures, retarded the movement. The old quarrel of which Plato speaks [38] between Poetry and Thought was fairly started—started by Homer himself, and to both combatants Homer gave the impulse.

[38] *Republic*, x. 607 B.

IV

THE BEGINNINGS OF GREEK CRITICISM

THE Homeric age of Greece passed—that is a statement no one will dispute; but how it passed, few will care to say with any tone of certainty. It may be that the Achæan invaders, as happened with the Normans in England and the Highland regiments in Quebec, were merged in the peoples they found, by the slow but sure processes of intermarriage. It may be that this had already happened when Homer made his poems. It may be that a destroyer, Minos, overwhelmed the old civilisation of the Aegean basin—that Homer's Agamemnon and the Mycenaean king of the Archaeologists both met murder and sudden death. I at least cannot speak of those times; what we call a dark age followed them—dark in any case to the historian, dark enough and full of ominous change for the men of the day.

One man of that age of change, whatever his century, was Hesiod the poet, a man born to trouble. His brother, he says, robbed him in the division of their inheritance, with at least the hope of aid from bribe-devouring princes.[1] Hesiod appears to suggest some fair arrangement which may disappoint the false judges. Whatever was done, Hesiod gave a great deal of good advice to his unfriendly brother, with what effect we do not know, though we may guess. Their father "was wont to sail in ships, seeking a goodly livelihood: who also on a time came hither, traversing a great space of sea in his black ship from Aeolian Kyme, not fleeing from abundance nor

1 *Works and Days*, 27 ff.

from riches and weal, but from evil penury, which Zeus giveth unto men. And he made his dwelling near Helicon in a sorry township, bad in winter, hard in summer, never good." [2]   Thucydides long after said the Hesiod was murdered by the people of the Locrian Nemea.[3]   So, waiving all the later legends, there we have a picture of the times—penury, bad towns, shipping, trade, settlers, robbery, unjust judges and murder. "The earth is full of evils," he says, "and full is the sea." [4]   It is the picture we have glanced at already, but drawn by a gloomy man, "a dour son of the soil," [5] whose one voyage was across the Euripus, a sea-passage to be measured in yards.[6]

Looked at more broadly, it is a period which sooner or later saw great movements of races. Cimmerians and Treres, and later on Scythians, broke into Asia Minor and swept through it, away to Gaza and to Mesopotamia, and back again to Lydia. Kingdoms and nations rose and fell—Hittites, Phrygians and Lydians westward; and eastward, Assyrians, Babylonians and Medes. The Greeks of the Asian shore, in walled cities, on peninsulas, or bays girt by hills, lived a kind of island life, trading and travelling to escape from "evil penury," and with a desire already to see the world. They built their ships and learnt their seas and coast-lines, watching the stars above and the eddies and currents of the sea below them, and grew into that self-reliance which the sailor always needs and generally develops, and into that individuality which made the Greek race outstanding among all the tribes of man. The sailor-people were for democracy in their home-towns, as against the land-holders, and the long series of Greek experiments in government went

2 *Works and Days*, 633 f.
3 *Thucydides*, iii. 96.
4 *Works and Days*, 101.
5 Cf. C. H. Moore, *Religious Thought of the Greeks*, p. 28.
6 *Works and Days*, 648 ff.

vigorously on. We find men from these Asian Greek cities discovering Gibraltar,[7] fighting at Babylon,[8] carving their names on the legs of colossal statues at Abu-Symbel, hundreds of miles up the Nile. In these cities began Greek philosophy. The period before us is a long one, from Homer, whose date I do not know, though I suspect it to be earlier than thirty years ago it was fashionable to say—down to the Persian wars—let us say, to the battle of Salamis in 480. There will be every temptation to linger and to wander in a period so long and so full of interest of every kind; we must try to remember that our subject is Progress in Religion, but not quite to forget how much this is conditioned by social and economic environment. We must remember, too, the forces working for and against progress—how sentiment, ignorance and terror retard it, how enquiry and thought and clearness, which are Greek habits of mind, promote it. Greeks had one advantage over Indians and over later Semites, Jews and Moslems, in not having sacred books. Homer wrote no Vedas; and when the nearest things to Vedas that Greece knew came into being, the habits of the race were formed, and Homer was there to overshadow all sacred and theogonic poetry. His genius kept the Hellen in the open air.

Hesiod, however, is our present concern—named, as we saw, by Herodotus (ii. 53) as one of the founders of Greek tradition about the gods. He tells us himself, what Homer never did, how he became a poet—a small hint of a new significance of the individual. "The Muses of old taught Hesiod sweet song what time he tended his sheep under holy Helicon. These words first spake to me the goddess Muses of Olympus, daughters of aegis-bearing Zeus: 'Shepherds of the fields, evil thing of

7 Kolaios of Samos; Herodotus, iv. 152.
8 Antimenidas, brother of the poet Alcaeus.

shame, bellies only! We know to speak many lies like
unto truth; we know, when we will, the truth to speak.'
So spake the daughters of mighty Zeus, clear of speech;
and they gave me a rod, a shaft of lusty laurel that they
had plucked, wondrous to see; and they breathed into me
a voice divine that I might tell of things to be and of
things aforetime. They bade me sing the race of the
Blessed that live forever, and always to sing themselves
first and last." [9] And he won a prize for song, a tripod,
on his one journey to Euboea, and offered it up to the
Muses; and Pausanias saw it on Helicon in the second
century A.D. or one that passed for it.[10]

Hesiod devoted himself to the collection and ordering
of the traditions of the gods. His verse and language
show the influence of Homer,[11] his cosmogony and
theology other strains than the Homeric, just as his
scheme of life comprises more taboos and more veiled
suggestions of magic.[12] He pursues his gods into a
remoter past. Chaos, Earth and Eros come first; Chaos
engenders Darkness and Black Night—Night is mother
of Aether and Day. Earth bore Heaven and the Mountains and the Sea, and many more children by Heaven
—monstrous and odious children, till Cronos mutilated
Heaven and there was an end of it.[13] The gross old
story must be very old; but the steady systematisation
of all is very modern; it is next thing to criticism; and
such accommodations of criticism and the uncriticised
prepare the future. The old myth and the new allegory,
the Titan, the monster and the personified abstract noun
(Memory, for instance, and Lying Speeches) will not go
together; they belong to different stages of thought, and
a system that puts them on one footing has written upon

9 Theognis, 22 ff.
10 *Works and Days*, 648 ff; Pausanias, ix. 31, 3.
11 Chadwick, *Heroic Age*, pp. 214, 230.
12 J. E. Harrison, *Themis*, p. 94.
13 Theognis, 160 ff.

it its own certain resolution into its elements. The tales of grossness and fear were to live long; but some of the newer ideas also were to thrive.

It is in Hesiod that we first find the distinction drawn between gods and those intermediate beings which later Greeks call "daemons"—beings more like the later Hebrew "angels" than the "daemons" of primitive agricultural Greece. These midway beings were the very keystone of later Greek theology, and Plutarch blesses the man who introduced them, whether Zoroaster or Orpheus or an Egyptian; he remarks that Homer used "gods" and "daemons" as synonyms, and that Hesiod was the first clearly to distinguish the four orders of gods, daemons, heroes and men.[14] It was in Hesiod, Dr. Adam notes, a symptom of the tendency to remove the Supreme God from direct part in men's affairs. And perhaps something may be put down to poetic feeling. "For near at hand, among men, Immortals take note who by crooked decisions oppress each other, heeding not the gods. For thrice ten thousand Immortals are there on all-feeding earth, warders of Zeus over mortal men, who watch over justice and harsh deeds—clad in darkness, passing to and fro over earth. Yea, and there is the maiden Justice, born of Zeus, glorious and worshipful among the gods that hold Olympus. And when one injures her with crooked reviling, straightway as she sitteth by Zeus her father, son of Cronos, she telleth him the mind of unrighteous men."[15] A line or two later he heightens what he has said: "The eye of Zeus, that hath seen all and marked all, looketh on these things too, if he will, and he faileth not to behold what manner of justice our city keepeth within."[16] Here at least heaven

---

14 Plutarch, *de dejectu oraculorum*, x. 414 F–415 A. *Conflict of Religions*, pp. 97, 98.
15 *Works and Days*, 249, 250.
16 *Works and Days*, 267-269.

is more righteous than in the *Theogony,* where the gods are frankly non-moral and gross to a degree unknown in Homer.   Here a step forward, and a great one, is taken or chronicled.

The poet wavers as he looks at the bad world he knows.   "Wealth is not to be seized: god-given it is better far.   For if a man take great gain by the violence of his hands, or plunder it by the tongue—as often befalls when Gain deceiveth the mind of men, and Shamelessness treadeth Shame (*Aidos*) underfoot—yet lightly the gods abase him and make that man's house decay, and his gain attendeth him but a little while.   He that wrongeth a suppliant, and he that mounteth upon his brother's bed, and he that in his foolishness sinneth against fatherless children, and he that chideth an aged parent on the evil threshold of old age with harsh words —it is all one.   Against him surely Zeus is angry, and in the end for his unjust deeds layeth upon him a stern recompense." [17]   Conversely for those who deal justly by strangers and citizens, Zeus sends peace "the nurse of children"; they know not famine; the earth beareth them much livelihood, acorns on the oak and bees within it, sheep heavy with wool, children like their parents, "nor do they go on ships." [18]   Wherefore, continues Hesiod, "with all thy might do sacrifice to the deathless gods, in holy wise and purely, and burn glorious meat-offerings withal, and at other times propitiate them with libations and with incense, both when thou liest down and when the holy daylight cometh, that they may have to thee a gracious heart and mind, that thou mayest buy a lot of another, not another thine." [19]   The whole passage is fiercely attacked by Plato [20]—"the noble

17 *Works and Days,* 320-334.
18 *Works and Days,* 225-237.
19 *Works and Days,* 336-341.
20 *Rep.* 363.

Hesiod!" he exclaims with contempt; but Xenophon says that the first line was a favourite quotation with Socrates.[21] But after all, Hesiod is not sure. Things go from bad to worse; he lives in the iron age; there is no loyalty left, no truth, no honour for the aged nor respect for the guest; and evil ways are growing. "Then shall Shame (*Aidos*) and Awe (*Nemesis*) veil their fair faces with their white robes, and depart from the wide-wayed Earth unto Olympus to join the company of the Immortals." [22]

After Hesiod, though how long after him I do not guess, came the poets of the seventh and sixth centuries B.C. They represent something quite different from either Homer or Hesiod. If Homer wrote for princes and Hesiod for peasants, these men and women wrote for themselves and of themselves, individualists all of them, self-conscious, restless, reflective, Greek, and more like the later Greeks than their two great predecessors. Few poets could be more personal than Archilochus and Sappho. "Soul, my soul, with troubles invisible surging," begins a fragment of Archilochus; and it was the legend of antiquity that the poet "battened on hatreds," [23] trouble at Paros, trouble at Thasos, trouble with the father-in-law-to-be. Of Sappho's two short poems—the three stanzas of passion translated by Catullus and the ode to Aphrodite—I need not speak; though the latter seems to me less of a religious character than some would have it—splendid, but hardly piety. Theognis writes of the political changes of Megara, moving about in worlds not realised: "Kyrnos, this city is still a city, but the folk are other folk, who knew not aforetime justice nor law, but wore about their flanks skins of goats, and lived without this city like the stags; and now they are the gentle-

21 Xenophon, *Mem.* i. 3, 2.
22 *Works and Days*, 174-201.
23 Pindar, *Pyth*, ii. 54.

folk; and the old highborn are base."[24] "O my soul,"
he cries, "amid all thy friends show a nature of many
hues. Have the mind of the folded polypus, who on his
rock, wherever he cling, is even such to see" (213 ff.).
So far away are the days when Odysseus could chide
Thersites and smite him.[25] We have to deal with men
thinking their own thoughts, wondering what traditions
will hold, and doubting of all. The times are times of
question and movement.

In such times men think of the gods in new ways—
they handle them more brusquely, they make peace with
them more abjectly. Life for Homer's heroes was so
good that the best life in Hades was incomparably worse
than the meanest above ground; but life is not so good
now. The gods leave everything in confusion. "Dear
Zeus," cries Theognis, "I marvel at thee. Thou art
King of all; thou hast honour and great power; thou
knowest well the mind and thought of every man; and
thy power is supreme over all, O King! How then, Son
of Cronos, doth thy mind endure to have wicked men and
the just under one fate ($\mu o \acute{\iota} \rho \eta$), whether a man's mind
be turned to self-rule, or to insolence, as they trust in
unrighteousness? Neither is any distinction made by
god for mortal; nor a road, whereby if a man travel,
he may please the Immortals."[26] "Father Zeus, would
it might be the pleasure of the gods that insolence delight the wicked! And would that this too were their
pleasure; that whoso contrived hard deeds in his mind
and heart, recking nought of the gods, himself should
pay again for his evil deeds, nor the follies of the father
be thereafter a curse to the children! and would that the
children of an unjust father, who think justice and do
it, regarding thy wrath, O Son of Cronos, and from

24 Theognis, 53 ff.
25 Iliad, ii. 245, 265.
26 Theognis, 373 ff.

childhood love justice amid the citizens, should not pay for the sin of their fathers!" [27]   Dr. Adam compares the striking passage where Jeremiah puts in his way, more piously but no less insistently, the same question: "Righteous art thou, O Lord . . . yet would I reason the cause with thee.   Wherefore doth the way of the wicked prosper?" [28]   The answer, toward which Jeremiah led the way for Israel, was not that given by Greek thinkers.

But there are pious souls who dread to challenge the gods with such questions, but who feel the questions none the less, and go about getting an answer in another way. They will surrender, and look again into that dark world which interested Homer so little.   There had been those who maintained that justice is done, who did not feel the distinction that Theognis draws between the sinner and his kin.

Solon, traveller, poet and legislator, had dealt sturdily with the problem in lines of real beauty.   Judgment comes like a devouring flame from a little fire: "Zeus seeth the end of all things; and on a sudden, as a wind in spring quickly scatters the clouds, stirs the depths of the barren wave-driven sea, and over the wheatlands lays waste the fair work of men, and cometh to the high heaven, the abode of the gods, and makes the clear sky to be seen, and the might of the sun shines forth over the boundless land, beautiful, nor is there a cloud left to behold; even so is the vengeance of Zeus, nor is he, like a mortal man, quick to anger at every deed.   But never doth it for ever escape his notice, who hath a sinful soul, and surely at the end it appeareth.   One payeth forthwith, another thereafter; and if themselves escape, if the doom of the gods light not upon them, yet it cometh none the less, and their children pay for their

[27] Theognis, 731 ff.   [28] Jer. xii. 1.

deeds, or their race after them." [29]   That had satisfied
Solon, but it does not satisfy Theognis.   The matter
must be carried further.

But before we go on, one or two points should be
noted.   The individual has come to be himself, and, as
already suggested, his children are individuals; the
family has ceased to be a unit; it is on its way to modernity.   Behind such views as Solon's, which we also
find in some of the Hebrew psalms, was a long tradition,
dim with age and soon to die—that ancestors and
descendants are one—that the living and the dead are
not without influences on one another; the old worship
of ancestors may have gone, but something is left that
proclaims the family to be an integer, and makes justice executed on the grandson balance the sin of the
grandfather.   This idea died slowly, if it ever quite died.
Perhaps it is truer to say that ideas have ghosts that
haunt the minds of mankind—intangible as the ghost of
Patroclus or of Hamlet's father, yet not without power.
But by the end of our long period when Theognis lived
each man is himself; *he* must be rewarded or punished,
himself and not another.   Nothing else would be justice.
This is a new phase of the long-growing demand for
morality in the gods and in men.   What we have noticed
from time to time already, assails us again here in the
unhappy complaints of Theognis—that emphasis on personality and morality which makes for Progress in
Religion.

Let us turn now to the god to whom Theognis addressed his complaint.   It is still Zeus—the Zeus of
Homer, of Hesiod and of Solon.   But, generally, it is
remarked in the lyric poets that Zeus is gaining a greater
ascendency.   We have only fragments to deal with, so
that our negative statements will hardly be as secure as

29 Solon, iv. 12 (4), 14 ff. (Bergk).

what we can say positively. The negative first, then.
There is an absence of reference in our fragments to the
old scandals of Olympus, a refraining from some of the
things said to Zeus and about him in the Homeric poems.
On the positive side, while the other gods survived, while,
as we know from other sources, they were worshipped,
Zeus is gaining at their expense. When a man questions,
it is the government of Zeus that he questions. Zeus
is hardly so personal as he was in Homer; he is more
like Providence, or Ultimate Justice, or the power behind
nature—all of which he became in time under Stoic
teaching.   The Greeks are still a long way from
Monotheism, but the old society of heaven is breaking
up. Local gods and local goddesses—and one great god
over all; this with some reservations, when one thinks of
corn and crop and the world of the dead, seems the picture of heaven that the period gives us.

Two points, then, are outstanding. Divine Justice and
Monotheism are not yet established, but in one way and
another men are beginning to ask for them; in the one
case they are quite clear in their feelings, that it is imperative to show the heavens more just. In the other,
an instinct, not yet thought-out, an instinct which
scholars tell us was in Israel as far back as our records
will reliably take us—an instinct which Tertullian seized
upon as a witness to the soul being by nature Christian,
which Muhammad found even among heathen Arabs—
is quietly impelling men to think in the terms of a single
supreme god. Fear, tradition, and the sense of solitude
compel them to supplement that one god; but, when we
survey from a distance the completed story of Greek
thought, we recognise here the beginnings of Monotheism. But there is another impulse, of which we have
so far had little evidence in what is left us of early Greek
literature.

Men ask for Justice in God; and an instinct, which works more slowly, drives them to conceive of him as One. But what St. Augustine summed up in his most famous sentence has plenty of evidence outside the range of Christian experience as well as within it. "Thou hast made us for thyself, and our heart knows no rest until it rests in Thee." [30] The thought is not one that seems to fit in with Homer or the Greek philosophers of the sixth century B.C., but it is quite clear that the impulse to seek peace with heaven, to find some rest for the heart on the basis of some relation with the gods, was powerful in the centuries under our present survey. *Primus in orbe deos fecit timor,* said Statius; [31] but, even if fear was the first factor, or even the only one, that drove men into religious thought and rite, fear was allayed by an effective relation with the gods. If the right prayer were said, if the right offering were made, the god would take the fear out of the human heart, either by going away himself or by helping the man to overcome it; and, whichever was the way, it was managed by intercourse; and that depended on the assurance that god and man understand each other.

When we were considering the Homeric gods, we saw how natural and how inevitable is the movement to Anthropomorphism. The gods must be rational and intelligible, must be interpretable in human terms. But they must also be just in their dealings with men, and moral and perhaps dignified in their relations with one another. And here the gods of the *Iliad* and the *Odyssey* might seem defective to people whose minds moved more slowly than Homer's, who were framed (let us say) in a more pious mould. Athene, Apollo and others of them are too like the Greek tyrant; intelligible enough,

30 Augustine, *Confessions,* I, I.
31 *Thebaid,* iii. 661; Petronius said it before him, fragm. 27 (Bücheler).

they are, however, "outside the ordinary thoughts," [32] one of which is the sense of responsibility. So, without renouncing these brilliant creatures, men turned elsewhere when they wanted gods who took a quieter view of life. It may not be quite the whole story, to say that they turned to gods less completely humanised.

Demeter and Dionysos had escaped the touch of Homer's imagination, and remained indeed less human, but what gave them their significance was something else —something about each of them that remained unexplained. Demeter was kind and good, the giver of crops and of life, the giver of laws; her ways were in the main very calculable; but her power was one of the most mysterious things on earth. Why should grain grow by being buried? Why should anything grow? How does it? Dionysos is different. How far he is to be regarded as initially a god of vegetation or of the vine, I do not know. I lean to the idea that he owed much of his significance to the play of primitive Psychology upon psychopathic phenomena, which it could not understand.

The Eleusinian Mysteries have piqued the curiosity both of ancient worshippers and modern archaeologists; and it is probable that if we could have a complete history of their origin and development, let us say from Demeter to Justinian, we should have a complete revelation of everything that stirred in Greek religion. For we have again to remind ourselves at this point that religion is never quite static. No religion ever was *semper eadem*. Every religion is always being re-translated, re-interpreted. Even the most orthodox speak the dialect of their day; and, as they of all people are least alive to the strange ways of words, they think in the dialect of their day and never realise that they are doing it; so they also re-translate their faith. Trans-

[32] Herodotus, iii. 80.

lation never leaves an idea unchanged; least of all when it is unconscious translation.

For us the definite history of Eleusis begins with the so-called Homeric *Hymn to Demeter,* which is not from the immortal hand and eye that framed the *Odyssey.* Thucydides thought, or assumed, with the men of his day that Homer wrote the hymns, but the great Homeric scholars of Alexandria did not.[33] The hymn to Demeter is generally allowed to belong to the beginning of the sixth century B.C. The rest of our evidence is later, some of it very late indeed, and, what is worse, of uncertain date. If our business were to write the history of Eleusinian faith and practice, it would be a long and difficult task to trace the growth of the mass of myth, legend and fable, the development of ritual and the transmutation of ideas associated with the mysteries, and to find the sources Thracian, Egyptian or Philosophic from which those ideas were reinforced. But our task is much simpler. The hymn tells us a good deal about the religion at the date when it was composed—a good deal but not all. Like other writers of hymns, the author, and perhaps his revisers, chose what he would emphasise, and assumed that those who would use the hymn knew more than he wrote, *e.g.,* about the ritual. They had the advantage of us there; but history, archaeology, and anthropology have given the modern student data and criteria that the worshippers hardly wanted. It seems generally agreed that behind the hymn, a long way perhaps behind it, was a ritual on the border-line between Magic and Religion—a ritual which would promote the growth and health of crops. Some vague daemon of vegetation was involved—daemon or daemons, but the matter could not be left there. The ritual needed ex-

---

33 Andrew Lang, *Homeric Hymns,* pp. 3, 4. Allen and Sikes, *Homeric Hymns,* p. 54.

planation, and an anthropomorphising instinct played upon the daemon or daemons; and out of the double process came the beautiful myth of Demeter and Persephone, which at last the hymn gives us with a new beauty and tenderness of its own, fixing its outline and its details and making it immortal, not without some hint of kinship with Homer and the gods that Homer drew. Something more followed, which is briefly told us at the end of the Hymn.

When the goddess had sent up the grain from the rich glebe, and the wide earth was heavy with leaves and flowers, she showed unto Triptolemus and Diocles the charioteer and mighty Eumolpus and Celeos, leader of the people, "the manner of her rites, and taught them her holy mysteries, which none may violate, or search into, or noise abroad, for the great curse from the gods restrains the voice. Happy is he among deathly men who hath beheld these things! and he that is uninitiate, and hath no lot in them, hath never equal lot in death beneath the murky gloom." [34]

The corn ritual, the corn daemon, Demeter the Mother, Persephone and the pomegranate—and then Immortality and Joy for the initiate. Even if, with Sir James Frazer, we were to say Demeter began as a pig—and he prefers a lowly origin for gods, as some people do for self-made men, though for the opposite reason—we have left the pig a long way behind; and Mr. Andrew Lang tells us it was never on the main track at all.[35] We have reached a point at which men are definitely fixing their eyes and their attention upon Eternity, and a differentiated Eternity—a religion intensely personal. It is not suggested by the poet that a man's moral character will bear directly on his immortal life; that seems to have been a gap in

[34] Lang's translation.
[35] *Homeric Hymns*, Intr., pp. 63-66.

the teaching of the mysteries throughout. The indignant question of the Cynic philosopher remains: "Shall Pataikion the brigand, because he was initiated, fare better after death than Epameinondas?"[36] It is plain enough that the priests of the mysteries made little inquiry as to the character of those they initiated. Mr. Lang would not allow the view of Lobeck that there was no ethical teaching in the mysteries; he urged that everywhere primitive peoples have associated moral instruction with mummeries and rituals, and that this association may have survived. "Holy" and "pure" are words with long and strange histories, and their exact meaning at any stage must be learnt before we can do much with them. In any case the strongest moral impulses have not been given to mankind by the guardians of ritual and sacrament; they have come from without; that at all events is true in Greece. Little can be added to what Aristotle says: "The initiated learned nothing precisely, but they received impressions and were put into a certain frame of mind, for which they had been prepared"— and evermore," adds Omar,

> "Came out by that same door where in I went."

As we saw before, however, moral effect is sometimes not quite to be measured by moral purpose, and whatever the purpose of the writer of the *Hymn to Demeter,* the poem must have contributed to the education of Greece in some of the things that matter most.

There were other mystery religions in Greece, and one of the most important movements of Greek religious thought now demands our attention. But one or two points may be recalled, and perhaps developed, first. We have seen the growing self-consciousness of the Hellen

---

[36] *Diogenes Laertius,* vi. 39.

as the world about him becomes more and more complex
and unintelligible, and we must not omit to notice that
the *Hymn to Demeter,* in that epilogue about the world
beyond, recognises the individual and his personal outlook on religion in a way that is almost modern. A' man
chose to be initiated, or remained uninitiated by choice.[37]
In other words, a change has come in religion, though its
implications are not broadly recognised as yet.   Once
to share in a cult had implied a blood relation (real or
presumed) of the whole tribal circle worshipping, and
the possession of the god by the tribe or group of tribes
·—he was "our god"; or the cult was a local one jealously
guarded; and in any case everybody belonging to the
tribe, or the group of natives of the place, was *ipso facto*
a subject for initiation and was initiated.   But the sixth
century bears witness to an innovation—choice in religion; and this carries with it, in germ, a good deal—
the weighing of the claims of conscience, heart, tradition
and philosophy, and the habit of reflection in religion,
of speculation.   Eleusis, further, was practically international, or became so.   "Demeter," writes Isocrates,[38]
about 385 B.C., "came to the country and gave two gifts,
the greatest of gifts—the crops which have saved us
from the life of mere animals, and the rite, whereof who
partake have sweeter hopes for the end of life and for
all time; and our city in piety to god and man, grudged
not but gave to all what she had received."   He implies
a tradition dating from the incorporation of Eleusis in
Attica perhaps in the seventh century, and the opening
of the rites to all Athenians.   A universal religion, then,
is in sight, and one in which the individual speaks the
decisive word—he will, or he will not, have it.   Meantime, the normal and established religions or cults are

37 F. B. Jevons, *History of Religion,* p. 328.
38 *Panegyric,* xxviii.; Jevons, *History of Religion,* p. 359.

not felt by their maintainers to be in any way challenged by the new development.   This was partly because polytheism never is endangered by the acceptance of an extra god, and partly because there was really nothing revolutionary about the ceremonies at Eleusis; all was old and traditional, as the goddess had given it; there could be no harm in it.   The dangers for a local religion that we now see to be involved in a universal religion, for a religion wholly tribal in one where the individual chooses, were not obvious at the stage reached; indeed, they never were very serious till the universal religion became definitely monotheistic.   India has assimilated or tolerated every religion except Islam and Protestantism.

Orphism [39] is the greatest religious movement of the age under our consideration.   It is a complex of many elements, assimilating ideas that perhaps had little to do with it in its earliest form, and adapting itself to them. The tradition was that it began in Thrace, among communities admittedly savage; and some of its features confirm this.   The tearing to pieces of living animals was a rite of several primitive religions, notably among the Semites; it is found to-day among Indians in British Columbia.[40]   To the Greeks this was startling enough, and not less were the other accompaniments of the religion, its influence upon women, who left their homes, ranged the hills, cried their god's name, and showed a heightening of muscular strength along with trance and hallucination—symptoms which we group to-day as psychopathic and consider to be of no intellectual or religious value.   In those days the phenomena had, as they have elsewhere to-day, only one explanation—viz. god-possession.   They were evidence of the presence of a god

39 See John Burnet, *Greek Philosophy*, pp. 85 f.; Bury, *Greek History*, i. pp. 316-318.
40 Or perhaps yesterday; my statement rests on a paragraph in a Kingston, Ontario, paper in the autumn of 1896.   The animal used by the Indians was a dog.

and of his effectual union with the natures of the persons affected.[41] There can be little doubt that the phenomena so explained were the first cause of the great spread of Orphism. The modern psychologist tells us how such waves of impulsive social action originate among people who have least inhibitory control, and how they spread by imitation, intensifying as they go. The ancient explanation undoubtedly contributed to the spread, and the contagion swept all over Greece, so irresistibly that the older shrines had to recognise the new god, who proved himself of such power. Apollo admitted his "brother" to Delphi; and he found a place at Eleusis, at Athens, at Sicyon.

Then fresh elements appear, whether due to another movement or not, or to a teacher identifiable with Orpheus; and the religion, which began with psychopathic disturbances, is equipped with myths, a theology, a philosophy of the soul and its origin and destiny, a system of life and ritual a good deal quieter than the original one, and an extensive literature.[42] Here again it is hard to make out an order of events; the Orphists put Orpheus earlier than Homer, which Herodotus rightly would not believe.[43] Among them they developed a Cosmogony, not free from variants;[44] they told, for instance, how Ocean first married Tethys his sister and begot various gods, how Dionysus-Zagreus, the child-god, was mutilated and devoured by the Titans, but was rescued by Athene and swallowed by Zeus to re-appear as the new Dionysus, while from the ashes, to which the Titans were reduced by a thunderbolt, sprang man, of twofold nature, god and Titan, an uneasy union of good and evil. Another similar myth tells how Zeus swallowed Phanês, in

41 Even this vague statement may be too precise. "Union" and "nature" are words that raise many questions.
42 The innumerable books, cf. Euripides, *Hipp.* 954: Plato, *Rep.* 364E.
43 Herodotus, ii. 55.
44 Dieterich, *Abraxas,* § 9, pp. 126-135.

whom, as the offspring of the world-egg, were all seeds
or potencies; and how, as a result, sky, sea, earth, ocean,
Tartarus, rivers, gods and goddesses, all that was or
would be was in the belly of Zeus, in confusion.[45]   The
soul, so the Orphics taught more certainly, was not at
home but in prison in the body, buried as it were (σῶμα,
σῆμα), but desirous of freedom.[46]   Sin before birth
sent it there, for the transmigration of an immortal soul
was among their tenets.   Herodotus (ii. 123) attributes
to the Egyptians the credit of first teaching the immortality of the soul; and perhaps the doctrine was only incorporated in Orphism after Pythagoras.   It seems that
the full Egyptian doctrine differed in essential particulars
from the Orphic; Egypt appears not to have taught
transmigration; nor is the Orphic doctrine precisely what
we find in Hinduism.   Orphism taught a possibility of
escape on other lines than Rāmānuja's.

If our ancient evidence is indistinct as to dates and
origins, a series of discoveries of small gold tablets buried
with the dead gives us a sure foothold.   In one the soul
of the dead is bidden (in Greek hexameters) to say: "I
am a child of Earth and of Starry Heaven; but my race
is of Heaven.   This ye know yourselves.   And lo, I am
parched with thirst and I perish.   Give me quickly the
cold water flowing forth from the Lake of Memory." [47]
In another, he says:—

"Out of the pure I come, Pure Queen of them below,
Eukles and Eubouleus and the other Gods Immortal,
But I also avow me that I am of your blessed race
But Fate laid me low and the other Gods Immortal,
[Some words omitted by } starflung thunderbolt. [accusative]
the Greek engraver] }

[45] Cf. Eugen Abel, fr. liii. 121, 122, 123, quoted by Adam, *Religious Teachers*, p. 96.   Cf. Aristophanes, *Birds*, 693; Plato, *Timaeus*, 40D; and see passages set out in Diels, *Vorsokratiker*, vol. ii. 66B.
[46] A favourite idea with Plato.
[47] J. E. Harrison, *Prolegomena*, pp. 574 and 586.   Diels, *Fragmente der Vorsokratiker*, vol. ii. No. 66, p. 480.

I have flown out of the sorrowful weary wheel.
I have passed with eager feet to the Circle desired.
I have sunk beneath the bosom of Despoina, Queen of the
    underworld.
I have passed with eager feet from the Circle desired.
Happy and Blessed One, thou shalt be god instead of mortal.
    A kid I have fallen into milk."

Eusebius, in his *Preparation of the Gospel,* and some
other writers quote a poem of Orpheus,[48] which, of whatever date, gives a striking portrayal of Zeus. "Zeus was
the first, Zeus last, lord of the thunder; Zeus head, Zeus
midst.[49] From Zeus all things are made, Zeus was male,
Zeus was the immortal feminine; Zeus foundation of
earth and of the starry sky; Zeus breath of the winds,
Zeus rushing of tireless fire; Zeus root of the sea; Zeus
the sun and the moon; Zeus king; Zeus himself source
of all beginnings. One might, one daimon was he, great
leader of all, one royal body, wherein all these revolve,
fire and water and earth and aether, night and day. And
Wisdom, first begetter, and Eros manifold of delight.
For all these things lie in the mighty body of Zeus";
and so forth.

Let us sum up what we have so far gathered, and
ignore the question as to the part of Pythagoras in
Orphism. Here is a religion linked with most primitive
rites and witnessed to by phenomena quite inexplicable
till explained by modern Psychology—a religion which
teaches a thorough-going pantheism, the divine origin of
the soul and its immortality and deliverance. To find a
parallel we must, I think, go to Hinduism. Orpheus,
whoever he was—Orphism has left the Homeric Zeus
with his golden chain on his Olympus, and teaches another more wonderful, but markedly less personal.

48 Abel, *Orphica,* fr. 123; *Praep. Ev.* iii. 9.
49 The form of the Greek appears to support the idea that Plato quotes this
line, *Laws,* 715E. Cf. Diels, *Vorsokratiker,* ii. 66 B6.

Homer had said that the wrath of Achilles sent many souls of heroes to Hades, but gave *themselves* to dogs and birds. Here the soul is the real thing; and an explanation, perhaps more than one, is offered of its situation and its difficulties in the body along with a clear promise of its release. Life is brought under the discipline of religion to this end; there is ritual, there is rapture and identification with the god; there is ascetic practice and abstinence from animal food. We are not told by the Orphics, as in India, that metempsychosis is the reason for vegetarianism; but a caustic quatrain directed by Xenophanes against Pythagoras helps us to that conclusion.

So the soul is asserting itself; the immortal personality of the man is getting recognised. God is somewhat stripped of his personality, but there is a suggestion of Justice about what is left of him, so far as Pantheism allows or needs him to be just, and so far as emphasis on ritual allows a place for justice. And the Thracian stories witness to the unquestionable reality of the god who inspires the Macnads, and to an effective union with him. The old tribal and local lines of division are growing blurred, this religion is universal and it gives the individual freedom of choice. But there were marked drawbacks about it. It stereotyped the primitive; it emphasised the irrational as the highest manifestation of God; and, whatever it may say about purity and holiness, by its attention to taboo, to ritual, to ascetisicm and the external, it shifted the interest of its worshippers away from the moral law and from the spiritual side of life; and finally, by its myths and its symbolism it militated against clearness of thought. There are those who hold that there was a danger of Orphism swamping Hellenism,[50] as Hinduism has swamped and sterilised Indian

50 Cf. Bury, *Greek History*, p. 316 f.

life and thought; but I do not find evidence for this. Orphism re-emphasised in its way the need of the individual human soul and its instinct for God, its craving to find rest in Him—so much must be conceded—but there is the testimony of Plato and of the greater Christian fathers that the *via prima salutis* is in another direction.

For the time, it is clear that the set of opinion was all for sacraments, initiation and holiness. There was no organised church or priesthood to formulate teaching, to regulate ceremony, or to ordain ministrants; and there was an immense demand for special intercourse with heaven. From what literature we have that bears on the age, we can see how the world began to swarm with priests and prophets, initiating, purifying, and bringing men by private ways to terms with the gods. Old rites were revived, as happens at such times; and often the more savage and primitive they were, the more repulsive and bizarre, the more virtue lay in them. Many of them were disgusting—natural *perhaps* for the savage; but the times were civilised. Then the state stepped in, accepted the new gods and the new notions, the new individualism, and controlled the new rites, as at Athens the Thesmophoria and the Dionysia, and the ceremonies of Eleusis were regularised if not regulated by the governing powers. It recognized *thiasoi, eranoi, orgeônes*—groups of initiates. In historical Athens we do not hear of the Thracian psychopathic phenomena. But the state did not eliminate what may be called the naturalistic element in these cults—the filth and indecency. A state is not often morally ahead of its citizens.

The criticism came from elsewhere. "If it were not in honour of Dionysus," says Heraclitus,[51] "that they were ordering their procession and singing a song of

---

51 Heraclitus, fr. xv.; Diels, *Fragmente der Vorsokratiker*, vol. i. 12B. 15.

phalli (he is more explicit), their conduct would be utterly shameless.   Hades is one with Dionysus, for whom they go mad and celebrate."   "If they are gods," he asked,[52] "why do you mourn for them as dead?   If you mourn for them, count them no longer gods."   So much for living and dead gods and men's worship of them. Xenophanes looked at the legends—"Homer and Hesiod fastened upon the gods everything that is shame and blame among men—theft, adultery and trickery."[53] Xenophanes suggested a question that went deeper yet— "The Ethiopians make the gods flat-nosed and black; the Thracians make them grey-eyed and red-haired"; and cows and horses, no doubt, if they had hands, would make the shapes of the gods like their own.   How are we to conceive of God?   Certainly not, these thinkers would urge, as immoral; certainly not as asking indecency and calling it worship.   The moral sense of Greece had waked and reached manhood.   The story of Greek religion shows extreme reluctance to give up the old rites and the old myths; it turns to them again and again, explains them, apologises, allegorises, but in vain. From Xenophanes and Heraclitus through Plato to the Christians the same indignant reaction is to be traced against associating God in any way with immorality, whatever holy name it wears.

The great gain that the new philosophy brought to Greece was the direct look at the world.   The mystic's mind tends to take a "knight's move;" but whatever may be allowed in chess, neither the bodily nor the spiritual eye can see round a corner; and symbolism is essentially an attempt at that.   The mystic sought to save his soul —to be comfortable about it; but these great pioneers sought truth first.

---

[52] Heraclitus, fr. 127; Diels, *l.c.*, 12B 127, a doubted fragment.
[53] Xenophanes, fr. 11, 16, 15; Diels, *l.c.*, vol. i. 11B.

It is wonderful to realize how great a world these men grasped, over what a range of space and time their minds moved. Xenophanes hit upon the true explanation of the fossils in the Sicilian hills; and Geology may lend a steadying hand to Theology. They meant to know and to understand the universe taken as a whole and as a unity. "Nature tries to hide herself" (fr. 123); and "eyes and ears are bad witnesses to such as have barbarian souls" (fr. 107), said Heraclitus. The harmony of all things will not be obvious; indeed "a hidden harmony is better than an obvious" (fr. 54). But, in any case, underlying the variety of things is unity; and they speculated, with a boldness amazing then or at any time, as to what that unity is. Is water the substance of all things, or fire, or the vaguer "infinite"? They extended the reign of law to all phenomena. Think what a god the sun was; think of the grim, avenging figures of the Erinnyes in art and legend; and then think of this saying of Heraclitus: "The sun will not overstep bounds; but, if he does, the Erinnyes, helpers of Justice, will find him" (fr. 94). We are in another world from that of the Orphic—a world of larger spaces and of air more open; and, as the proverb says, "nothing of all this concerns Dionysus." Anaximander held that "there are created gods, rising and disappearing at long intervals, and that these are the innumerable worlds."[54] Xenophanes, whose caustic criticism we have seen upon the forms of his country's gods, is not only destructive. Four short fragments,[55] perhaps of the same poem, speak of another god than Greece had yet adopted or conceived, though we have had hints of him.

> One God there is 'mid gods and man the greatest,
> In form not like to mortals, nor in mind;—

---

[54] Cicero, *de Nat. Deorum*, i. 25; Adam, *Religious Teachers*, 187.
[55] Xenophanes, fr. 23-6.

He is all eye, all mind, all hearing he;—
He without toil rules all things by his will;—
Ever unmoved, in one place he abideth,
Him it befits not here and there to go.

Points of contact are noted here with Orphism, but the
scorn he poured upon Pythagoras for recognising the
voice of a lost friend in the cry of a beaten dog (fr. 7),
and his quarrel with Epimenides, the professional purifier
from Crete, suggest the same independence of mind that
we find in him throughout.   There has been much controversy about the phrase "greatest among gods"; but
James Adam, using parallels from the Hebrew psalms,
concludes that he meant definitely to affirm the unity of
God in opposition to Homeric polytheism, and that further this God is the visible world, but yet perhaps a personality.

As for the soul of man, "the bounds of soul," said
Heraclitus, "thou couldst not by going discover though
thou didst travel every road; so deep a *logos* hath it"
(fr. 45). *Logos* is one of Heraclitus' chief contributions to philosophy, a cosmic principle, actively intelligent and thinking, and operative in man and in all nature,
rational and divine.   And here he led the way for Plato
and the Stoics, for Philo and the fourth Evangelist.

Now, in conclusion, to survey what we have seen. The
Greek world has travelled far from Homer. Heraclitus
and the philosophers have a new outlook altogether, see
a new world, a world vaster, more ordered, more thinkable, but a world, as they admit, of problems. "Guess
is over all," said Xenophanes (fr. 34). The Orphic has
his philosophy of all existence, but a practical problem
occupies his energies—the management of something
with the gods that will save his own soul and give him
peace. The two groups are looking different ways—not
without some contempt for each other; and from now

onward the endeavour of some of the greatest teachers of Greece is to bring them together. Religion may be reformed; its squalid fears, its sensual sacrifices, its phallic songs and foolish myths and symbols might be swept away—or, if not quite swept away, explained away or toned down. Plato stands for thorough reform, Plutarch for explanation and apology. And Philosophy might be brought to bow the knee to Religion, to find a justification for cult and tradition, to humanise itself to the extent of recognising the poor frail soul of man, unequal to high thought and speculation, full of fears and in desperate need of God or of something it can persuade itself to be God, on which it might lean in its uneasy transits through a world of daemons and dangers. But neither will quite take the trouble to understand the other. The abstract world-soul will not do for the devotee, and "truth or something that might pass for it" revolts the philosopher; the one does not realise the passion for truth and the other hardly grasps the passion for personality in God.

V

EARLIER ISRAEL

THE contrast between Greece and Israel is perhaps nowhere more marked than in the story of their religious development, but certain tendencies are to be traced alike in both. Greece and Israel, each on its own way, knew the impulse to moralise religion and to personalise the divine; both felt the drive to monotheism, both grew more and more conscious of the significance of the individual, and both pursued his story beyond the gates of Hades. The greater, then, the contrasts, the more important is the common experience, the more suggestion too for us, when we find the minds of men so different in race, in outlook and habits of thought, responding in the same way to human experience.

It is some ways a great deal harder to follow the course of the story of Hebrew religion than of Greek, because the history has been confused. The Greeks theorised about their ancient history, but they never deliberately rewrote it. Plato denounced the influence of Homer as a religious teacher, but he never got the *Iliad* and the *Odyssey* expurgated or remodelled. But in Hebrew literature the hand of the reviser is everywhere; nothing escapes him but by accident; and the sound principle that the detail must be explained by the general tenor has been misapplied by the commentator, who failed to remark that his documents were not in anything approaching their original form. Luther, four centuries ago, however, "denied the Mosaic authorship of part of the Pentateuch; he declared *Job* to be an alle-

gory; Jonah was so childish that he was almost inclined
to laugh at it; the books of *Kings* were 'a thousand paces
ahead of *Chronicles* and more to be believed.' *Ecclesiastes* has neither boots nor spurs, but rides in socks, as
I did when I was in the *cloister*." [1] It was two centuries,
however, before Astruc made the suggestions from which
date the modern methods of criticism that have brought
what order is possible into Old Testament History. We
are now taught to recognise four or five hands, where
once that of Moses alone was seen—four or five at least,
with corrections and modifications by more still. I do
not need here to speak in detail of the Jehovist and the
Elohist, whether individuals or schools, the Jehovist's
work completed, as some think, by about 840 B.C., the
Elohist's by about 775 B.C.; nor of the man or men who
fused the two narratives into one. Deuteronomy, which
existed at least in nucleus about 620 B.C., marks a stage
in the religious development of Israel ahead of the other
two. The Priestly Code, which grew in and after the
exile, only concerns us for the purposes of this lecture
in a negative way; we have to beware of the influence of
its authors in every quotation we make. For, last of all,
by men of letters or by school, the great combination
that we know as the Pentateuch was formed of all these
very diverse materials—and, fortunately for the modern
scholar, the work was not very efficiently done. Com-
pilers and harmonisers are not apt to do their work well;
if they had the literary sense needed for their task, they
would have as a rule the instinct to be doing something
else.

One tendency marks all the documents with which we
have to deal—a tendency with two distinct features.
We, all of us, unconsciously re-create the past in the
light of the present, import the present into the past and

1 Preserved Smith, *Life and Letters of M. Luther*, p. 268.

find the ideas of to-day operative there, see our own convictions in our spiritual ancestors and our political and
religious opponents in those who opposed them. This is
natural, and it is more legitimate than some historians
allow, for the past was at least once alive, and its greater
minds were in fact more modern than contemporaries
could imagine, or than matter-of-fact historians understand. On the other hand, controversy always seeks
weapons from the armoury of the past, and a great point
is made when it is shown, or even asserted, that the innovation of which our opponents complain is "the oldest
rule in the book." Hebrew history was re-written with
a purpose, and it was profoundly altered. "See," writes
Wellhausen, "what *Chronicles* has made out of David!
The founder of the kingdom has become the founder of
the temple and the public worship, the king and hero at
the head of his companions in arms has become the singer
and master of ceremonies at the head of a swarm of
priests and Levites; his clearly-cut figure has become a
feeble holy picture, seen through a cloud of incense. . . .
He has had now to place his music at the service of the
cultus and write psalms along with Asaph, Heman and
Jeduthun, the Levitical singing families." [2]

Disentangling the history as best we can, with the help
of modern scholarship, the main movements become
fairly clear for us. The detail, as ever in stories of
religious development, is often very far from clear.
Words, as we have seen, even when we have no doubt
of their authenticity, are ambiguous witnesses. Here we
are always haunted with the doubt as to whether our witnesses are personated. But still, when we take a survey
of centuries together, the main points stand out; and it
is these that we want.

The Greeks, as we saw, in obedience to a universal

2 *Prolegomena*, p. 182.

instinct personalised their gods; and under the stress of
what seems a necessity of thought they moved toward
some sort of ultimate monotheism; but almost in proportion as their god grew to be One, he lost personality and
sank into being a principle. Here is the first and perhaps
the most striking contrast with Israel. The Hebrew
moved much more definitely, and it would seem more
naturally and at an earlier stage, to monotheism; and
with each step—till we reach the end of the prophetic
period—the personality of Jehovah grew more distinct,
more individual, and more intensely real and significant
for every worshipper. The Greek monotheist was a
philosopher and in intellectual habit an aristocrat; he
never believed that the people could take in the conception of One God or that they would be content with it
if they did. He conceded polytheism to the vulgar and
with it idolatry—with the result that his monotheism remained a paradox or an irrelevancy, a discussion of the
schools, not a conviction of the market-place. When the
Greek philosopher became Christian, he carried his habit
with him—and, convinced that the vulgar would never
be satisfied with One God, he once more conceded a
practical polytheism in the worship of the saints; and
heathen Artemis yielded her functions to her own geni-
tive case transformed into Saint Artemidos.[3] So the
world saw the religion of Jesus infected with image-
worship. The Hebrew monotheist was a man of the
people, even when he was a priest or a land-owner. One
of the most striking of the prophets was a herdsman.
The Hebrew, then, assumed that his people could perfectly well take in the idea of One God, and he was
proved right by the history of Israel and even more
remarkably by the history of Islam. So far from mono-

---

3 Hamilton, *Incubation*, p. 174; J. T. Bent, "Researches among the Cyclades"
(*Journal of Hellenic Studies*, v. p. 46).

theism being unintelligible to the vulgar, it becomes a glorifying and ennobling passion; there is no god but God, and Muhammad and countless millions are his prophets, fervid and clear, every one of them. And with Hebrew monotheism there developed a hatred of idolatry. When the Hebrew became Christian his new religion saw him still a passionate monotheist, a hater of idols; and wherever a genuine pulse of the Old Testament religion still beats in Christendom, there is the monotheist still, uncompromising.

On the other hand, the contrast is only less surprising between the Greek and the Hebrew in their views of the individual man. One might well have expected to find Egyptian influences potent in Hebrew religion; but where Egyptian thought and usage laid most emphasis the Hebrew laid none at all. The elaborate care which the Egyptian took of the dead, the mummy, the "Book of the Dead," the pyramid—they all point back to a theory, a conviction of a personal immortality; and the Hebrew is hardly interested in it at all. We are told that there are only four clear allusions to immortality in the Old Testament; stranger still, none of them is in Jeremiah, and Jeremiah was as individual and self-conscious as Archilochus or Sappho, and the interest of his life centred in his personal relations with Jehovah. Eventually the idea of immortality developed, as we see in Apocalyptic literature, but how late, when we think of the Homeric hymn to Demeter, of the mysteries of Eleusis and of Plato's *Phaedo*!

I know of no explanation for these contrasts. Renan once spoke of a primitive Semitic tendency to monotheism; but that is no explanation, it is a mere restatement of our problem—to say nothing of the verdict of modern and perhaps less rhetorical scholars that it

cannot be maintained.[4] The historian, confronted with
the Hebrew prophets, turns almost by instinct to the
earlier history of Israel to find at least the germs of their
amazing monotheism. He will ask: What is the origin
of this Jehovah? What makes him so different from
Chemosh, the god of Moab? In view of Greek and
Hindu amalgamations of their gods, how could this God
escape being swamped among the Baals of Canaan, and
identified with them? We know that there was at times
a strong probability that this would happen; and it did
not happen; but why? An Egyptian king, Amen Hotep
IV (Ikhn-Aton), established a very remarkable monotheism as the state religion of Egypt, and it lasted till
the end of his reign and was gone; the Egyptian people
would not have it.[5] Why would Israel have Jehovah?
To reply that Jehovah began as their own tribal god is
not to answer the question (cf. p. 46). Athene was
perhaps the cantonal goddess of Athens, but she did not
keep out Dionysus or dozens of other gods either. Why
did the monotheistic worship of Jehovah capture Israel?
Why, to put the question differently, were there
always monotheists in Israel, enthusiasts for Jehovah?
And finally, why and how did Jehovah manage to remain
so personal, when Zeus became a dogma, an abstract
noun? It is again not a complete answer to say that
there were many Zeus-es, each so personal, that, when
they were all fused, the resultant Zeus was impossible,
a negation of all decency. Jehovah was not fused with
other gods; he annihilated them; and slowly the people
of Judah recognised this. The wonder is that it happened at all.

Of course, it is clear that the agents by whom all

[4] G. A. Barton, *Semitic Origins*, p. 321.
[5] See the interesting chapter (with the King's hymns) in Breasted, *History of the Ancient Egyptians*.

was achieved with the prophets. Then they have to be explained, and I find a Semitic scholar of note conclude a long and learned research into Semitic origins with the admission that "the moral standards of the prophets and their conceptions of God are utterly unaccounted for by their environment." [6] The explanations which I have seen attempted seem to me to fail in two ways: they rest a great deal too much on conjecture; and their authors do not appear to realise that it is a question of dynamic, and they offer nothing with force or life enough in it to be the real source of what we have to explain. This is not to dispute their reconstructions, I am not qualified to do that; they may be right in every particular; but the sum of their particulars seems to me to omit just what I want to find. I am not prepared with a hypothesis myself; in the Cambridge caste to which I belong, to advance a great theory outcastes a man, and though I should, I hope, be ready for that, it could only be when I am a great deal surer of my ground. At present I do not propound a theory; but even my caste allows me to ask myself a question.

When we reach the prophets, the question of Moses at once rises; it rises, and, like so many more, it waits an answer. The modern student must often echo the cry of the Israelites: "As for this Moses, we wot not what is become of him" (Ex. iii. 21). Once he was as clear and well-known a figure as Agamemnon; but since then, like Agamemnon, he has had his very existence doubted. To-day, however, scholars in a good many fields incline to accept the existence of the great law-givers of the peoples; perhaps even Lycurgus, stripped of every legend, may struggle into history again. We have at least to ask what may be said of Moses and his work that will stand the test of historical criticism.

[6] G. A. Barton, *Semitic Origins*, p. 306.

The Hebrews believed that they owed their escape
from Egypt and the foundations of their religion to
Moses, and to these modern scholars add the beginnings
of the nation. Moses, they suggest, gave the various
tribes—some of them—the beginnings of that process
which saw them for two reigns a united people. So
much would probably be conceded in the case of a nation
known to what used to be called secular history. The
book of Deuteronomy, dated about 621 B.C., implies a
very strong tradition; but if the date of Moses is about
1300 B.C., we have a long gap to fill. Working back, we
find Elijah about 850 B.C., who does not indeed mention
Moses, but whose story implies what is really of more
concern to us, a sense that for Israel to worship another
god instead of Jehovah is a national apostasy. As the
habit of worshipping other gods along with Jehovah was
an ingrained temptation with the Hebrew people, we are
carried back a good deal farther. The narratives of
Jehovists and Elohists which tell of Moses are dated 300
years after his death.[7] Working downward, we find in
Judges (xviii. 30) the adventures of a grandson of
Moses—adventures so discreditable to the descendant of
the founder of the religion as later conceived, that, while
we can understand the quiet emendation of the grandfather's name, the improbability and unsuitability of the
grandson's conduct go some way to guarantee the grandfather. It is what a modern scholar in another field
would call a "pillar-text." The foundation seems a slight
one; but we have to remember that epochs of thought
and epochs of national life are normally the work of
some significant man, of some hero, as Carlyle called
him; and in this story we have both kinds of epoch associated with a name, embedded firmly in national memory.
Despite the case of Persia, which forgot the Achaemenids,

7 J. P. Peters, *Religion of Hebrews*, 85.

this weighs a good deal with scholars. Moses may well leave Agamemnon in the limbo where Odysseus found him and come back into History—not as the hero of a hundred episodes, but as a national hero of long ago, who gave a people a new consciousness of itself and a new sense of relation to its god.

The god was Jehovah, and he is associated with the tradition of the exodus from Egypt; but whose god Jehovah was before that, or what his relation to Israel, is disputed. The Old Testament, as it stands modelled to ultimate Jewish orthodoxy, refers Jehovah's first dealings with Israel back to Abraham; but Abraham raises more problems than we need wait to solve, and scholars to-day emphasise some curious passages in Exodus. The Elohist and the Priestly Code narrate that the God who spoke to Moses told him that he had not previously been known by the name Jehovah; [8] the patriarchs had known him as El-Shaddai, and the Elohist says (Joshua xxiv. 14) that in Egypt the Israelites were idolaters. It is maintained, too, with some plausibility, that Jehovah was the god of the Kenites, into which tribe Moses married (Ex. xviii.), and that Heber the Kenite "officiated as though introducing Moses into a new cult"; and the covenant between Israel and Jehovah follows. For centuries Sinai was regarded as the home of Jehovah, far away from his people's land, from which mountain he swept down to aid them in battle, as the ancient poem of Deborah tells us. The Kenites, moreover, to the south of Judah remained loyal to old ways of the desert, to old religion, down to the day of Jeremiah (xxxv.), and they had lent a hand to Jehu in the extirpation of Baal-worship in Northern Israel (2 Kings x. 15). Though conscious of a distinct descent, they were reckoned as in Judah;

8 G. A. Barton, *Semitic Origins*, p. 276; E in Ex. iii. 13 f.; P in Ex. vi. 2 f.; J. P. Peters, *Religion of the Hebrews*, p. 89; Budde, *Religion of Israel*, p. 13 ff.

and the Jehovist document, which is supposed to be of Judaean origin, shows no consciousness of Jehovah-worship being anything but primeval. Jehovah was a god of war, and he carried the people covenanted with him to victory; and so began the great development which we find on far loftier heights in the prophets.

Such is the reconstruction of modern scholarship, not indeed unchallenged, but strongly supported.[9] I am not competent to offer an opinion on its value, and happily it is not of first importance to us to determine if Moses or Abraham first realised Jehovah. Here as with the Greeks, and as Aristotle pointed out, the end is the explanation of the beginning and of more consequence. Nor need we spend time on the Decalogue of Moses; that he was a law-giver is the tradition of Israel, and there is no improbability in this. Whether he had reached the stage to give his people the familiar Decalogue, has been much debated. It is pointed out that it comes in the Elohist's section (Ex. xx.), while an alternative decalogue is given by the Jehovist (Ex. xxxiv.), a series of commandments dealing much more with ritual and much less with ethics, and therefore more likely to be primitive. The second commandment, "Thou shalt make thee no molten gods," seems a protest against luxurious and costly images rather than a prohibition of all images whatever. In any case Hebrew religion took a long time in reaching the observance of this law.

Little need be said here of the origins of the Hebrew people. They hardly concern us, except as showing the strange and confused elements from which a nation may arise; and it may be noted that such fragments of fact as we get do not throw much light on the early history of Jehovah. Among the Tel-el-Amarna tablets [10] (which

9 See G. A. Barton, *Semitic Origins*, p. 275.
10 Cf. G. A. Barton, *op. cit.*, p. 273 f.; Budde, *op. cit.*, p. 5; Skinner, *Genesis*, p. xvi.

are written in Babylonian script, and are dated about
1400 B.C.) are some letters of Abdikheba of Jerusalem,
which tell of people called Khabiri invading Canaan.
There are references to Egyptian over-lordship over a
crowded land full of walled towns of Babylonian culture
and full of war—not such a land of pastoral spaces as
we had pictured from the story of Abraham and Isaac.
We learn also of places called Jakob-el and Joseph-el.
A stele of the Egyptian king Meren-Ptah (discovered
by Flinders Petrie in 1896) places Israel among enemies
whom the king destroyed in Palestine—roughly about
the date of the exodus.   These fragments of fact are
a little difficult to adjust to the Pentateuch as it stands.
Possibly the Khabiri were not the Hebrews, but a tribe
of the same type.   In Greek history we have odd and
perplexing hints of tribes and peoples, whose numbers
and movements we do not know, engaged in war and
migration about the Aegean lands, and at last Homer
comes out of the confusion.   So it is with these Hebrews;
their origins we do not know (what people's origins do
we know?), and then we find them in Palestine, more
or less masters of the country—tribes of perhaps various
stocks, but not incapable of settling down into a common
race, as Angles, Jutes, Saxons, Celts and Danes made
English.   Some at least of the tribes had been in Egypt,
and had come triumphantly away.   Gad was at once the
name of one of the tribes and of the Aramaean and
Phoenician god of Luck; A'sher may be a divine name
or a place-name.   As sometimes happens in such matters,
the twelve tribes are a little difficult to adjust, as the
number is obviously an arbitrary one, and at least thirteen tribes formed Israel.   Our oldest documents upon
the tribes are the Song of Deborah, which is contemporary with the events it describes, and the Blessing of
Jacob, which is old and obscure but belongs to a period

centuries later than the date of Jacob, if he had a date at all.

So far we have been moving in a world only dimly revealed to us in fragments and guesses; but when Israel, in some general sense of the name, enters Canaan, we find some agreement among our guides, Jehovist, Elohist, the author of the Priestly Code, and the modern scholars. Not about everything—not about Joshua, nor even David, but about that struggle between the worship of Jehovah and the cults of Palestine which ended in the victory of prophetic religion. It is agreed that now the issue was whether Jehovah was to be merged among the gods of the land. Whether he was known to Abraham first or to Moses does not greatly matter; nor if neither of them knew him at all. The period before us shows a people who do know Jehovah, but are uncertain so far as to his position and his character.

Scholars have little difficulty in giving us the general outlines of Semitic religion, and much that they tell us is found far beyond the range of Semites. The great literature of Babylon, the archaeological remains of Canaan, reveal peoples akin to this Israel which now concerns us. There are great differences among them in culture, and some in outlook, as a result of their different experiences in settlement and wandering. Life in the desert differentiates a tribe from its agricultural or town-dwelling kindred; and their religions will show the reaction of the circumstances. Israel's religion, by its separation and desert-life, had, we gather, escaped some features which had developed in Canaan. But now Israel was to live in Canaan, and the conquest was such a conquest as, we are gradually learning, generally accompanies a settlement in a new land. The Achaean did not exterminate the "Mediterranean race," nor the Saxon the Celt, nor the Norman the Saxon, nor the

Spaniard the Inca. In every case it was amalgamation,
slower or quicker; and in Canaan, we learn, it was amalgamation. The Deuteronomist, six hundred years later,
represents Moses as inculcating extermination just as he
represents him emphasising worship in that place alone
which the Lord shall choose; [11] but in both cases he is
re-moulding history nearer to his heart's desire. Inter-
marriages, it is evident, if only from the story of Ruth,
were frequent, and that is a constant source of religious
change. Intermarriage went on down to the days of
Nehemiah. And when the stock of religious ideas on
both sides comprised so many held in common, the wonder grows that the religion of Jehovah was not swamped
altogether.

Semitic religion covered a wide range of beliefs and
superstitions and practices.[12]   The Semites, like other
primitive peoples worshipped the dead (cf. Deut. xxvi.
14), sacred stones, sacred trees, sacred wells, sacred animals, and spirits of all sorts—of birth and disease, of
the house and the desert. They honoured the objects
of their devotion with sprinkled blood, by circumcision,
by offerings of milk and hair, by kissing,[13] by feasts,
and sometimes by human sacrifices. A story, thrown
back into patriarchal times, tells how in the persons of
Abraham and Isaac God forbade human sacrifice.
Scholars generally agree that this rite is not strictly
primitive, and is more prevalent among the semi-civilised
than among savages. It rests on several beliefs—*e.g.*
that the gods want attendants, or are appeased by the
death of a wrongdoer, or that they like human flesh; and
the rite becomes a form of insurance, in war, in famine,
in time of plague, and it recurs in history when trouble
gets past a certain point. Children were buried under

11 Deut. xii. 5.
12 See Addis, *Hebrew Religion;* Marti, *Religion of O. T.,* p. 80 ff.
13 1 Kings xix. 18.

foundation stones, as the archaeologists have shown.

Canaan was no new-found land; it had been long inhabited, and it was like such lands, full of holy places. "Bethel and Beersheba, Dan and Gilgal, were the principal, but Mizpeh, the top of Tabor, and Carmel, perhaps Penuel, were also conspicuous among the countless *high places* of the land." [14] Gilgals were many—ancient stone-circles, and Mizpehs, which were watch-towers, seers' stations. Beth-el was a house of God, Beersheba had a sacred well, where Abraham planted a "grove" (or tamarisk: Gen. xxi. 33) ; and all over the land were standing stones, at Shechem, Gilead, Gibeah, En-rogel and elsewhere—Massebas—at once altar and idol in one,[15] perhaps at last a god's abode. And groves and sacred trees meet us at every turn, till the prophet indignantly declares that there is idolatry "under every green tree"—much as we see it in India still. When a place is once holy, it is apt to remain holy. There are Moslem holy-places in Asia Minor which have been Christian and were heathen before that. Invaders, like the Israelites, take over such places—*cromlechs,* holy wells, pillars, trees and graves, from the people they conquer, and take with them the cult and ritual of each place. Sometimes the suggestions of the place are changed to suit the ideas and preconceptions of the newcomers. Sometimes it is the other way. The Elohist writes of Bethel and other places, sacred to the mind of Northern Israel, and gives them new legends; his story of Bethel is a beautiful one, but Bethel must long have been a holy place (Luz, Judges i. 23). But long before the legends were re-made, Israel took over shrine and cult, and the thoughts of the god that went with the cult. "Even the technical terms connected with sacrifice were in great

14 G. A. Smith, *Twelve Prophets,* i. p. 37 f.
15 W. Robertson Smith, *E. R. S.,* p. 205 ff.

part identical. The vow, the whole burnt-offering, the thank-offering, the meat-offering, and a variety of other details appear on the tablet of Marseilles and similar Phoenician documents under their familiar Old Testament names, showing that the Hebrew ritual was not a thing by itself, but had a common foundation with that observed by their neighbours." [16]

Every holy place had its Baal, or lord, the god who gave the land its fertility, to whom therefore was due the tribute of first-fruits and worship along the lines of the fertility he gave.[17] This, too, Israel took over, and learnt under the name of holiness an uncleanness he had not known in the desert. Temple harlots are a feature of Semite religion, as of Hinduism, and a prohibition in Deuteronomy (xxiii. 17) is a sure sign that Israel knew them—temple harlots and worse, and all in the worship of God. *Qedesha*—dedicated or "holy woman" —is a tell-tale word. It was one of the iniquities associated with religion against which Amos and Hosea inaugurated the protest.[18] Jerusalem was a new shrine, but the power of the influence of Canaanite and Phoenician religion is seen in the things that Josiah did away with in his reformation—vessels dedicated to Baal, priests who burned incense to Baal, to sun and moon and planets, and all the host of heaven, the "grove" or sacred trees, the sodomites, the horses of the sun, and all sorts of altars and images, and "he defiled Topheth which is in the valley of the children of Hinnom, that no man might make his son or his daughter pass through the fire to Molech" (2 Kings xxiii. 4-14). The later associations of the names Tophet and Gehenna have thus some historical justification. The history as we have it tells us that other kings before Josiah made similar clear-

16 Robertson Smith, *Prophets,* p. 56.
17 Robertson Smith, *E. R. S.,* p 94 ff.
18 G. A. Smith, *Twelve Prophets,* i. p. 259; Amos ii. 7; Hosea iv. 13.

ances, and the evils came back, as they seem to have done after Josiah's reformation too,[19] in honour of the Queen of Heaven.

It may well be asked how in such an atmosphere the religion of Jehovah was to survive; or if the truer question be, how was it to emerge, it is no easier to answer. The problem, age after age, is to find a religion that will avail for a world in flux—a religion which will safeguard mankind against its own old impulses, freer, it would seem, age by age by the wearing down of old sanctions, and stronger as every generation grows more conscious of power and of individuality. A fixed religion for a world of change is not the wisest thing; for a religion must keep pace with the demands upon it, and these grow greater as man realises himself. Here, then, was a people stepping from the desert into a comparatively old civilisation with a religion which we may call older still. The temple harlot was perhaps the last squalid memorial of a social morality long outgrown. Canaanite and Babylonian had reached the conception of the sanctity of marriage, if their gods and goddesses had not; for them religion was no longer a force purifying life, it was corrupting it, and giving the sanction of God's name to vices that revolted decent thinking men and women and that tended to make human society impossible. The effect of it upon newcomers must have been twofold—to fascinate and to repel; but it was the way of the gods of the land.

Israel by entering Canaan transformed themselves to an agricultural people; and their religious festivals changed their character to meet the new situation. It is not sound to say that the desert promoted monotheism, but the cultivated land at least made the complexity of life greater and introduced men to new fields

19 H. P. Smith, O. T. History, p. 336.

of wonder and reflection. But Canaan, as we have seen, was no mere prairie-land; it had known the neighbourhood of two great lands of culture—Babylonian and Egyptian had already fought over its length, and had sought to possess or to control it; for, apart from anything it had of its own, it was the pathway to regions of more importance. When the armies ceased to waste it, the traders would follow—ministers of change no less potent. Philistines, too, had come from Caphtor, as the Old Testament tells—not the barbarians suggested by the German slang which Matthew Arnold naturalised, but, as we should expect of people coming from prehistoric Crete, and as archaeologists now assure us, a race with a culture of their own, and a religion which gave them an epithet of distinction from the Semites. If David's ancestress was a Moabite woman, his early associates and his guards to the end were Philistine. Solomon married an Egyptian princess, and other foreigners after her. Eighty years after Solomon's death, Ahab married a princess of Tyre and fought against the Assyrian at the battle of Karkar (854 B.C.). New modes of domestic life, the field instead of the desert, intercourse with the city-folk of Canaan and Philistia, *Weltpolitik* involving them with Egypt, with Tyre, with Syria and Assyria—all these things make for comparison, for criticism, and for change. If Israel brought a pure or even a potential monotheism into Canaan from the desert, it was bound to be tested fiercely in the surroundings, and in spite of the Kenites it is almost certain that any tendencies that Israel had toward monotheism were as yet faint and undeveloped.

Jehovah, we are told, would hardly have demanded exclusive worship. He was the god of the federation, and there would be gods of the home. If there was a Decalogue at all in those days, whether the command-

ment forbade molten images only or all images molten
and graven and every other kind, the accepted story
makes it clear that there were images none the less, and
plenty of them, public and private. If Moses' degenerate
grandson—though there is no suggestion in the tale that
he was so reckoned—was an apostate from his grandfather's religion when he ministered to the *teraphim,* or
graven image, stolen from Micah and set up in Dan
(Judges xviii. 30, 31), David at least is a hero of Jewish
story, and in his house was another *teraphim,* of considerable size, and mistakable, in a bed, for the hero himself (1 Sam. xix. 13). In the eighth century the Elohist
tells how Rachel, the ancestress, stole her father's
teraphim and sat on them to prevent his recovering
them; and she incurs no censure (Gen. xxxi. 19), even
if they are to be counted as among the "strange gods"
put away a little later (Gen. xxxv. 24). These all look
like private gods, gods of a family.

It is more startling when we realise that, in spite of
the familiar denunciations of Jeroboam, the son of
Nebat, who "made Israel to sin" by setting up golden
"calves" at Bethel and at Dan and making "priests of
the lowest of the people which were not of the tribe of
Levi," [20] it was in reality long before any feeling mani-
fested itself that it was unsuitable to worship Jehovah in
the form of a bull. "The state worship of the golden
calves led to no quarrel between Elisha and the dynasty
of Jehu; and this one fact is sufficient to show that, even
in a time of notable revival, the living power of the religion was not felt to lie in the principle that Jehovah
cannot be represented by images." [21] The Elohist takes
pains to associate Bethel, the seat of this "calf" worship,
with Jacob the founder of the race and with his God.

20 1 Kings xii. 31.
21 Robertson Smith, *Prophets,* p. 63; cf. J. P. Peters, *Religion of the Hebrews,* p. 100.

What is more surprising is that Amos himself, though he denounced the cult at Bethel, did not accuse Israel on the score of idolatry or polytheism, or suggest that in this way they had really apostatised from the true God's revelation of himself.[22] Hosea, some years later, appears to be the first prophet to denounce idolatry.[23] Jeroboam himself, according to the story, called his son Abijah— "Jehovah-is-his-father"—a name which does not suggest conscious apostasy; so that it is possible to accept the suggestion that he was moved by zeal for the God of Israel when he dedicated to him images in accord with the accepted symbolism of the times.[24]

We need not give too facile a belief to the orthodox Jewish account of Jeroboam's priests. It bears the mark of controversy, and there is little to show that they were much worse or any better than other priests of a people at that stage of culture. The evolution of the priest is an interesting theme. The patriarchs generally did without priests, unless Melchizedek's kingship is secondary to his priesthood. Saul, David and Solomon built altars and sacrificed for themselves; and Samuel, priest or prophet, was an Ephraimite, not a Levite. The Hebrew priests, we are told, were primarily seers; they interpreted oracles and consulted Jehovah on behalf of his people, and revealed his will in *Tôrôth*—and his will bore directly upon every form of calamity. Urim and Thummim are not very lucid words to us to-day, but a hint of their use lies behind the text of 1 Sam. xiv. 42, implied by the Septuagint. "O Jehovah, God of Israel," prays Saul, "wherefore hast thou not answered thy servant this day? If the iniquity be in me or in Jonathan my son, O Jehovah God of Israel, give Urim; and if it

---

22 H. P. Smith, *O. T. History*, p. 215.
23 I find it hard to trace an allusion to the Decalogue in his words, Hosea iv. 1, 2.
24 H. P. Smith, *O. T. History*, p. 181.

be in thy people Israel, give, I pray thee, Thummim."
But the day came when Jehovah answered Saul "neither
by dreams, nor by Urim nor by prophets" (1 Sam. xxviii.
6); and Urim and Thummim become the right of priest
and Levite—"and of Levi he said, Let thy Thummim and
thy Urim be with thy holy one" (Deut. xxxiii. 8).
There were of course other ways of learning the gods'
will—the flight of birds or the whisper of the trees.
The priests were, naturally, in charge of the shrines—
Canaanite shrines, as we have seen—and of the ark while
it existed, and at an early date we can see the beginnings
of their insistence on privilege; they claimed a part of
the sacrifice (1 Sam. ii. 13-16), and eventually a
monopoly of the right to sacrifice, till at last, as sacrifice
came to fill a larger place in religion, the priest became
central in religion. Ceremony and ritual were in his
hands, and he "taught for hire" (Micah iii. 11). When
we reflect upon all this, and remember his associates at
many of the shrines, the *Qedesha* and her like, we shall
not expect to find in the priesthood the impulse that
transformed Jehovism into the purest and most fervent
of monotheisms. Broadly speaking, we find all over the
world that the priest's business is rather the maintenance
of established beliefs and the performance of accepted
rituals than the development of fresh aspects of religious
truth. That is left for the prophets, but not for all of
them.

For even in those earlier times Israel had prophets—
Nebi'im—and in some considerable numbers. A story
of the reign of Ahab numbers the prophets of one god
and another by hundreds (1 Kings xviii.). The Deu-
teronomic prohibition of "any one that useth divination,
or an observer of times, or an enchanter, or a witch, or
a charmer, or a consulter with familiar spirits, or a
wizard, or a necromancer" (Deut. xviii. 10, 11), coupled

not insignificantly with "any one that maketh his son or
his daughter to pass through the fire," tells a tale in its
negative.   There were such people—men who, as Robertson Smith puts it, had on the physical side of their
being relations with the godhead—"in the mysterious
instincts of their lower nature, in paroxysms of arti-
ficially produced frenzy, dreams and diseased visions." [25]
The words of Balaam picture the type: "Balaam the son
of Beor hath said, and the man whose eyes are open hath
said: he hath said, which heard the words of God, which
saw the vision of the Almighty, falling down but having
his eyes open" (Num. xxiv. 3, 4); and the narrative tells
us that he spoke after "the spirit of God came to him."
By ventriloquism the wizards made those who consulted
them hear, or think they heard, the voice of ghosts rising
from the world of the dead (1 Sam. xxviii.; Isa. xxix.
4); and they were paid for their trouble.   Saul consults
Samuel as to lost asses, and has a quarter shekel ready
for him (1 Sam. ix. 8).   There is nothing peculiar to
the Semites in all this; it is found all over the world, a
potent agency for fraud and cruelty.

When all their neighbours knew *Nebi'im*, it is not to
be supposed that Israel could be ignorant, even before
the entry into Palestine.   Of that period our records are
slight and uncertain, but when History begins to speak
with clearer utterance, we find the first king of Israel
powerfully affected by the *Nebi'im* associated with Jehovah.   More than once we read how the sight of them
prophesying worked upon him: "the spirit of God was
upon him also, and he went on and prophesied, until he
came to Naioth in Ramah.   And he stripped off his
clothes also, and prophesied before Samuel in like manner, and lay down naked all that day and all that night,"
king of Israel as he was (1 Sam. xix. 23).   It is plain

25 *O. T. J. C.,* p. 285.

from the narrative of Saul's life that he was mentally
unstable; and insanity is still associated by the Arabs
with a peculiar relation to God. One of the most brilliant of English explorers in Arabia, it is said, owed a
good deal to the Arabs supposing him to be mad. Music
in Saul's case, and in Elisha's, is mentioned as having
a powerful influence on the man's state. The prophet
who anointed Jehu made the impression on Jehu's
friends of a "mad fellow" (2 Kings ix. 11), though they
quickly accepted his suggestion. Professor D. B. Macdonald's friendly account of modern dervishes in Egypt
gives a picture closely parallel,[26] and makes it clear that
sincerity is or may be an element in this form of approach to the unseen. Muhammad, he points out, was
himself a pathological case, and his revelations came to
him in trance; like all trance-mediums he had strangely
perverted ideas, but an impostor he certainly was not—
not at least till the last ten years of his life.[27] He compares the actions of the dervishes, whom he saw, with
the tumultuous shrieking, leaping and crying aloud upon
their god by the priests of Baal and the cutting themselves with knives; and adds, "it was all perfectly
genuine." [28] More strangely, a convert to Christianity
told him that there had been a certain element of spiritual
advantage in it all—"then I was a saint; but now I am
a Christian," he concluded—"with a plainly regretful
if also humorous tone in his voice." [29]

We may form our own opinions of the spiritual value
of such practices—the East is against the West on this
question, but the East's interest in it has been less scientific, because the East has accepted possession and trance
as direct evidence of contact with God and has not com-

26 *Aspects of Islam*, Lectures V. and VI.
27 *Ibid.*, pp. 72, 74.
28 *Ibid.*, p. 95.
29 *Ibid.*, pp. 170-172.

pared or cross-examined its witnesses. If I am right in accepting the view (to which I think the bulk of the evidence—all the evidence—leads a candid mind) that in every case of trance or mystical state a man becomes conscious of what he has met before, and in no case gains fresh facts or fresh knowledge—however much he maintains that to see the old in a new way is to make a new discovery—then we may conclude that the *Nebi'im* of Jehovah depended upon suggestions that had reached them in their normal state, and we may draw something from our conclusion. The heightening which trance gave to their conception of Jehovah, trance gave also to the conceptions that others have had of Baal, of Kali, of the Virgin Mary—the same heightening, the same conviction, with this result that we must look elsewhere for the real values.

The *Nebi'im* of Jehovah were saved from morbidness, we are told, by their enthusiasm for Israel;[30] but probably, if we knew more, we might find the same nationalism among the *Nebi'im* of Chemosh, only with Moab for its centre. National feeling is not always a sure guarantee of sanity or of truth. *Nebi'im* play a large part in public affairs in Hebrew history, advising and deposing kings, urging to revolt, to murder and to war. The real progress of religious thought, however, will come from the stable rather than the unstable; or if a man is both by turns, as sometimes happens, it will come from Paul when he is *not* speaking with tongues.

Something the *Nebi'im* must have done, as the Orphics, so like them in Greece, did. They detached religion in some degree from its established sanctuaries and from its officials; they bore a confused and doubtful witness to Jehovah—doubtful, for Baal had witness as good, and they kept alive the tradition of a national wor-

30 G. A. Smith, *The Twelve*, i. p. 25.

ship, of a national god, of which saner heads were to
make a great deal more.

Man was wrestling already with the problems that
always face him. Baal was clearly obsolete in his morals;
a normal man would not wish his own wife or daughters
to be attached to Baal's shrine, whatever a desperate
man might do; and what people in desperation about
children will vow in India, we know. Let us stick to
the normal man. He thinks out moral problems quietly,
and one day he will be ready for a great lead, he will
follow a new prophet who, on the basis of moral sense,
proclaims a revolution in religious thought. Religion
in old Israel had its usual varieties—it was local, national, liturgical, ceremonial; it was merry-making before
the Lord; and here and there it was personal. The spirit
of Jehovah came upon a man—sometimes through the
influence of a prophet band—sometimes in solitude; and
where the man was strongly founded on ethical thought
and observation, both morality and Jehovah-worship
gained by it. Jehovah so far had little to say or to
suggest about a world beyond the gates of Death; it
was very long before Jehovism looked so far. Jehovah,
again, was admittedly a god among gods; every people
had its god, its Chemosh or its Dagon. Israel had Jehovah, though he, unlike some of these gods, had his
seat, not in the land which he gave to his people, but
away upon Sinai. One thing more we can say of Jehovah even at this early period which we have not evidence to let us say of the other gods. His cult was not
inconsistent with the moral development of his people.
The abominations of religion which we have noticed
might be incorporated in his worship, but they belonged
elsewhere more properly. Michal's indignation at
David's ecstatic dancing before the ark [31] is a hint of

31 2 Sam. vi. 20.

a change of mind coming over the Hebrews—curiously, here, on the women's side, for in religion the pioneers have been most usually men.

Our inquiry has not taken us very far. The future of the world's religion lay with Israel, but Israel had not so far realised Jehovah. That was to come, and its coming is as mysterious as all the deepest things in man's story. Meanwhile Jehovah wakes a real poetry in his people and gives a promise of greater days. Then sang Deborah [32] :—

I, even I, will sing unto Jehovah.
I will sing praise to Jehovah, the God of Israel.
Jehovah, when thou wentest out of Seir,
When thou marchedst out of the field of Edom,
The earth trembled, the heavens also dropped,
Yea, the clouds dropped water.
The mountains flowed down at the presence of Jehovah,
Even yon Sinai at the presence of Jehovah, the God of
      Israel. . . .
O my soul, march on with strength.

[32] Judges v.

VI

THE HEBREW PROPHETS

ISRAEL began with the two old Semitic convictions about his God—that Jehovah was the God of Israel, to stand or fall with Israel and involved in maintaining Israel—and that Jehovah's religion was essentially one of ceremonial, of rites and sacrifices, and that when these received due attention, all was well in a normal way.[1] There might be searchings of heart in days of darkness, but religion was a clear and straightforward thing, and normally a happy and cheerful affair, its centre a jollification with the God. If there was, as we are sometimes told, a bias toward the ethical in Jehovism from the beginning, so there is, we observe, in every religion where the religious reflect upon life and experience. The real interest of the Old Testament for the modern student lies not in the evidence it offers of yet another people with a religion of a common type—national, ceremonial and sacramental—but in the emergence of men who protest generation by generation against the beliefs of their countrymen, and who, though an insignificant and unpopular minority, compel their people, by the sheer weight of their teaching and their personality, to rethink every conception they have formed of God, till Israel reaches a faith without parallel in the ancient world.

The use of images in worship was an axiom in ancient religion. This is shown by Tacitus' epigram, when Pompey entered the Holy of Holies and found in it nothing

1 G. A. Smith, *The Twelve*, i. p. 102.

whatever, *vacuam sedem et inania arcana*,[2] a grotesque
discovery to make in a shrine so much talked of all over
the world. It is shown further by the instinctive feeling
of the ancients in spite of centuries of philosophers, that
the Christians must be atheists, since they had no temples,
no altars and no gods. Elijah and Elisha, as we have
seen, had no quarrel with the "golden calves" at Bethel.
Men of real religious instinct to-day in India have as
little quarrel with their countrymen's regard for the
sacred bull and the still stranger things which India has
to show. To Western minds nothing can be more repulsive than the worship of the *lingam* and its use in personal names; and nothing more unintelligible than that
pure-minded people can make it the centre of their religion. The explanation appears to be that the thing is
so familiar that no one realises what it is, no one thinks
about it. In spite of the interpretation put by the established text upon Jeroboam's religion, it would appear
from the story about Aaron that the bull had been from
time out of mind the standard, or a standard, embodi-
ment of Jehovah. It seems likely that the brazen serpent
was another of the kind at Jerusalem. The trouble taken
in the Pentateuch to explain it gives a new and perhaps
suspicious significance to the phrase in Kings—"the
brazen serpent that Moses had made." [3] Jehu (840
B.C.) was a champion of Jehovah against the Baal-
worshipping house of Ahab. Ahab had not, however,
renounced Jehovah but named his sons for him, and Jehu
maintained the bull-shrines.

The legends of Elijah and Elisha are supposed to have
been reduced to writing about 800 B.C.; the author of the
Elijah story, at least, writes with an ease, a grace and

---

2 Tacitus, *Histories*, v. 9.
3 "A very ancient emblem of an original serpent worship, later converted into
an emblem of Jehovah." So J. P. Peters, *Relig. of Hebrews*, p. 238; see Kings
xviii. 4, Num. xxi. 4 ff. Cf. H. P. Smith, *O. T. History*, p. 239.

a vividness that appeal to every reader. He moves in the atmosphere of miracle. Fire comes from heaven at the prophet's call; the dead are raised, and leprosy is inflicted with a word. Fifty years later Amos writes down his own prophecies—a herdsman, whom Wordsworth might well have quoted in support of his views of language, a master of form, whose style is as clear and direct as his thought. He deals in no miracles; he sees and thinks like a modern, watches events, reasons from facts, and trusts the truth of his message to find its way to the consciences of men. We are in a new age—a world as modern as that of Pericles or Napoleon—one generation away from a Middle Age of miracle. We have reached a period of suffering and of hard thinking, when religion gained a new profundity and took on a new character, when it became in large measure what we still hold it to be.

The period falls into two parts; the dividing point is the fall of Samaria in 721 B.C. Before that we are concerned with Northern Israel and the prophets who spoke to a kingdom unshaken and prosperous. After that Northern Israel passes utterly out of history and is absolutely lost to us—unless the guess, a mere guess, is right that the Beni-Israel of Bombay Presidency are a last surviving handful of them.[4] Thereafter all the interest shifts to Judah, a smaller kingdom, with a century and quarter before it full of unspeakable menaces without, of reformation, reaction and despair within; and then it too falls in 586 B.C. Cyrus indeed "restored" the Jews in 538 B.C., but the exile and the restoration come at a later point in our story.

Jeroboam II. reigned over Israel for forty-one years (783-742 B.C.), "and Jehovah said not that he would blot out the name of Israel from under heaven; but he

4 See p. 242.

saved them by the hand of Jeroboam." [5] Whatever be
the historical value of the detail added, it remains that
Jeroboam II. was a warlike and prosperous prince, that
Syria was decadent, and Israel, outwardly at least,
flourished exceedingly in his reign. But long and successful wars with small neighbours did not build up the
national strength; they told heavily on the poorer free-
men, and war, famine and plague left the country all the
weaker to face the Assyrian.[6] Twenty years of usurpers
followed, and then Sargon took Samaria; he records how
he transported 27,290 of Israel, and the Hebrew narrative adds how he put foreigners from Babylonia and
elsewhere in their place (721 B.C.). Twenty years later
abject submission did not save Hezekiah of Judah from
seeing his land ravaged, two hundred thousand of his
people carried away, and his city besieged. How his city
escaped capture is recorded in the book of Isaiah (ch.
xxxvii.), and something analogous is told by Herodotus
(ii. 141). Meantime a new power was rising in Egypt.
Psammetichus, Herodotus says (ii. 152), received an
oracle that vengeance would come from the sea, when
bronzen men appeared; and they did appear—Ionian
Greeks and Carians in armour; and they enlisted in his
army and remained the strength of the Egyptian forces
till Cambyses conquered Egypt. The Egyptian king in
turn comes into Judah's story and defeats and kills
Josiah at the battle of Megiddo (608). Herodotus also
tells us of Scythian invaders of Asia, to whom Jeremiah
refers.[7] They spared Jerusalem, but they were the ruin
of Assyria. That great nation, great in war and conquest, had worn itself out, and in 606 B.C. Nineveh was
taken by the Medes. The prophet Nahum has a picture
of the siege and the fall that throbs with passion. He

5 2 Kings xiv. 27.
6 Robertson Smith, *Prophets*, p. 95.
7 Herodotus, i. 104-106; Jer. iv. 5-26.

sees the warriors in red, the horses prancing, the rush of
the chariots; and then:

> The river-gates burst open, the palace dissolves,
> And Hussab is stripped, is brought forth,
> With her maids sobbing like doves,
> Beating their breasts.
> And Nineveh! she was like a reservoir of waters. . . .
> Plunder silver, plunder gold,
> Infinite treasures, mass of all precious things!
> Void and dread and desolate is she.[8]

After Nineveh came Babylon, and twice Jerusalem was
stripped of her best, and the Babylonish captivity began.

This is a poor, short summary of great events. What
a challenge to easy orthodoxy four years of world-war
can make, we know; and at no moment in those years
were the issues so awful for thinking men as throughout
the long period we have surveyed in these few para-
graphs. What the condition of the people was, with an
Assyrian army in the land, the boasts of Sargon and
Sennacherib hint. But take things at their best in Jeroboam's reign, and look at the life that Amos describes,
its contrasts of splendour and oppression. Here are the
rich. "Ye that put far away the evil day, yet bring near
the reign of violence; that lie upon beds of ivory, and
stretch themselves upon their couches, and eat the lambs
out of the flock, and the calves out of the midst of the
stall; that sing idle songs to the sound of the viol; that
improvise songs like David's; that drink wine in bowls,
and anoint themselves with the chief ointments, but they
are not grieved for the afflictions of Joseph" (Amos
vi. 3-6). And "they have sold the righteous for silver,
and the needy for a pair of shoes, who trample to the
dust the head of the poor and pervert the way of humble
men; they lay them themselves down beside every altar

8 G. A. Smith, *The Twelve*, ii. 107, 108; Nahum, ii.

upon clothes taken in pledge, and in the house of their
God they drink the wine of them that have been fined"
(ii. 6-8). "Gather upon the mount of Samaria and see!
Confusions manifold in the midst of her; violence to her
very core! Yea, they know not how to do uprightness,
saith Jehovah, who store up wrong and violence in their
palaces" (iii. 9, 10). Religion flourished bravely in all
this time of splendour. Pilgrims sought the shrines, and
enjoyed their visits to them, with feasts and temple
women—"whoredom and wine and new wine," said
Hosea (iv. 11). In the south it was much the same.
After the fall of Israel, Judah plunged uneasily into
reformation and reaction by turns. If reformation failed
to get all they wanted from Jehovah, they would try
elsewhere—

Flectere si nequeo superos, Acheronta movebo.

The joyousness of the old religion was gone, and men
turned to god after god in desperation at the national
outlook; their temper is shown by their persecuting. The
very refugees in Egypt tell Jeremiah that, while they
burnt incense to the Queen of Heaven, "then had we
plenty of victuals, and were well, and saw no evil. But
since we left off to burn incense to the Queen of Heaven,
and to pour out drink offerings unto her, we have wanted
all things and have been consumed by the sword and by
the famine" (Jer. xliv. 17, 18).

Here, once again, we have the factors which we saw
in the Greek world after Homer—saw or thought we
saw, for the records were fewer and more confused; but
the same Scythians at least were there, and the same
upheaval of life, peoples in movement, rich and poor in
conflict; and the agony of a nation going down, city by
city, before the power of Lydia—misery, scepticism and
devotion; and the deeper minds driven to inquire why

Zeus keeps his world in such confusion, neglects the good, rewards the bad, and perplexes men's hearts so with doubt and fear. Something more is asked of Zeus, and something more is asked of Jehovah, some explanation, some principle.

The Hebrew prophet and the Greek philosopher are concerned with the same problems:

To justify the ways of God to men.

There are differences between them, but there are great likenesses. There is the same emphasis on clearness of thought; the same feeling that righteousness matters; Homer "deserved to be whipped and driven out";[9] the same instinct for a unity in the world and all its affairs, for law and principle. The Greek seeks his way along the lines of a common substance underlying all things and a reign of law, to the One in Many. The intellectual problem moves him most; indignation he leaves to the leader of the Demos. The Hebrew is more stirred by the sight of moral wrong, of undeserved suffering, and he goes direct to Jehovah and cries aloud for explanation. Neither is much interested in cult or ritual, neither in initiations and sacramental revelations. The Greek reckons on reaching God by analysing God's intellectual processes, mind discovering mind by natural affinity; the Hebrew feels that righteousness is the key to understanding God.

It will be hard not to digress into the study of the characters of one or two of the prophets, but that is rather aside from our purpose. Something, however, must be said of the type of the prophetic mind. In the "Cotter's Saturday Night" Burns speaks of

The rapt Isaiah's wild prophetic fire;

9 Heraclitus, fr. 119 (Bywater); cited by Diog. Laert., ix. 1.

and plenty of readers make nothing whatever of most of the prophets. What threads or clues there ever were to the prophet's thought—and such natures, it must be allowed, drop their links—are obscured for us by the desperate state of the texts and the blank inadequacy of word-for-word translation to convey any meaning. And then, in modern commentary, the rapt Isaiah appears as a shrewd statesman and Amos as a socialist. The fact is that both Burns and the commentators are right. The prophets are thinkers who will have their facts in clear, hard outline, intelligible to the utmost, and who insist on men returning to facts, and facing them, and thinking them out. But there is another quality, or faculty, about them. They do not report facts they have amassed and deductions they have drawn. They are men—some of them, at least—of the type upon which a whole situation will flash at once, like a country-side in a storm of lightning at night, men to whom things speak—no, to whom God speaks Himself authentically and unmistakably. The book of Amos begins: "The words of Amos, who was among the herdsmen of Tekoa, which he *saw*"; and the third verse starts, "Thus saith Jehovah." The point must be remembered, but it should not be over-emphasised. In the spiritual ancestry of Amos are the *Nebi'im,* men convinced of the immediacy of their contact with Jehovah. They are not in the pedigree of Heraclitus. However we may criticise our fathers, we inherit from them a habit and a vocabulary which react on each other.

"The characteristic of the true prophet," writes Robertson Smith,[10] is that he retains his consciousness and self-control under revelation." The prophets are always emphasising knowledge and reflection. "Israel doth not

10 *O. T. J. C.,* p. 289.

know, my people doth not consider," says Isaiah (i. 3).
"My people perish for lack of *knowledge,*" says Hosea
(iv. 6), and "Ephraim is a silly dove without brains"
(vii. 11).   They eliminate the irrational from all that
concerns religion, from intercourse with God.   Not
ghosts, and familiar spirits, but God, says Isaiah (viii.
9).   Not wizards that peep and mutter, not the leaping
and howling psychopathic votaries of Baal, but men
sobered by the words of God.   God "speaks to his
prophets, not in magical processes or through the visions
of poor frenetics, but by a clear intelligible word addressed to the intellect and the heart." [11]   "I have heard,"
says God to Jeremiah, "what the prophets have said, that
prophesy lies in my name saying, I have dreamed, I have
dreamed—even the prophets of the deceit of their own
heart. . . . The prophet that hath a dream, let him tell
a dream; and he that hath my word, let him speak my
word faithfully.   What is the straw to the wheat? saith
Jehovah.   Is not my word like as fire? saith Jehovah;
and like a hammer that breaketh the rock in pieces?"
(Jer. xxiii. 25-29).   The mark of the prophet is that
he will, in Cromwell's great phrase, "speak *things.*"
"It is a fundamental principle with us," wrote John
Wesley, "that to renounce reason is to renounce
religion, that reason and religion go hand in hand, and
that all irrational religion is false religion." [12]

Such a habit does not lead to the easy solution of problems; it is rather apt to multiply them, for clearness
always emphasises our ignorance.   In a passage that recalls one we have seen of Theognis, Habakkuk [13] asks
the same urgent question, in weariness and perplexity:—

How long, O Jehovah, have I called? and Thou hearest not.
I cry to Thee, Wrong! and Thou sendest no help.

11 *O. T. J. C.,* p. 289.
12 Quoted by Davenport, *Primitive Traits in Religious Revivals,* p. 145.
13 Hab. i. 2, 3, 12, 13.

Why dost Thou make me to look upon sorrow,
And fill mine eyes with trouble? . . .
`Art not Thou of old, Jehovah, my God, my Holy One,
Purer of eyes than to behold evil,
And that canst not gaze upon trouble?
Why gazest thou upon traitors?
Why art thou silent, when the wicked swallows him that is
    more righteous than he?

His contemporary, Jeremiah, deals with God as explicitly: "Righteous art thou, O Jehovah, when I plead with thee; yet would I reason the cause with thee. Wherefore doth the way of the wicked prosper? Wherefore are all they at ease, that deal very treacherously?" (xii. 1). In very striking words Habakkuk answers himself; he will, in modern phrase, take a wider outlook, he will take time and trouble to know.

Upon my watch-tower I will stand,
And take my post on the rampart.
I will watch to see what he will say to me,
And what answer I get back to my plea.

Hesiod, as we saw, speaks of the Muses meeting him and speaking to him; and this was the source of his matter-of-fact poetry. But one wonders what element of inspiration at all lies behind the pleasant story; is it just an amplified imitation of Homer's invocation? The Hebrew prophets speak of a call of God Himself as the ground of their action in going with His message to their people. Isaiah tells us how he saw Jehovah high and lifted up, and how the sight filled him with a sense of his own uncleanness (Isa. vi. 1-5). There is no gay adaptation of the conventional about that; it is a story wrung from the heart. Jeremiah confesses to having resisted the call; he was not the man for the task, a mere child; but he had to obey—and obedience again and again, we can see, meant misery and humiliation to that gentle and sensitive spirit (Jer. i. 6; xx. 9). Amos in a brief parallelism (iii. 8) says simply: "The lion hath roared, who will not fear; the God Jehovah has spoken, who can but prophesy?" And in a memorable and vividly-drawn scene he tells the priest at Bethel that prophecy was no trade of his; he was a herdsman; but he had no choice; "the Lord took me" (vii. 14). It is hard to imagine experience more authentic in the history of religion; there is nothing psychopathic here, the men are what Carlyle called "sons of fact"; they draw their materials from "conscience and history." [14]

The habit of seeing fact and of basing oneself on principle is not yet so common that we should suppose the prophets to be representative men. I have heard a minister praised as "more sympathetic to the common opinions of the day" than another—a eulogy which it is notorious the great prophets never achieved, and never sought. "Behold, now," said an envoy of the court to an earlier prophet, "the words of the prophets declare good unto the king with one mouth; let thy word, I pray thee, be like the word of one of them and speak that which is good." [15] "As Jehovah liveth, what Jehovah saith unto me, that will I speak," is the answer, and it is the badge of all his tribe. They are pioneers, who penetrate to the mind of God; and the common opinions of the day are irrelevant. They were not popular, but neither was Socrates. "The possession of a single true thought about Jehovah," says Robertson Smith,[16] "not derived from current religious teaching, but springing up in the soul as a word from Jehovah Himself, is enough to constitute a prophet, and lay on him the duty of speaking to Israel what he has learned of Israel's God." This brings us to the teaching of the prophets,

14 Mazzini, quoted by G. A. Smith, *The Twelve*, i. p. 89.
15 1 Kings xxii. 13, 14.
16 *Prophets of Israel*, p. 182.

to those ideas of God which they set forth and which to some extent were assimilated in the thought and life of Israel, though not wholly—ideas which in spite of the teaching of Jesus himself are still very largely foreign to the minds of men, unintelligible and repugnant.

Let us start with Amos, with whom the roll of the great prophets begins. From the wilderness of Tekoa, the very verge of civilisation, he suddenly appears at Bethel, the holy place of Northern Israel, and he makes a series of announcements from Jehovah—startling in their character and impressive in their form. "Thus saith Jehovah: For three transgressions of Damascus and for four, I will not turn it back." What was *it*? There is something that moves in the vague *Quos ego* of the formula, which comes with each doom. Twenty years later the Assyrians explained what it was. "The people of Syria shall go into captivity." A judgment upon Syria was not a message to trouble Israel. The prophet went on: "Thus saith Jehovah: For three transgressions of Gaza and for four, I will not turn *it* back . . . the remnant of the Philistines shall perish." Still a message likely to be popular, for these were the hereditary enemies, North and South. Then came the turn of Tyre, a slave-trading town like Gaza, selling human beings in herds to Arabia and to the west; and then of Edom and Ammon; and then Moab; and always the same prelude, "For three transgressions and for four," and always the same awful menace, "I will not turn *it* back"—a stirring series of God's judgments, good to hear, good to dwell upon—but the prophet was not done.

"Thus saith Jehovah: For three transgressions of Judah and for four, I will not turn *it* back." [17] Judah, too, was an enemy from time to time; but let us hear the sins of Judah. The sins of the other peoples were

[17] Some critics think the doom upon Judah a later addition here.

the common barbarities and treacheries of Semitic warfare—mere outrages on humanitarianism. It was odd
perhaps that Jehovah should be so squeamish, especially
when, in the case of Moab, it was Edom and not Israel
that suffered. But what had Judah done? "They despised the law of Jehovah; his statutes they did not observe; their false gods led them astray. But I will send
fire upon Judah and it shall devour the palaces of Jerusalem."   And then, "Thus saith Jehovah: For three
transgressions of Israel and for four, I will not turn *it*
back. They sell the honest man for silver, the poor man
for a pair of shoes; they trample to the dust of the earth
the head of the poor and pervert the way of the humble
folk. A man and his father will go in to the same temple-
woman, to profane my holy name. By every altar they
lay themselves down on garments given in pledge, and
the wine of those that have been fined, they drink in the
house of their God" (ii. 6-8). So doom, the prophet
thinks, is to come upon Israel, for a mere matter of
social righteousness.

The most brilliantly civilised of Greek states, when she
sacked Melos, Histiaea, Scione, Torone, Aegina—and,
the historian adds, many other towns of the Greeks—
killed the men and sold the women and children for
slaves, and when she fell, it came home to her what she
had done: "that night no man slept." Plato deprecated
such treatment of Greeks by Greeks; it might serve for
barbarians. Amos drags it into the cognisance of Jehovah; it matters to Jehovah—this common usage of
war which all states understand and practise when they
can. "They sold the captives; they ripped up the women
with child—to enlarge their territory." And God, Amos
says, judges,—"I will not turn *it* back." More still, for
barbarity in war is not charged against Israel at this
point—we know that David practised it—Jehovah is con-

cerned with the oppression of the poor, with the cold
and hunger to which the needy are exposed, with the lust
and uncleanness associated with His temples. He has
His eye upon the palaces where the great "store up violence and robbery," on the tribunals and the judges with
itching palms. And all the piety and devotion of His
people go for nothing—for less than nothing, for they
anger Him. "Come to Bethel," He says in irony; "come
to Bethel and sin; come to Gilgal and multiply transgression! Every morning your sacrifices, every three days
your tithes! and offer a sacrifice of thanksgiving"
(iv. 4). "I hate, I despise your feast-days, and I will
not smell your sacrifices in solemn assembly. Though
you offer me burnt-offerings and meat offerings, I will
not accept them; your thank-offerings of fatted calves,
I will not look at them. Take thou away from me the
noise of the songs; for I will not hear the melody of
thy viols" (v. 21-23).

We have remarked among Greek thinkers—and perhaps more still is it to be remarked among the plain
people of Greece, men who loved their wives and daughters, and gave themselves to making men of their boys—
an instinct which grows slowly to a conviction, that
morality and religion do belong together, that Zeus must
be just, that the gods must be clean. To that feeling in
Greece we shall return at a later point. But, after all, in
Greece the conviction grows slowly; it comes up like a
quiet tide. In Amos it sweeps upon Israel like the inrush
of the whole sea at once after an earthquake. Religion?
Jehovah hates and despises your religion; smell and
smoke and tinkling tunes, and robbery and uncleanness.
He is not interested in priests and shrines and rituals.

> From vice, oppression and despair
> God save the people!

Plato and Amos reach the same point. Religion without morality is a lie, and Gods damns it. Plato's subject in that sentence may be vague or plural, but the predicate is definite enough. With Amos it is the subject that has all the emphasis, terrible as the predicates are; "thus saith *Jehovah.*" "Woe unto you that desire the day of Jehovah! to what end is it for you? The day of Jehovah is darkness and not light; very dark, and no brightness in it."

It is little wonder that Amaziah, the priest of Bethel, was for sending Amos away. "O thou seer, go, flee thee away into the land of Judah, and there eat bread [there the priest speaks by his trade]; prophesy there. But prophesy not any more at Bethel; for it is the king's chapel and it is the king's court" (vii. 12, 13). And with the doom of that priest the personal history of Amos ends. But his clear association, his identification of religion with morality, rings on through all the great religious teachers of Israel—for Israel and for all who hear.

Ethics, however, are very well in the abstract, but the issue lies always with religion; that at least is practical. And in religion, all turns on how men conceive of God. Without attempting to deal with the prophets in detail, any more than elsewhere with the poets and philosophers, let us push to the conclusion of the whole matter—what do they make, individually and collectively, of Jehovah?

The first point to be noted is made appallingly clear by Amos. He links Israel with Gaza and with Tyre for judgment, in one and the same formula. Jehovah is not tied to Israel. "Are you not as the negroes, the children of Ethiopia, unto me, O children of Israel? saith Jehovah. Did not I bring up Israel out of Egypt? Yes, and the Philistines from Crete, and the Syrians from Kir" (Amos ix. 7). This was to give the lie direct to

144 PROGRESS IN RELIGION

all early notions of the inter-dependence of god and
tribe. Jehovah can do without Israel—a terrific discovery, and a very unpatriotic one. It is remarked that
Amos never calls Jehovah "God of Israel"; He is God
of Hosts.[18] Amos has little hope of Israel; "hate the
evil and love the good; it may *perchance* be that Jehovah,
the God of hosts, shall be with you, as you say" (v. 14).
They said so, and here is Jehovah's reply, detached
enough: "You only have I known of all the families of
the earth. Therefore I will punish you for your iniquities. Can two walk together, except they be
agreed?" (iii. 2). The covenant of Jehovah with Israel
had apparently two sides; there was a predominant
partner. And Jehovah, as we saw, will punish Moab for
what Moab did to the doomed people of Edom (ii. 1).
The prophets look further afield than the patriots. Isaiah
recognises in Assyria a tool of Jehovah's—it is difficult
for us to grasp the extreme daring of the thought, the
bold extension of Jehovah's sovereignty far outside His
own land, and the insight that subordinates the intolerable menace of Assyria to the purposes of God. The
language is contemptuous beyond translation: "In the
same day shall Jehovah shave with a razor that is hired
—viz. the king of Assyria—the head and the hair of the
feet, and it shall also consume the beard" (Isa. vii. 20).
Ezekiel, in language of more sympathy, says of the next
great oppressor of Israel, that Jehovah announces: "I
will strengthen the arms of the king of Babylon, and the
arms of Pharaoh shall fall down, and they shall know
that I am Jehovah, when I shall put my sword into the
hand of the king of Babylon, and he shall stretch it out
upon the land of Egypt" (Ezek. xxx. 25). Later on,
the second Isaiah hails Cyrus: "Thus saith Jehovah to
his anointed, to Cyrus, whose right hand I have holden,

18 Wellhausen, *Prolegomena*, p. 472.

to subdue the nations before him. . . . I will go before
thee to make the crooked places straight, I will break in
pieces the gates of brass and cut in sunder the bars of
iron . . . for Jacob my servant's sake, I have called thee
by name, though thou hast not known me. I am Jehovah,
and there is none else; there is no God beside me" (Isa.
xlv. 1-5). Small wonder the early Christian read *κύριος*
for *κῦρος* and applied the great language to another.
Amos struck the keynote, and the crown of all is in that
second Isaiah:[19] "Have ye not known? have ye not
heard? hath it not been told you from the beginning?
have ye not understood from the foundations of the
earth? He that is enthroned above the circle of the
earth and its inhabitants are as grasshoppers, that
stretcheth out the heavens as a curtain, and spreadeth
them out to dwell in. Behold, the nations are as a drop
of a bucket, and are counted as the small dust of the
balance; behold, he taketh up the isles as a very little
thing; he hath measured the waters in the hollow of his
hand. Lift up your eyes on high, and behold who hath
created these stars, that bringeth out their host by number: he calleth them all by names by the greatness of his
power; not one faileth. Why sayest thou, O Jacob, My
way is hid from Jehovah? Hast thou not known, hast
thou not heard, that the everlasting God, Jehovah, the
Creator of the ends of the earth, fainteth not, neither is
weary? there is no searching of his understanding."

"The sun will not transgress bounds; or else the
Erinnyes, avengers of Justice, will find him out," said
Heraclitus[20] about this time, using the language of old
poetry to express the reign of law, for "Nature loves to
be hid."[21] The Hebrew boldly asserts the personal rule

---

19 Verses not quite in order, from Isaiah xl.
20 Heraclitus, fr. 94 (Diels, *Vorsokvatiker,* i. p. 75); fr. 29 (Bywater);
Plutarch, *de exilio,* ii. p. 604.
21 Heraclitus, fr. 123 (Diels); fr. 10 (Bywater).

of Jehovah, and we have seen how the prophets have built up that personality—how it has been revealed to them, they would say. Jehovah, as Amos saw, stands for law and for morality; for the great law that sways sun and star, as the second Isaiah saw, and for a greater law in accordance with which He punishes—He and no mere Erinnyes—the nation and the man who do evil and call it holiness, who omit to see justice and dream that religion can matter without it. He is, as Habakkuk of the Watchtower said, "of purer eyes than to behold evil, and cannot look upon iniquity" (Ha. i. 15). The Hebrew, however, knew the shrinking of the Greek from a crude anthropomorphism. The Elohist, we are told,[22] reaches a higher level of reflection than the Jehovist in dealing with the old legends of his people; he tones down his theophanies, he has a more spiritual conception of revelation, while on the human side he strikes a deeper vein of subjective feeling; he finds the sense of tears in things, feels the appeal of tenderness, and is more careful in his treatment of right and wrong. Both varieties of sensitiveness are felt in the prophets, and they escape the depersonalising tendency that undid philosophic religion among the Greeks, because that sense of the pathos of human life never leaves them. "Thou shalt *love* Jehovah thy God" is the eventual Hebrew religion. Not so spoke the Greek. "Friendship or love," says Aristotle,[23] "we speak of where there is return of love; but love of God admits neither return of love nor indeed love at all. For it would be an odd sort of thing if a man were to say he loved Zeus." It would, indeed; but Jehovah was thought of on other lines. And this began in earnest with Hosea, one of the most remarkable of

22 Skinner, *Genesis*, pp. liii. and xlvii.
23 Aristotle, *Magn. Mor.*, ii. 11, 1208 b., 28 ff.

the prophets. Hosea and Jeremiah may be called the tenderest spirits in Hebrew religion.

It is not necessary to tell again the dreadful story of Hosea, more miserable and more splendid as one feels one's way into it. He has the prophet's habit of basing himself on fact, and an eye for nature comparable to that which we find in Jeremiah and in the parables of Jesus. It is remarkable that he was, it would appear, the first to observe the effect of national licentiousness in diminishing population.[24] He was also a psychologist, and to some effect, who read deeply in the human heart. He found that his wife was unable to stand alone, too animal a nature to choose purity or too weak to hold to a resolve; that she lacked character and personality; and that her one chance lay in his helping her, not once, but always; that if he let her go, there lay nothing before her but ever deeper infamy. He found, too, that he himself was not unwilling to help her; that he could not, in fact, do anything else; that he could not let her go; that he could forgive her and keep her whatever she had done. He asked, it would seem, whence came these feelings? And he drew the greatest of all inferences—that Jehovah Himself, Maker of all, is the source of tenderness, that Jehovah must therefore be good and tender beyond man's dream. He applied this to Israel—to Israel unable to stand alone, to be true or loyal, ever in need of fresh forgiveness and of perpetual support. "How can I give thee up, Ephraim?" he hears Jehovah say. "How can I cast thee away, Israel? My heart burns within me, my compassion is all kindled. I will not execute the fierceness of my wrath, I will not turn to destroy thee; for I am God and not man, the Holy One in the midst of thee" (xi. 8 f.).

24 G. A. Smith, *The Twelve*, i. pp. 233, 284; Hosea ix. 11, 14, 16.

"O Israel, return unto Jehovah thy God. . . . I will heal their backsliding, I will love them freely, for mine anger is turned away from him. I will be as the dew to Israel; he shall bud forth as the lily and strike his roots as Lebanon" (xiv. 1 f.). "O Israel, thou hast destroyed thyself, but in me is thy help" (xiii. 9). The language is so extraordinarily personal that it is hard to realise that it is addressed not to an individual but to Israel, to the nation. The fuller place of the individual in the thoughts of Jehovah comes with Jeremiah.

Hosea, however, is a pioneer in the exploration of God, who has marked several points which remain for ever. He was the first of the prophets to recognise the malign significance of idols. To Amos the calves were a part of that cult which he saw that Jehovah despised. To Hosea they are symbols of apostasy—"and now they sin more and more, and have made them molten images of their silver, even idols according to their own understanding, all of them the work of the craftsmen; they say of them, Let the men that sacrifice kiss the calves" (xiii. 2). With the horrible symbolism before him, in which the ancient religion expressed the relation of heaven and earth, rites of fertility, and with his own domestic parable in his heart, he uses the metaphor of marriage to describe the union of Jehovah and Israel, and in the idols he sees the lovers for whom Jehovah's wife has forsaken him and "played the harlot" (iv. 15, 17).

He was, further, the first teacher of repentance. This involved a new treatment of the whole question of Sin— a subject on which the contribution of Israel to the thought of mankind is incomparably richer than that of Greece, and only approached by that of early Roman Christianity. The Greek practically omitted Sin, like M. Renan;[25] and when he put his mind to it, he treated

[25] See p. 58.

it in two ways. Sin might be a meddling with the whims
and fancies of a divine or daemonic being of no moral
qualities whatever; or it might be a blunder which involved a man in consequences entailed by a breach of laws
quite impersonal, as a short-sighted man's stumble may
entail breakage of bone or wrenching of muscle as a
result of man's natural construction and the hardness
(let us say) of stone steps. In neither was the act of
much import apart from its consequence; it did not carry
the whole man with it; and it did not, apart from daemons, bring him into collision with another personality—
and the daemons which might have to be reconciled were
only partly personal, much less so than the man himself.
The Stoic, indeed, coined the word "conscience," but it
was a religion of Hebrew ancestry that used it. The
Hebrew, where Hosea led the way, conceived sin as an
attitude of mind, apostasy, "harlotry" in the phrase of
Hosea, and on either side saw a genuine personality. If
"Israel" is not quite personal, the stories of the call of
Isaiah and Jeremiah show strongly the emergence of
the individual.

Sin is, then, for the Hebrew an attitude of mind de-
termining conduct toward God. The whole situation is
changed by the emphasis on the personality of God; it
is further changed by the strong conviction that God is
righteous and moral, which the common gods of Greece
never were; the third development follows, when Hosea
brings forward, as a necessary implicate of God's personality, His personal affection for His own, His tenderness and His yearning desire to have His own again.
"How *can* I let thee go?" Sin stands in a clearer light
than ever before, interpreted by this psychologist who
could not get over his love for a disastrous wife. Repentance, then, is a change of mind—and that is one
reason why Hosea so constantly emphasises knowing and

not-knowing and understanding. Israel has "rejected knowledge" (iv. 6) and "the people that doth not understand shall be overthrown" (iv. 14). And his appeal is: "Oh, Israel, return unto Jehovah thy God . . . take with you words and return unto Jehovah; say unto him, Take away all iniquity and accept that which is good; so will we render as bullocks the offering of our lips" (xiv. 1)—a change of attitude which means a new type of religion, not one of external gifts, of slain bullocks, of blood out-poured and incense burnt, but one where the inner man meets God face to face—a change of attitude which involves an entire re-modelling of conduct and makes it possible for Jehovah to give in the spirit and on the scale which the prophet sees to be His desire. Hosea is the forerunner of the New Testament doctrine of Grace—the "greatest of all Catholic doctrines," as Renan said.

The contrast of all this with the highest thought upon God that we find among the Greeks is more remarkable as we study it more. Once again I find it hard to discover anything like it in the earlier history of Jehovah-worship, as it is generally described. Even if the later developments are in the traditional way put down to Abraham and his age, the change of century does not make the facts less strange. The whole habit of mind and outlook of Hosea and Jeremiah is irreconcilable with the conceptions on which early religion as a rule rested; and one feels the justice of Professor Barton's conclusion, already quoted, that the moral standards of the prophets and their conceptions of God are not accounted for by their environments.[26]

The slow recognition of human personality was one point in which we saw that the Hebrew differed from the Greek — and very surprisingly. One wonders

[26] P. 109; Barton, *Semitic Origins*, p. 306.

whether the scholars can be right who assure us so definitely that all the messages of Jehovah are for the nation. It is quite clear at last that the individual had his
messages too. The call of the prophet is as intensely an
individual transaction as a proposal of marriage to-day.
It is inconceivable that Jehovah, with such a character
of tenderness as Hosea draws, could call a man and use
a man, and have no further interest in him. That point
is made good by Jeremiah, whose whole life is, in a way,
a dialogue with Jehovah. In the long run, he extends the
relation of Jehovah to every man, and two things may
be traced as contributing to this. His own personal religious life, a deeply individual life of battle, despair and
divine grace and re-consecration, will take him a long
way. Jeremiah, too, like Amos, saw that God is not tied
to people or place—if He can do without Israel, He
can do without Judah. If Jerusalem escaped Sennacherib, it is not necessarily sound thinking to talk on
about "the temple of the Lord, the temple of the Lord,
the temple of the Lord" [27] (Jeremiah's iterations are not
accidental). Jehovah can do without His temple; He is
not dependent on Jerusalem. Temple and tower may go
to the ground, and Israel may go into exile. Amos told
the priest he would die "in a polluted land"; for Jeremiah there is no polluted land; he sees that the religion
of Jehovah is detachable from Jerusalem:—

> Where'er we meet Thee, Thou art found
> And every place is hallowed ground.

Yes! and it is detachable from race as well as from place.
God has, in a sense, failed with Israel. Israel will not
have Jehovah. But is Jehovah baulked of his purpose by
a foolish people? Amos thought not. Sheer ruin, failure, disaster and collapse are the drastic teachers of

[27] Jer. vii. 4.

Jeremiah; they drive him into deeper and deeper research into the ways of Jehovah. He discovers the individual to be the key to God's thoughts. Men talked of people and of family—the life of Israel, the continuity and unity of the family. Their proverb ran that "The fathers have eaten sour grapes, and the children's teeth are set on edge" (Jer. xxxi. 29). Jeremiah denied it—"every man that eateth sour grapes, his teeth shall be set on edge"; and then he goes on to unfold what is implied in this new individuality of the individual. The passage which follows has had a great history in religion and in literature, and gave its name to the most famous of all books some centuries later; for its meaning was seen at last.

"Behold, the days come, saith Jehovah, that I will make a new covenant with the house of Israel and with the house of Judah, not according to the covenant that I made with their fathers, in the day that I took them by the hand, to bring them out of the land of Egypt; which my covenant they brake, although I was an husband unto them, saith Jehovah. But this is the covenant that I will make with the house of Israel: After these days, saith Jehovah, I will put my law in their inward parts, and in their heart will I write it; and I will be their God, and they shall be my people. And they shall teach no more every man his neighbour, and every man his brother, saying, Know Jehovah: for they all shall know me, from the least of them unto the greatest of them, saith Jehovah: for I will forgive their iniquity and their sin will I remember no more" (Jer. xxxi. 31 ff.).

Beautiful words! no wonder the early Christians laid hold of them and quoted them so often! And the inference of personal immortality seems to lie so near, and he did not draw it! One thing, however, was assured. When the day came that Jews would draw the inference,

there were certain fixed points. The personality of God
and the personality of man were established, and their
inter-relation made it clear that the inference would not
take the form of transmigration of souls. Mankind was
to have an alternative to the cycle of eternal re-dying, the
"sorrowful weary wheel."

Let us sum up what the prophets did. A religion is
always conditioned by the character it gives to God. The
Hebrew prophets kept the personality of God—kept it
triumphantly, and abolished all other claimants to Godhead. God is personal, and God is one; God is righteous,
and God is kind—they are four great tenets on which to
base any religion, and they were not lightly won. They
were the outcome of experience, hard, bitter and disillus-
ioning—a gain acquired by the loss of all kinds of hopes
and beliefs, national and personal, tested in every way
that man or devil can invent for the testing of belief.
The prophets got the religion of Jehovah detached, or
detachable, from shrine and cult, just when the deporta-
tion and the exile in Babylon made it imperative that the
religion must do without shrine and cult or perish for
ever. They cut it clear from priesthood and tradition
and law-book, though their successors entangled it with
these again. They struck the blow of which idolatry
died. They made righteousness a thing no more of ritual
and taboo but of attitude and conduct and spirit. They
set religion free from ancient follies and reviving horrors. "Wherewith," says Micah (about 720 B.C.), "shall
I come before Jehovah, and bow myself before the high
God? Shall I come before him with burnt offerings,
with calves of a year old? Will Jehovah be pleased with
thousands of rams, or with ten thousands of rivers of
oil? Shall I give my first-born for my transgression,
the fruit of my body for the sin of my soul? He hath

showed thee, O man, what is good; and what doth Jehovah require of thee, but to do justly, and to love mercy, and to walk humbly with thy God? [28]

So wrote Micah—in impressive contrast with old Hebrew religion, with Greek religion and with what we find in the Roman Empire and in modern India. But there was another chapter of religion yet to write, and Hosea and Jeremiah saw what it would be about. They did not read, nor yet divine, all its contents; but they knew that it would turn, not on what Jehovah requires of man, but on what Jehovah will do for man, how He feels for him and what He will give him. For the days were coming when the Hebrew, like the Greek, would ask a great deal of his God—Immortality, for a beginning, and other things more wonderful.

28 Micah vi. 6-8.

VII

THE GREAT CENTURY OF GREECE

No period of ancient history has been more studied than the fifth century B.C., the great age of Athens; and yet one of the acutest thinkers in the classical field to-day tells us that "the beliefs of sixth and fifth century Greece are not yet fully ascertained. The country is but partially mapped out, and any one who sets foot in it risks losing his way." He points out that to-day so many forms of religion beside the Olympian have to be considered— "Orphic mysteries with a highly spiritual teaching, Dionysiac religion emotional and enthusiastic, and the propitiation of formidable Chthonian deities." [1] We are told elsewhere, with at least enough emphasis, that it is the three last forms of religion which are important; but Mr. Livingstone points out that the Olympian gods retained significance enough to draw upon themselves the successive attacks of Euripides and Plato, of the early Church, of Lucian of Samosata, and finally of St. Augustine, while Orphic and Chthonian worship escaped, in the main or altogether, the attention of reformer and satirist—an indication surely where the real strength lay. If the contention which we have been studying so far is valid—that some instinct or impulse, something natural within him and inevitable, drives man to personalise his god, we shall not be altogether surprised at this conclusion. However vague the religions of Dionysus and Demeter may have been at the beginning, and for long after the beginning (whatever and whenever that was), whether they are at first mere responses of fear and hope

1 *The Greek Genius and its Meaning for Us*, p. 49.

to observed facts of alterations of personality and the fruitfulness of the soil, both Dionysus and Demeter developed legends, and the very slightest touch served to link them to the hierarchy of Olympian gods. It may be that the superficial psychology of the common man, and his undeveloped wonder at natural processes, served to keep a basis of experience under these two divinities, which some gods lost early if they ever had it; none the less they too were Olympian and personal. The Chthonian powers may well have kept their significance for people who were tender or timid rather than reflective, just as water-spirits and (more vigorously) ghosts retain for long their hold on some types of mind, and luck and one's star keep it still longer. But they cannot be called very relevant to our immediate subject of Progress in Religion, unless obstacles are to be reckoned.

But no one, I think, who seriously studies ancient history, will contend that the real importance, the real value, of that fifth century B.C. is to be looked for in the worship of Chthonian gods. Matthew Arnold used to distinguish between the permanent and the historical value of literature; certain books were of moment to those who studied the period in which they were produced, but they had ceased to be living literature in any sense.[2] The student of the fifth century must indeed recognise that the Chthonian cults continued then, and no doubt for long after; superstitions die hard. Yes, they die hard, but there are things of more interest. There is an interest in the beast-lore of Elizabethan days—

> Spring-headed Hydraes, and sea-shouldring Whales,
> Great whirlpools which all fishes make to flee,
> Bright Scoolpendræs, arm'd with silver scales,
> Mighty Monoceroses with immeasured tayles—

2 *Essays in Criticism*, ii. No. 1., pp. 6 ff.: "the fallacy caused by the estimate which we call historic."

THE GREAT CENTURY OF GREECE   157

but the study of Nature is more interesting. My analogy
is not quite perfect; but my meaning, as I have tried to
say already, is that what matters at any stage is the movement, or impulse, or idea that makes for the next stage.
In the fifth century no one would claim that for Chthonian gods. Wherever and whenever they are in the ascendent, one may look for retrograde thinking and decline.

It was the age when Greece became more conspicuously
and gloriously Greece than ever before, when all the powers of the human mind flowered at once and then bore
fruit as they never had done in a period of the same
length nor perhaps did again till the early years of the
sixteenth century A.D.; and on that fruit mankind has
lived with a satisfaction always intense, and its seed has
in turn been fruitful in every civilised race. Our business now is to see what that age had to say for itself in
religion—not what it inherited and kept through filial
affection, timidity, or mere inattention, but what it
thought out on its own account and found interesting to
itself.

Many things went to make the fifth century alert.
There is a sense of power pervading all its men—a power
stimulated and made conscious by the subjection of the
world to man, by exploration and geographical discovery,
by trade and adventure outside the range of old knowledge. But exploration took place in other regions than
the Mediterranean; "the rise of mathematics in the Py-
thagorean school," we are told in a suggestive sentence,
"had revealed for the first time the power of thought," [3]
and mathematics were not the sole revelation of this.
Travel had brought Greeks into contact with men of
many minds and had raised many questions, difficult and
new; it had brought them face to face with customs not

[3] J. Burnet, *Greek Philosophy*, i. p. 67.

their own, with fauna and flora, rivers, mountains and lands full of wonder, and all to be explained. Criticism was born. The impulse to understand, the impulse to co-ordinate, were immensely quickened; and the habit grew, which marks all Greek philosophy at last, of taking one's stand as "the spectator of all time and all existence." [4] The phrase is Plato's, and the thought is developed by Longinus when he speaks of Plato—"for the contemplation and thought within the reach of man's mind not even the whole universe together suffices; but our conceptions often pass the bounds of space; if one were to look around upon life on every side, and see how in all things the striking, the great and the beautiful stand supreme, he will soon know for what we were born." [5] Longinus lived long after our period, but he interprets it aright. The range of the human mind was immensely increased, and the freedom with which it treated the hugest of conceptions and the subtlest of laws.

To this sense of power and to the widening of range we have to add an intellectual discipline far severer than any other race had ever known. Greek science, geometry, astronomy—and, I expect, medicine—went beyond the science of Egypt and Babylon, whatever they gave of stimulus. The mathematics meant discipline of thought, and they were accompanied by logic and dialectic, by criticism that became more and more acute and penetrating—in all, a training that makes every other race of mankind seem rather provincial.

Criticism and art do not often go together, but in this age of Greece they did. Whatever we make of the naïve notion of more commonplace Greeks that poets are pre-eminently teachers—Homer of tactics, Hesiod of farm-

4 Plato, *Republic,* vi. 486 A.
5 Longinus, xxxv.

ing, and so forth—the three great tragic poets of Athens were teachers indeed, and they taught things far beyond the practical. They put before the Athenians, and gradually before all Greeks, problems in human destiny, in character and conduct, and in such a way that the spectators must ponder them out even unconsciously. The fall of Agamemnon, the tragic results of Deianira's indirectness,[6] the moral grandeur and pitiful fortune of Hecuba in the *Trojan Women,* will occur to us at once. If tragedy declined into mere pathos and quibbling, as we are told, argument and fierce argument was at its heart from the first. "God's law or man's?" asks Antigone. "God's justice or man's interest?" asks Hecuba.

   If gods do deeds of shame, the less gods they!

cries a character of Euripides; and gods, so myth and legend and religion announced, had done many deeds of shame, and men began to feel it. There is argument there; but more potent was that appeal to moral instinct (*Aidôs*) which tragedy made; for by appealing to it tragedy developed moral instinct, and when once that awakens, there is nothing so educative. Men *said* the gods must be right, they *felt* the gods were wrong, and it was vain to urge that laws are made for the little and do not apply to the big. The gods had been human since Homer's day, and now men were coming to feel what that "human" meant. If pity and terror were purged by tragedy, once purified they reacted on men's religious belief—an awakened pity and an educated terror rose up with more sympathy for human pain and a grip on moral principle that robbed religious darkness of many of its vague alarms.

   But it was not only by starting intellectual problems

---

6 Sophocles' *Trachiniae* seems to me to turn, like his *Philoctetes,* on the tragic failure of indirect ways.

and moral problems that tragedy influenced Greek thought. Side by side with sculpture, it brought a new aesthetic sense to bear on all life. The influence of a feeling for beauty upon religions is extraordinarily subtle; it is very hard, or impossible, to limit its scope; it hurts and it heals and it transforms. The new Dissenting chapel that replaces the barn has curious effects upon ceremony, and ceremony upon thought; and when you reach Westminster Abbey you have travelled still further from the upper room in Ephesus where Paul talked half the night. The sharp edges of thought that squared with the barn seem out of place, and they are apt to go; and it is often an open question whether they ought to go. Right and wrong, heaven and hell, seem in sharper antithesis at the street corner than in the cathedral; and I think both Plato and Paul would say that they cannot be in antithesis too sharp. Why does art make us want to soften contrasts which philosophy counts vital? There we touch again "that ancient quarrel between Poetry and Philosophy" that troubled Plato.[7] If Art toned down old story, if it softened ancient prejudice, it made something immortal—but was the something true? Plato asked; and if it is not true, does Art help us? These are great questions, and that age raised them, perhaps for the first time; and as my illustration from English religion suggests, we have not quite solved them yet. But Art with all her magic was there, transforming gods and legends and fixing their form for ever—the friend and enemy of Religion in that exasperating and alluring way which troubles and charms us still. We cannot compute her influence; but we must not forget it. One thing we must note—that Art brought god and man so near together, gave to the god such human lineaments, whispered to man such hints of his own god-likeness, that

7 Plato, *Republic*, x. 607 B.

either Religion must be the most natural and at last most tender of all necessary modes of life, or it must be the most false and deadly of all drugs that bewitch the soul and lay waste the nature. Art drew men very close to the gods,[8] or with its "lies" and symbols it abolished God. Art stereotyped God, and that is the beginning of falsity; "there is no heresy but finality." [9]

So much for the effect of Art on one side of Religion; and I have only suggested a few of the questions and answered none of them. Art, however, is one of the most individualising of all man's gifts. If Art transforms Athene in the Parthenon, and gives her beauty and form for ever, what is its effect on the artist himself and on those who enter in any degree into his thought? He and they gain a new self-consciousness—partly power and partly claim. The journeyman may be put on one side; the real artist is the most individual of men in his sense of power, more still perhaps in his feeling that he must have the meaning of things, not an abstract general meaning, but what they definitely intend to convey to him. His mind—intellect, imagination, emotion, everything included—is the last great court of appeal. God or gods, ethics, nature, society, wait his interpretation; and as he interprets, they will be. Even those who are not great artists, who lack the force of mind and the moral qualities of the greatest, have the obvious gift of the artistic temperament. That it was not at all unknown in Greece, we are reminded by Plato's brilliant and amusing sketch in his *Ion*; the rhapsode there describes himself unmistakably as an artistic temperament, and has that strong sense of the supremely significant *Ego* which we know so well in the type. Those who dabbled in Art,

8 Cf. Dio Chrysostom, *Or.* xii. 53.   Pheidias' Zeus abolishes men's earlier conceptions of the god; Quintilian, xii. 10, 8: The beauty of his Zeus *adjecisse aliquid etiam receptæ religioni videtur;* Livy, xlv. 28: Aemilius Paullus, at the sight of the statue, *Iovem velut praesentem intuens motus animo est.*
9 G. Steven, *Psychology of Christian Soul.*

Sculpture or Poetry, and those who went deeper and understood the problems and the endeavours, came out, in higher degree or in lower, more individual than they went into it.

If there were those in whom Art failed to waken and to stimulate the *Ego,* the Sophists were there to take them a nearer way to the meaning of the individual. They did not in the long run bear a good name, but they contributed to the growth of the Greek mind, and incidentally, but inevitably, to the remoulding of Greek religion —a genuine contribution, and value, even if we discount their services for their excessive rationalism. But that danger is one that besets the young and the shallow, and Society is saved by the one growing in experience and by the other sinking into nonentity; and the great gains remain, of the emphasised Individual and of emphasised Reason.

Finally, on this part of our subject, there was the greatest Sophist of all, the Athenian public itself; and here we must not ignore the converse of Plato's condemnation.[10] Πόλις ἄνδρα διδάσκει, said Simonides long before, "the city teaches the man"; and Athens taught her sons to be themselves—"democratic men," if one likes to borrow Plato's dreadful picture, but something better, too. Who were the men she honoured? Not only those who echoed her ideas, but an Aeschylus, a Sophocles, a Pericles, a Protagoras—any one who would think something, or do something, or be something, distinctive. Εἰ δὲ τύχῃ τις ἔρδων[11]—"if one accomplish aught of doing"—that was it! Athens loved and honoured it, and invited her sons to *be.* The great funeral speech of Pericles, whether he spoke it or Thucydides wrote it, is a paean upon individuality.

10 Plato, *Republic,* vi. 492 A.
11 Pindar, *Nemeans* vii. 11.

Let us sum up what we find, then—an age full of
the sense of power, interested in ideas, full of contrast
and contest, absorbed in "the spectacle of all time and all
existence," and keen in its interest in every man who
was individual.   Such an age cannot keep altogether off
the question of Religion, and it will have something to
say worth hearing.   Its alertness and its experience will
give it a right to speak—if it be only to question—and it
will say more than was ever dreamed or mumbled in the
rituals of Chthonian gods.

Herodotus has been credited with a simplicity verging
on imbecility, and with a cynical humour to vie almost
with Gibbon; quite unjustly, I think, in both cases.   He
is a larger nature than some of his critics realise, and his
simplicity is that of genius.   He is open-eyed and open-
minded for all he hears about the gods, and he weighs
what he is told.   He does not approach the matter with
a theory; let that be our first point, and it is an important
one.   Around him are men who worship abjectly, and
men who blatantly proclaim their lack of interest.   Herodotus avows his interest, and he collects and notes facts
that bear on the question, and he comments on what he
gathers.   He notes things that suggest divine intervention—miracles, judgments, alleged theophanies, and,
above all, oracles.   But he does not commit himself to all
he is told; this or that "they said—which another may believe, but not I," he says sometimes; and again he emphasises that he tells what he has been told, *that* is his
function; but not necessarily to believe everything men
have told him (vii. 152).   He says frankly that he does
not say anything against oracles, that he does not allege
them to be anything but true (viii. 77), and he gives
telling instances of oracles fulfilled; but he recognises
that oracles have been faked or counterfeited (i. 66, 75;
v. 91; vii. 6).   He feels that the gods did intervene in

the Persian war; they sent the storm that wrecked the
fleet of Xerxes (viii. 13); he traces Providence in the
fecundity of certain animals—design in nature (iii. 108).
He has a sort of pious reticence in speaking of Egyptian
religion; but he makes shrewd comments on the evidence
it supplies as to the origin of Greek gods, cults and
theories.   He believes that Greece learnt the names of
her gods from Egypt after worshipping them for ages
without names (ii. 50-57).   He holds that the Egyptians,
first of all men, taught the immortality of the soul and
its transmigration—"certain Greeks have used that doctrine, some of old, some lately, as if it were their own.
I know their names; but I do not write them" (ii. 123).
Commentators suggest he means Empedocles, though
Pythagoras is the name of which one thinks first; but
he does not, we are told, speak of any but contemporaries
in this way.   It certainly looks as if he sympathised with
the Scythian criticism which he quotes upon Dionysus—
that "it was not fitting to invent a god like this who im-
pels men to frenzy" (iv. 79).   He was interested, too, in
Persian religion—"Images and temples and altars they
do not account it lawful to erect, nay, they even charge
with folly those who do these things; and this, as it
seems to me, because they do not account the gods to be
in the likeness of men, as do the Hellenes.   But it is their
wont to perform sacrifices to Zeus, going up to the most
lofty of the mountains; and the whole circle of the
heavens they call Zeus"; and so forth (i. 131).   This
was a stage in the history of Comparative Religion, which
was perhaps the child of Xenophanes.   Herodotus is
prepared to reconcile Geology and Religion; men said the
gorge of the Peneios was made by Poseidon; he thought
it looked like the work of an earthquake; well, Poseidon
is the author of earthquakes (vii. 129).   Once he raises
the whole problem of prayer.   While the storm raged

against the Persian fleet at Artemisium, the Magians did sacrifice and chanted and "stopped the storm; or else it flagged and dropped of its own accord" (vii. 191). On the other hand, he pulls himself up once at the end of some speculation—"now that I have said so much, may the gods and heroes be gracious!" (ii. 45). And when the Great King plans his expedition against Greece, Herodotus tells stories to show that the king was forced into it by divine agency, and the divine bidding was made clear to him in dreams (vii. 12-18).

There is in all this a good deal of wavering, and it answers to the feeling of the age. It was a question whether the gods did all they were credited with doing; did they look after the affairs of men, intervene in them, guide them? did they give oracles? did they even exist? Herodotus is interested in all these speculations; he is not the author of them, but they all wake something within him, and he keeps his eyes open, as I said, for evidence. He represents the age—eager for the odd event, the striking coincidence (as we call it, not without a theory of our own perhaps)—curious as to customs and the light they throw on origins—ready to speculate in a great way, as Herodotus' own reflections on the Geology of Egypt show—and yet not desirous to break with the gods, in case they are gods.

In spite of the movement of Illumination, which we associate with it, the fifth century had its strong under-currents of piety and orthodoxy. Cimon brought back the bones of Theseus from Scyros to Athens, and that this was not merely like the return of the dead Napoleon from St. Helena to Paris, is shown by the emphasis which Sophocles lays on the advantage to be derived by Attica from the dead Oedipus. "I will show thee," says Oedipus to Theseus, "the way to the place where I must die. But that place reveal thou never unto mortal man—

tell not where it is hidden, nor in what region it lies; that so it may ever make for thee a defence, better than many shields, better than the succouring spear of neighbours." [12]

Foreign gods came in with foreign settlers—Adonis, Sabazios, the Mother of the Gods, and so forth; but their significance for our present purpose lies in the fact that their worship was in Athens a matter primarily of private judgment—a point noted before in the case of the mysteries. Further, the Mother of the Gods, at all events, was destined to have a long and a great history; she was Olympianised more or less, but she remained a possible divinity for world-wide worship—a goddess of universal sway. For such there was a great rôle reserved, though the age was not ripe for them, in spite of tentative identification of Greek gods with Egyptian. They waited for Alexander.

It is sometimes said that Apollo exercised a wide influence for good in Greek morals and politics. I am not clear what the evidence is for this; but in our period the power of Apollo was materially weakened by his desertion to the Persians in the great invasion; and later on the definite support which he promised Sparta in the Peloponnesian war [13] must have made it still further clear how little basis the oracle really had in the divine, that it was an affair of priests who had their price. But a rationalism, political or religious, that cuts men off from heaven, is little joy. We even find Socrates sending Xenophon to consult the god as to whether he should go to Cyrus. And Apollo gave oracles down to Plutarch's day, who boldly said that the god had not lost his glory of three thousand years. Men wished to believe; and in times of fear not only wish but panic swept them back into a fierce orthodoxy. The expulsion of Anaxagoras,

12 Sophocles, *O. C.*, 1520.   13 Thucydides, i. 118.

the prosecution of anybody who could be suspected of the mutilation of the Hermai, the hemlock-cup given to Socrates, remind us how slowly mankind accepts progress in religion.   Yet progress there was, and not the less genuine for being largely unconscious—"veiled progress," as Professor Lewis Campbell called it.

We must now consider more specifically certain points that have occupied us already.   First we must see what the men of this time have to say of the gods; next, what are their thoughts as to moral law, righteousness and sin; and finally what hope or thought they had of immortality.   In every direction we shall find great development.

Dr. Adam grouped Pindar and Sophocles as the most religious of Greek poets—for reasons which I do not quite guess.   I should have said that Euripides had more religion in him than the pair of them.   Pindar, however, stands at the beginning of this century a great figure, a master of sound and colour, a poet who alternately amazes his reader with his wealth and with his poverty of thought.   His poetry is full, as we all know, of gods and myths and legends.   He is pious, aristocratic, brilliant, imaginative, and commonplace; and what he finally believes it is hard to divine—beyond the happiness of good fortune and good birth with wealth, the wisdom of prudence, and, of course, explicitly and fundamentally the supreme value of Poetry.   "God is in heaven and thou upon earth; therefore let thy words be few."   So the Hebrew thinker said (Eccles. v. 2), and Pindar might have borrowed his phrase.   A poet's words can hardly be few, however, and we do not ask of him the severity and immediate consistency of a philosopher.   He has many thoughts upon the gods; and of most of them we can at least say this—that they would not clash with what an orthodox patron would hold.

"God," says Pindar—and we may note at once the large general term, half monotheistic in its vagueness— "God accomplisheth every end whereon he thinketh, God who overtakes the eagle on the wing, and passes the dolphin in the sea, who bendeth the high-minded in his pride, and to others he giveth deathless glory" (*Pyth.* ii. 50). To express the abstract idea of omnipotence he uses pictures of power and speed that touch the imagination with a sense of the wonder of God. And in an age of change and chance and disorder, that omnipotence is inscrutable. "Why askest thou me?" says Cheiron to Apollo. "Thou, who knowest the certain end of all things, who knowest all paths. How many leaves the earth sendeth forth in spring, how many grains of sand in sea and river are rolled by waves and the winds' stress, what shall come to pass, and whence it shall be, thou discernest perfectly" (*Pyth.* ix. 44). Apollo "gave heed to his own wisdom, his mind that knoweth all things; in lies it hath no part, neither in act or thought may god or man deceive him" (*Pyth.* iii. 29). It is so that omniscience is brought home to the mind. All the gods are apt with Pindar to have all divine quality,[14] yet not to be exempt from impulses and passions that in men would be called lawless and animal. It is interesting to see that meanwhile Pindar tones down certain of the ancient legends. Men said that a god ate part of the shoulder of Pelops at the table of Tantalos. "Verily," says Pindar, "many things are wondrous, and haply tales decked out with cunning fables beyond the truth make false men's speech concerning them. . . . Meet is it for a man that concerning gods he speak honourably; for the reproach is less. Of these, son of Tantalos, I will speak contrariwise to them who have gone before me. . . . To

---

[14] L. Campbell, *Religion in Greek Literature*, p. 171; G. F. Moore, *History of Religions*, p. 480.

me it is impossible to call one of the blessed gods canni-
bal; I keep aloof; in telling ill tales is often little gain"
(*Ol.* i. 35 ff.). But tales of lawless love he tells many;
tales that Euripides set in their true light, naked, horrible
and cruel, in his *Ion*; Pindar feels no shame in them. He
wrote poems in honour of an unspeakable dedication to
Aphrodite at Corinth—Pindar, who will tell no ill tale
of God, omnipotent, omniscient. "Forget not to set
God above everything as the cause thereof" (*Pyth.* v.
23). "Zeus giveth this and that (good and evil); Zeus,
lord of all" (*Isth.* v. 52). It is a strange blending of old
story and new moral sense, of destiny over all, and the
gods of Homer and of the Semite. Pindar keeps gods
and men well together—sons of Zeus and daughters of
men produce heroes; man's deeds and end are of the
gods' giving and disposing. "One race there is of men
and one of gods, but from one mother draw we both our
breath, yet is the strength of us diverse altogether, for
the race of man is as nought, but the brazen heaven abideth, a habitation steadfast unto everlasting. Yet withal
have we somewhat in us like unto the immortal's bodily
shape or mighty mind, albeit we know not what course
hath Destiny marked out for us to run." [15]
    If the problems of God and destiny from time to time
rise before the mind of Pindar, they are the dominant
preoccupation of Aeschylus. Dr. Adam conceded to
Aeschylus "a greater intensity of moral purpose, and a
far profounder treatment of moral and religious problems, than either the subjects of Pindar's odes or the
peculiar quality of his genius allowed." [16] How this
should leave Pindar more religious, I do not see. Professor Lewis Campbell, indeed, found a progress in
Aeschylus' thought on these matters, as might well be

[15] Pindar, *Nemean*, vi. 1; cf. Adam, *Vitality of Platonism,* p. 39.
[16] Adam, *Religious Teachers of Greece,* p. 139.

with a man who gave himself so intensely to the greatest
of problems. For a man's mind grows with the tasks
he puts upon it and with the questions to which he conse-
crates it. In the *Suppliants* the legend of Io transformed
to a heifer almost jostles the conception of the Almighti-
ness of Zeus.

> That ancient saying declared aright
>   "The purpose of Zeus there is none may trace."
> To him lieth bare in his own fierce light
>   All—though he shroud it in blackness of night
> From the prying eyes of the earth-born race.
>
> The thing that Zeus by his nod hath decreed,
>   Though ye wrestle therewith, it shall ne'er be o'erthrown;
> For, through tangled ways and shadowy, lead
> The paths of the purpose that none may impede,
>   By no eye to be scanned, by no wisdom known.[17]
>
> *Suppl.* 86-95.

In the *Prometheus* the problem is one of reconciliation,
though the end is lost to us, as we have only one play
of the trilogy; but Fate and Zeus and Prometheus have
issues to settle, which can only be settled on the lines of
justice. In the *Persians*, with a deep sense of the Hellenic triumph and a sense still deeper that divine laws
were working through the conflict, the poet traces an
awful vindication of moral law in the defeat of Xerxes—
not accident, not the envy of the gods, but Justice de-
termines all.

> Zeus sits on high, a chastener of thoughts
> That soar above man's reach, a judge austere.
>
> *Pers.* 827.

The great sin of man is *Hybris*—"Jeshurun waxed
fat and kicked," is the contemptuous phrase of the Hebrew poet, and the very word comes in the *Agamemnon.*

17 A. S. Way, altered a little.

"Struck by the hand of Zeus!" ay, truth indeed,
And traceable: 'tis the act of will decreed
And purpose. Under foot when mortals tread
Fair lovely Sanctities, the Gods, one said,
The easy Gods are careless: 'twas profane!
Here are sin's wages manifest and plain. . . .

> The Rich man hath no tower,
> Whose Pride, in Surfeit's hour,
> Kicks against high-enthroned Right
> And spurns her from his sight.   *Agam.* 379.[18]

And in all the difficulties and perplexities which life
flings round a sentient nature—the fall and rise of fortune, the strife of good and evil—Aeschylus divines a
law of God, just and inevitable, and in it he finds comfort.

> Zeus whosoe'er he be—
>   In that name so it please him hear—
> Zeus, for my help is none but he;
> Conjecture through creation free
>   I cast but cannot find his peer;
> With this strange load upon my mind
> So burdening, only Zeus I find
>   To lift and fling it sheer.   *Agam.* 170.[18]

Justice he finds in God; but as he passes out of the
influence of old legend into the sphere of thought, the
turn of pious phrase "Zeus whosoe'er he be" more than
hints that it is a law rather than a personality that rules.
He has moved beyond Pindar; for he has felt more
deeply, and thought more intensely, and has suffered;
and he has reached a promise of peace. God, in whatever sense we use the name, is righteous; and that is a
discovery that bears on life in every aspect, that will take
men deep into new secrets of God, and that will re-create
at last the whole conception of God; the old legends will
have to go, and man's life will need to be thought out

18 Walter Headlam.

anew. This was the task of Euripides, heir, here at least, to Aeschylus.

But in the meantime there were other thoughts with which men had to reckon. A century earlier the philosophers had sought a primal unity into which to resolve the variety of the world and of all being—water or fire, it might be, or the vague "unlimited." These thoughts were not dead; they had gained currency. In this century Diogenes of Apollonia was pushing Air as the great original. "Air," he said,[19] "as it is called by men, seems to me to be that which has intelligence; all things are steered by Air, and over all things Air has power. For this very thing seems to me God, and I believe that it reaches to everything and disposes everything and is present in everything. . . . The soul of all living creatures is the same, viz. air warmer than the air outside us in which we live, but much colder than the air about the sun." Air he held to be "great and strong and eternal and knowing many things."[20] In other words, Diogenes holds a kind of pantheism, along the lines of matter. Adam called him a Stoic born out of due time. His contemporaries might have asked him, as Plutarch asked the Stoics, what became of God and righteousness on his terms; and what of the soul? and his answer must have satisfied them as little as the Stoics satisfied Plutarch. God, righteousness, and the immortal soul—all swept into matter and impersonality; Religion moves another way. The solution of Diogenes will fail, but it remains a challenge to religion.

Anaxagoras was the first Greek to try to distinguish mind and matter,[21] and that he impressed his times we can conclude from the fact that the wits of the Athenian

19 Adam, *Religious Teachers of Greece*, p. 226; Diels, *Vorsokratiker*, § 51, fr. 5.
20 Fr. 8.
21 See discussion by Adam, *Religious Teachers of Greece*, p. 259, and the evidence of Plato, *Phaedo*, 98 B.

streets nicknamed him *Nous,* and that the orthodox of
the anti-Pericleian party prosecuted him for impiety. But
the ground of the prosecution may have been his conclusion, after some study of meteorites, that the sun was
merely a large mass of incandescent stone. Anaxagoras
held that Mind, which "has all knowledge about everything," "has power over all things that have life" and
"owns no master but itself," "set in order all things that
were to be" and started that rotatory motion which made
the world. Plato represents Socrates as complaining that,
while Anaxagoras started well with his conception of
Mind, he fell back too soon on material forces and causes.

Philosophy, says Callicles in the *Gorgias,* is a good
thing up to a certain point; but you can go too far.
There were people in the fifth century who wanted to
see how it all bore on the gods and on religion; they felt
that religion really was something; everybody had said
so; now what did all this philosophy make of the gods?
Protagoras bluntly said he did not know; he did not even
know whether gods exist or not; his working scheme was
a hand-to-mouth pragmatism—"other people think differently," as we say in Cambridge; and there the thing
rests. Nobody can know, but then everybody can think;
and what you think is true for you, if it is false for me.
But everybody believes in gods of some kind. Prodicos
explained that "primitive man deified the sun and moon,
rivers and fountains, in a word, whatsoever things ben-
efit our life, on account of the services they render, just
as the Egyptians deify the Nile." Here was Comparative
Religion again; Egypt once more gave the clue, and the
physicists were still in the ascendent. Critias went further;[22] the gods were not, as Prodicos suggested, the
creation of a natural instinct; they were the contrivance

---

[22] Verses by Critias, quoted by Sextus Empiricus, *adv. Math.* ix. 54; Diels,
Vorsokratiker, vol. ii. no. 81, p. 620.

of an ingenious man who, because governments could not control everything, imposed them upon the vulgar as an invisible secret police, remarkably effective in maintaining decency—a lie, of course, but a very good one, with truth somewhere or other in it. Three centuries later Polybius is found with much the same idea [23]—and Polybius is a much less flippant figure than Critias. It will be noted for what it is worth, that this view associates the gods with morality.

If any of these views be right, what becomes of the gods? Thucydides was not a typical Athenian, but he shows how little the gods were conceived by ordinary Athenians as being concerned with morality, personal or international. Nicias was pious enough, and ruined Athens at Syracuse. The repulsiveness of the political immorality avowed by Athenian diplomats at Melos would not, the Athenians thought, alienate the sympathy of the gods. The common man, then, after all these ages of thought, was at the primitive point of view—that religion and morality have nothing to do with each other. And, one is tempted to add, there he is still, whenever he is really frightened.

The uncommon man took a different view.

> If gods do deeds of shame, the less gods they!

So said Euripides. He found "great confusion among things divine, yes, and mortal things too" (*Iph. Taur.* 572). Sometimes he seems to lean toward Diogenes of Apollonia and his identification of god and air:—

> Thee, self-begotten, who in aether rolled
> Ceaselessly round, by mystic links dost bind
> The nature of all things, whom veils enfold
> Of light, of dark night, flecked with gleams of gold,
> Of star-hosts dancing round thee without end.
>
> *Fr.* 593.

23 In speaking of the Romans and the pains of hell, vi. 6; cf. p. 294.

Pantheism is as susceptible of splendid language as the orthodoxy of Pindar, but to come to the brute facts of life, and they were many; "O Zeus!" cries Euripides,

> O Zeus! what shall I say? that thou seest men?
> Or that they hold this doctrine all in vain,
> And Chance rules everything among mankind?
>
> *Hec.* 488.

With relentless hand he drew gods doing deeds of shame—not new ones, but the old deeds of shame consecrated in legend—"these be thy gods, O Athens." It was quite clear that he was an atheist, as Aristophanes said; and he did well to go to Macedonia. A self-respecting nation is better without men who think for themselves; they only make trouble. So the Peloponnesian war taught the Athenians. "Dulness and modesty ($\dot{\alpha}\mu\alpha\theta\iota\alpha$ $\mu\epsilon\tau\dot{\alpha}$ $\sigma\omega\phi\rho o\sigma\dot{v}\nu\eta\varsigma$) are a more useful combination than cleverness and license. The simple sort generally make better citizens than the more acute." So said the great Athenian leader.[24] What does a nation engaged in a great war want with intellect? So Euripides went to Macedonia; but before he goes let us hear him once more on God and Righteousness—before the hemlock is given to Socrates and the last voice of all of this century is silenced.

> O stay of earth, who hast thy seat on earth,
> Whoe'er thou art, ill-guessed and hard to know,
> Zeus, whether Nature's law, or mind of man,
> I pray to thee; for, on a noiseless path,
> All mortal things by justice thou dost guide.
>
> *Troades,* 884.

Here are echoes of Aeschylus, and of Diogenes of Apollonia, perhaps—the cry, at all events, of a heart, racked with every question the mind ever framed, crying

24 Cleon, in Thucydides, iii. 37, 38.

aloud for God and Righteousness—the voice of one crying in a wilderness of problems and theories and darkness, alone, individual.

So much said about the gods, the outlines of the discussion of Righteousness, divine and human, are laid
down. The Greek conception of the state implied law;
but Greek thinkers had no term which quite answered
to ours. They called the laws of the state, *Nomoi*; but
Nomoi also meant customs—its more usual meaning at
first. Reflective Greeks saw the significance of this likeness of law and custom; "Custom rules all," says Pindar
as Herodotus quotes him (vii. 104). But in Nature, as
opposed to human society, they saw something else. "If
the sun pass bounds, the Erinnyes, aiders of Justice, will
find him," as we saw. That is poetic language; in plain
prose, Nature manages her business by compulsion, by
necessity, *Ananke*. Between *Nomos* and *Ananke* there
is a broad gulf—between Nature and usage. Where are
we to place what Pericles calls "those unwritten laws, the
transgression of which brings admitted shame"? [25] Where
are the sanctions and basis to be found for that social
morality on which the well-being of state and individual
so obviously depends? That was the question. Pindar
called Truth "the daughter of Zeus" (*Ol.* x. 2), and
Aeschylus, as we have seen, found the closest of associations between Zeus "whoever he be" and Righteousness. Even Euripides, with all his hesitations, had the
same feeling. But what if Protagoras is right, if Truth
is not the daughter of Zeus, but your own notion of the
moment, if right and wrong are exactly what you make
them? We reach the conclusion of Callicles, the practical
man in the *Gorgias*—echoed instinctively by many other
practical people in many lands and ages—that "Right is
the interest of the strongest." That was a sturdy Athen-

[25] Pericles, in Thucydides, ii. 37.

ian conviction which Plato had to refute; and it took
some refutation, for every ancient community rested on
slavery; and what justification was there, or is there,
for any slavery, however well disguised, but just this
"interest of the strongest"? It followed that Right and
Wrong are merely charms, *mantrams,* with which the
many humbug or hypnotise one another—sheer *nothings*
with no foundation in Nature or anywhere else.   Meanwhile the cults continued in the old way, with the old
notions—conspicuously *Nomos* all of them, mere custom, and more obviously unreal, as men entered into the
philosophic conceptions, pantheism, natural law, and the
relativity of all morals.   The priests and prophets made
money out of it, and talked about sin and holiness; but
what were sin and holiness?   The language was old and
unreal.   No doubt there was something in Sophocles'
praise of the "kindly soul" (*O.C.* 495); but then Sophocles always took the safe way and steered clear of the
questions that racked Aeschylus and Euripides.   "Hard
it is," said Simonides long ago, "to be good in truth,
hands and feet and mind foursquare, wrought without
blame."   It was harder than ever now.   And yet, in
spite of questions, or because of them, man's instinct
for righteousness was growing.   It was this that nerved
Euripides' attack on the current opinions of the gods, as
it inspired Plato's a generation later.   Only, a reasoned
and understood foundation had to be found.

The course of Greek thought is very different from
that of Hebrew—here, as in the matter of God's personality.   The Greek never developed any strong sense
of sin, as he never succeeded in making or keeping God
both personal and righteous at the same time.

Finally, on Immortality, what could be said?   The
cults went on as before, with their talk of things in
Hades; but if God and the soul are air, and death mingles

two wafts of air, where is the man? and what is the use
of initiation?   What can it do?   The "holy"—and the
meaning of that word was as essentially the creation of
Nomos as anything; it had nothing to do with Nature,
or Righteousness, or anything recognisable—the "holy"
were on one side and the reflective on the other.   Pindar
in his second *Olympian* drew islands of the blest, round
which ocean breezes blow, where golden flowers are
glowing, where the good, set free from labour, possess
a tearless life, with the honoured of the gods, whosoever
had pleasure in keeping of oaths, whosoever were of good
courage and refrained their souls from all iniquity.   Wonderful vision! but, says Euripides in his *Hippolytus*:

> But if any far-off state there be
> Dearer than life to mortality;
> The hand of the Dark hath hold thereof
> And mist is under and mist above;
> So we are sick for life, and cling
> On earth to this nameless and shining thing.
> For other life is a fountain sealed,
> And the deeps below us are unrevealed,
>   And we drift on legends for ever."

In the curiously explicit phrase of the Greek here, Pindar's pictures fail "through non-demonstration."

Let us sum up what Greece has reached in the centuries so far, and not forget the Hebrews.   Greece at
least has discovered the individual, and made him the
centre of all religion.   With all that men tell us of Greek
conceptions of the City and the State, it is remarkable
that the religious thinkers of Greece had so little to say
of State or City; they offer no very clear account of the
relation of the ultimate divine to anything but the universe and the individual.   When the world broke up
under the successors of Alexander, these were the two

26 Euripides, *Hippolytus,* 191; Gilbert Murray's translation.

fixed points with the Stoic. All Greek history and literature was a preparation for the Stoic emphasis on the individual. The Stoic indeed coined the terms for "conscience" and "will," and much else, but the individual was a discovery of earlier days.

The Greek talked much of God and gods; he personalised his Pantheon and left it behind. He did not listen to God as the Hebrew prophets did; he never had a "Thus saith the Lord." The ultimate divine was too impersonal to speak; it was not Lord; it was hardly interested in any man or in any thing. But Law in one form or another the Greek discovered. Law or Reason, or both, ruled Nature. Morality was written in Nature, and the Stoic at last made the centre of his teaching the Law of Nature.

Greek religion failed. Religion and philosophy parted company. The Greeks looked outside themselves for religion, and one and another religion they found, and intellectualised them, in turn. But great as their influence has been they left the centre of things vague and abstract, and the heart of man will not have it so.

So far as we have reached, we have so much. Man has an inward instinct, a drive within himself, to unify his experience, to personalise God, to ask morality of his God and to impose it upon himself, and finally to demand of God the recognition of his personality and of all that it implies. Greek and Hebrew move toward the same goal, propelled by the same impulses. The whole world, as Paul said, groans together in travail. The cost is great, as prophet and philosopher found; but what is once gained is never quite lost again. Slow and fluctuating, there is a progress in man's conceptions of God, and mankind moves forward with a surer hope of reaching Truth.

VIII

PLATO

THERE is a certain audacity, not unlike the violence of
those who take the Kingdom of Heaven by force, an
audacity almost shameless, about a mere historian who
will endeavour out of the thoughts and the impulses of
a "myriad-minded man" like Plato to make a single
chapter in a story of Progress in Religion. Professed
Platonists will count it irreverent; they will find the treatment inadequate; and they may not hold it a sufficient
apology when the historian pleads guilty to their charges.
But Plato has been the study of centuries, men have given
their lives to him, and it is not wanting in reverence to
use their results, their judgments and conclusions. And
there are other lines of defence. Plato was not the
writer of a coterie; he took pains to write in such a way
as to charm his readers, and, when he has captured them,
to put forward certain lines of thought with such clearness and power that his readers cannot miss them, and
with such life that he starts trains of reflection in their
minds, which work on independently of books. The
Greek world lost the manuscripts of Heraclitus; it nearly
lost Aristotle's; but it kept Plato, read him, submitted
to him, and transmuted him into Greek life, and thence
into much else. Like St. Paul, Plato was a mind irre-
ducible to a system, too progressive through eighty years
to be harmonised with itself by smaller minds. Indeed
with such men it is common to find that they hardly attempt this task themselves; they are more keen to discover and to assimilate truth, reality, nature, than to

reconcile their own views past and present. The endeavour is always there to make unity of all they find; the conviction remains that all reality is in unity with itself; but they outgrow and discard their own thoughts and move onward. It is this habit of mind that above all gives them their influence and makes it wide-reaching. For, like St. Augustine, Plato is the father of many schools; the mystics of antiquity, of the Middle Ages and of the Renaissance, found their stimulus and their exemplar in him, while he gave mankind the real impetus to overcome or to correct mysticism in his insistence on the rational basis and inter-relation of all that is, and on its intelligibility to the human mind.

It is not necessary to tell at length the story of his life or to attempt to date his works; but certain outstanding factors may be noted in passing. He was the child of the great period of Athens and of Greece; and like other children of genius he criticised home and parents as genius only can. To get his point of departure we must recall the grandeur of that fifth century—its sense of power in every sphere that appeals to the human mind. The Greek had conquered sea and sky, navigation, astronomy, geography; he had triumphed over the foreigner; he had tasted empire. He drank too deep of power, and his sense of power led him away from reality; and the reaction against Greek and Athenian perversion of power and truth is to be seen in Plato as well as in Euripides. The most gifted community that the world had seen or has yet seen gave the hemlock-cup to Socrates—and this in its hour of sobriety and reformation, and on the proposal, not of the wilder demagogues, but of quite respectable citizens. Democracy had failed under the test of the Peloponnesian war; and here was a worse failure. Again and again, as we have seen, the forward steps in religious thought are taken under the stress of social breakdown, of human failure on a large scale. Plato's nature was not so easily satisfied as that of Anytos, who impeached Socrates; democracy, human nature, Greek achievement failed to content him, and the old problems of God and righteousness, of society and the soul, rose again.

This time they were handled by a man of genius beyond comparison with anything that Greece had seen. It was his ideal to be "spectator of all time and all existence," [1] to understand, and to base himself on reason; and, at the same time, in him, as Dr. Caird says, "the poet generally spoke before the philosopher." [2] A Puritan with a sense of humour, with an intense feeling for beauty, an inexorable reasoner, a man of friendships, a human being sorely tried by national and personal suffering and humiliation, and a man of genius whose very mistakes are more fertile than another man's escapes from error—he could leave nothing as he found it. He must handle "the whole tragedy and comedy of life," [3] and what he made of it must change the thinking of mankind. It was part of his contribution to human progress that he knew when he had not completely solved a problem. His myths have had an immense influence; to some they were revelation; to others they meant rather the holding of the door open, the suggestion that Reason would at last discover what Intuition divined. Euripides refused, or tried to refuse, Intuition; Plato used it, but he was as clear as Euripides that, however akin to Reason, it is not Reason.

So far, in following the movements of religious thought, we have remarked from the first a progressively strong tendency to emphasise the unity of experience, the

---

1 *Republic*, vi. 486ʌ A.
2 E. Caird, *Evolution of Theology in the Greek Philosophers*, i. p. 93.
3 *Philebus*, 50 B.: τῇ τοῦ βίου ξυμπάσῃ τραγῳδίᾳ καὶ κωμῳδίᾳ.

unity of the universe, to bring, in Plato's own phrase
already quoted, all time and all existence under one survey.   That assumed, men go on to attribute personality
and at last unity to the god-head; they bring God and
man and the universe under one law of righteousness,
and they make more and more of man's personality till
finally they demand for him a full and real immortality.
When one reflects upon these things, one is half tempted
to think them taken directly from Plato himself, so large
a place do they occupy in his thought.

In one memorable phrase after another Plato brings
out that the unity of all things is no accidental quality,
no mere fact, but the essence of their being.   The doctrine of ideas, of the spiritual counterpart, of "the pat-
tern in the heavens," brings the phenomenal into closer
relation with the real world than was ever achieved before.   When he relates all ideas to the idea of good, he
carries this essential unity of all things further still. Man,
he says, is "a heavenly plant, not of the earth"; [4] he too
belongs to the realm of the unseen and the eternal.
"God," says Plato, "made soul prior to body and older
than it." [5]   World-soul and man's soul are all of God.
"When he framed the Universe, he set Reason in soul
and soul in body, in order that he might be the author
of a work that in its nature should be as beautiful and
good as possible." [6]   That is how he looks at all time
and all existence, and the conception of the unity of all
things glows with warmth and colour in a new way.

A man's religious outlook, and not necessarily less if
he be a great man, is affected by the current religious
ideas of his day, whether he sympathise with them or be
repelled by them.   We have seen already something of
the various attitudes of ordinary men and philosophers

4 *Timaeus*, 90 A.
5 *Timaeus*, 34 C.
6 *Timaeus*, 30.

toward the gods. Socrates was given the hemlock because he did not satisfy an Athenian court that his teaching about the gods was correct. They knew that many
of the philosophic teachers, if not downright atheists,
were what we now call agnostic—that was avowedly the
position of Protagoras; they suspected that Socrates had
gods of his own, not those of their city; and they had
evidence of the most dreadful and unmistakable kind
that his pupils were enemies of god and man, were men
of corrupted mind and nature, whoever had corrupted
them. The Athenians were steadily loyal to a traditional
piety which bore no relation, apparently, to astronomical
or other scientific discovery, and still less to any morality
of a progressive kind. Homer was still learnt by heart,[7]
and many people were in their religious thinking still at
a pre-Homeric point of view. The mysteries still gave
men and women what they supposed to be revelations
of the gods, and by exciting certain feelings inspired them
to believe that their immortal happiness was assured.
Orphic priests and others of their kind held more private
initiations and offered reconciliation with the gods on
lines independent of the intellect and of morality, and
on terms tainted with the sordid suggestion of money
profit. Not all Athenian religion was of this rather primitive and emotional type. For when Xenophon represents
Socrates as believing in constant and reliable relations
between gods and men, and as holding "that the gods
know all things, what is said, what is done, what is
planned in silence, they are everywhere present and give
signs to men about all the affairs of men," [8] as recom-
mending Hesiod's famous line:

Give all thou canst in sacrifice to heaven,[9]

[7] Xenophon, *Symposium* 3, 5-6.
[8] *Mem.*, i. 1, 19.
[9] *Mem.*, i. 3, 2; Hesiod, *Works and Days*, 336.

it is clear that he is trying to show how closely in line
his great teacher had been with what the best Athenians
counted real religion.   With all these types, atheist and
traditional, charlatan and genuine, Plato was brought
into contact, and sooner or later into conflict.

When Plato wrote the *Laws,* he traced all unholy acts
and all lawless words to one or other of three beliefs
about the gods; a man who acted or thought amiss must
have supposed one of three things—either that the gods
did not exist; or, secondly, that if they did exist, they
took no care of man; or, thirdly, that they could easily
be appeased by sacrifices, or turned from their course by
prayers.[10] Perhaps even more explicitly he said the same,
in earlier days, in the *Republic* :[11] "Still I hear a voice
saying that the gods cannot be deceived, neither can they
be compelled.   But what if there are no gods? or suppose
them to have no care of human things—why in either
case should we mind about concealment?   And even if
there are gods, and they do care about us, yet we know
of them only from tradition and the genealogies of the
poets; and these are the very persons who say that they
may be influenced and turned by 'sacrifices and soothing
entreaties and by offerings.'[12]   Let us be consistent, then,
and believe both or neither.   If the poets speak truly,
why, then, we had better be unjust, and offer of the fruits
of injustice; for if we are just, although we may escape
the vengeance of heaven, we shall lose the gains of injustice; but if we are unjust we shall keep the gains, and
by our sinning and praying and praying and sinning the
gods will be propitiated, and we shall not be punished.
'But there is a world below in which either we or our
posterity will suffer for our unjust deeds.'   Yes, my
friend, that will be the reflection, but there are mysteries

10 *Laws,* x. 885.
11 *Rep.,* ii. 365 D.
12 Referring to the passage quoted before in 364 D from *Iliad,* ix. 497-501.

and atoning deities, and these have great power. That
is what mighty cities declare; and the children of the
gods, who were their poets and prophets, bear a like
testimony."

Thus the conception of God is not an abstract thing,
a question of the study; it becomes the most practical
thing in the world, the centre of all life; and on it depend character, righteousness, and the very existence
of society. Accordingly nothing is so relevant to the
statesman or to any one who has the good of the state
at heart as "the type of divine tale" [13] commonly told to
the young. "God," Plato says, "must always be represented as he is, whatever the sort of poetry we write,
epic, hymn or tragedy." [14] This was to introduce a new
principle, at once into theology and into education; for,
so far, speculation and belief about the gods had not
commonly been considered in relation either to conduct
or to the training of the young. The orthodoxy of Aristophanes, of popular legend, of the mysteries, was not
inconsistent with the ascription of the most disgusting
savagery and obscenity to the gods. Heraclitus [15] had
made caustic comment on the combination of piety and
filth which still prevailed and was to prevail long after
Plato's days; but Plato was more in the heart of society
than Heraclitus, he was less a critic from without and
more constructive in both instinct and attitude. If the
ideal life of men and women and states is to be attained,
the first thing is to "represent God as he really is."

The very foundations of education were thus to be
changed. Plato left no shadow of doubt about his meaning. Such tales as that of Hephaistos binding his mother
Hera, or that of Zeus sending him flying for taking his
mother's part when she was being beaten, and all the

13 *Rep.*, ii. 379 A.
14 *Rep.*, ii. 379 A.
15 See chap. IV, p. 99.

battles of the gods in Homer would not be admitted at
all in an ideal state.[16] Nor must we listen to Homer or
any other poet who tells us that two jars stand at the
threshold of Zeus, full of lots, one of good and one of
evil, and that, drawing from these as he will, Zeus is
dispenser of good and evil to us; for God is not the
author of evil at all.[17] Nor does God prompt to lies or
to strife; nor, though Aeschylus said it, does God plant
guilt among men when he desires utterly to destroy a
house.[18] Nor does God change shape or take disguise,
or indeed submit to variation at all; for God is no wizard,
and God will not lie;[19] nay, God cannot lie: "the superhuman and divine is absolutely incapable of falsehood;
God is perfectly simple and true both in word and
deed."[20]

This was to give the lie direct to that teaching of
Homer in which the majority of Plato's contemporaries
still believed, and to all poets who modelled themselves
on Homer. There was "an ancient quarrel between
poetry and philosophy"[21]—there always is—so, though
"a certain friendship, a reverence, from the days of boy-
hood" checks Plato when he would speak of Homer, he
speaks none the less; and his conviction carries him further into a condemnation of a great deal of poetry and a
great many poets. "We will fall down and worship him
[this genius in "imitation"] as a sweet and holy and
wonderful being; but we must also inform him that in
our state such as he are not permitted to exist; the law
will not allow them. And so when we have anointed him
with myrrh, and set a garland of wool upon his head, we
shall send him away to another city. For we mean to

16 Rep., ii. 378 D.
17 Rep., ii. 379 E; Iliad, ii. 69; xx.; Rep., ii. 379 C, D, referring to Iliad,
xxiv. 527.
18 Aeschylus, fragm. 160.
19 Rep., ii. 381 E.
20 Rep., ii. 382 E.
21 Rep., x. 607 B.

employ for our soul's health the rougher and severer
poet or story-teller only." [22]

To this criticism of Homer there was already current
a type of reply which long survived.   There were hidden
meanings in the great poet.   Theagenes of Rhegium
about 525 B.C. began the allegorical interpretation of
Homer; Hera was the air, Aphrodite was love; moral
and physical meanings intermingled and confused the
story.[23]   This was a game at which everybody could
play—and did play, more and more as men grew progressively uneasy about the truth and value of the traditions and legends inherited from the ancient days; and
the method passed from Greek students of Homer to
Hebrew students of the Old Testament and to the Christian church.   It flourishes independently in India to-
day; the legends of the gods and their representations in
art may strike the uninitiated grossly, but they are renderings of philosophic and mystical truth.   And the same
retort avails, and admits of no reply.   "Shimga goes
but its songs remain," is the Marathi proverb about the
festival of the god of Kondoba; mystical or not, the
songs are obscene and have their effect.   "We must not
receive" the stories of Homer "into our state," says
Plato, "whether they are allegories or not allegories." [24]
A young man cannot judge what is allegory and what is
not; and anything that he receives into his mind at that
age is hard to wash out, and is unalterable.   So it is the
more important that what they hear first should be stories
of beauty that direct the mind to "excellence."

Plato's thought centred upon God; and he realised, as
any man will who is serious, how God outgoes our best
thoughts.   In a long life of eighty years a mind so active

22 *Rep.*, iii. 398 A.
23 See Gomperz, *Greek Thinkers*, i. pp. 379, 574; C. H. Moore, *Religious
Thought of the Greeks*, p. 350.
24 *Rep.*, ii. 378 D, E.   It seems that Plato's contemporary Metrodorus, a
pupil of Anaxagoras, explained that Agamemnon was the aether.

must have many conceptions of God; and it is possible to say that not so much any single conception, or even an attempt to link and harmonise as many as may be of those conceptions, is so significant as the fact that the man is in the great succession of the "God-intoxicated," that he is always thinking of God, that God is his centre, his atmosphere, his universe. Commentators will of course vary, age by age, in their interpretation of his ideas, as they do in Paul's case; all depends on what element in the teacher's experience touches most closely experience of their own. It was Plato's belief, Professor Burnet says,[25] that no philosophical truth could be communicated in writing at all; it was only by some sort of immediate contact that one soul could kindle the flame in another. The novelist William de Morgan put Plato's idea in the language of our day—"the congenial soil in which the fruit of Intelligence ripens is Suggestion, and the wireless telegraphs of the mind are the means by which it rejoices to communicate."[26] A good deal depends on the "receiver"; if that instrument has defects— and most have—the message will not be complete; things will not be in the same proportion as when transmitted. Plato and Paul have "communicated" to all sorts of "receivers," and the emphasis has been found all over the message, now here and now there. This clash of interpretation is supremely of use; it tells of the teacher's greatness and variety, and it means quickening. "The Maker and Father of this all," says Plato, "it is a hard task to find; and when a man has found him, it is impossible to declare him to all men"[27]—a significant confession which the sympathetic Clement of Alexandria loved to quote.

I do not propose to discuss in its variety and pro-

25 Burnet, *Greek Philosophy*, Part I. p. 1.
26 William de Morgan, *Somehow Good*, p. 331.
27 *Timaeus*, 28 C.

fundity the teaching of Plato upon God; but, by recall-
ing a few outstanding features of that teaching, by quoting again a few well-known sayings, to try to show how
they bear on the line of inquiry which we have been
following. So far, we have seen Greek gods achieve
personality, at the cost of coming under a law of righteousness which made them progressively impossible; and
we have seen philosophers speculating, with little thought
of the divine as men conceived it, as to what was the
origin of the universe, what underlies it, what it is. They
leaned a great deal to physical substance—"Water is
best," quotes Pindar—sometimes to what we should call
force, for "fire" is surely what our physicists call "heat,"
though the conceptions are not quite the same. Anaxagoras lifted the subject to a higher plane when he said
"Mind," and then left it there, as Socrates complains, to
decline to the discussion of "air and ether and water and
other eccentricities." [28]

Now, whatever the commentators conclude to have
been the eventual relation of God and "the idea of good,"
the very suggestion that there might be any relation at
all between them is an immense step forward; for it links
God at once with all existence and on its most spiritual
side, and it gives to the universe a moral unity and intelligibility, a certain warmth too and value, which it had
not had before. Plato's contribution may be measured
when we compare his view with that of Diogenes of
Apollonia a generation or less earlier, that Air is the
basis of all and has intelligence and is good.[29] At all
events God was not to be swamped in physical theory;
and here it is well to recall that the Pantheism on which
the Stoics were continually falling back, in spite of splendid maxims which seemed to imply the personality of
God, Plato counted as equivalent to atheism. God is

<hr>

28 Plato, *Phaedo*, 97, 98.   29 See p. 174.

PLATO 191

not a "form" but a soul, the self-moved mover of the best motions.[30] We touch here the borders of the most difficult of the problems of thought, questions hard enough for us still, that wake in ourselves the cry of Plato that "it *is* hard to find God"; but enough is said, perhaps, to show how the whole question has been moved forward by the long work of Plato.

The ancients were divided as to whether the *Timaeus* was to be reckoned with the myths of Plato, or was to be taken literally, whether it represented Plato's own doctrine or not. In any case it was a fertile work. In it Plato explains why God made (as we say) or took in hand the universe: "He was good, and the good has never at any time a feeling of jealousy towards anything, so he wished everything to become as like himself as possible" (29 E). Three points here may receive comment. Greeks believed for ages that "the divine is envious," but Plato says with emphasis here and elsewhere that "Envy stands without the divine chorus." [31] Likeness to God is, according to Plato, the end and object of creation, and it is the aim of every man who sees aright to become like God. Protagoras had taught that "man was the measure of all," truth was what a man made it, the individual was his own standard. With this doctrine in his mind, Plato in the *Laws* (iv. 716 C) says explicitly that "God would be measure of all things most really and far more than any man, as the saying goes." God being the measure or the standard, creation moves to his likeness, and man, "heavenly plant and not of earth," finds his true nature in "likeness to God." "He who would be dear to God," Plato continues after his allusion to Protagoras, "must, as far as possible, be like him and such as he is. The man who rules himself

30 Burnet, *Greek Philosophy*, Part I. p. 337.
31 *Phaedrus*, 247 A.

is the friend of God, for he is like him." "As far as possible"—the phrase recurs, for Plato finds a refractory element, an "errant cause" πλανωμένη αἰτία) in the universe, which resists the efforts of God and man. Mind is confronted by Necessity, *Nous* by *Ananke*; "even gods cannot fight with necessity," Simonides had once said (viii. 20); and the word comes again in Plato, hard to interpret exactly, but not far from our experience. "Evils, Theodorus," says Socrates in the *Theaetetus* (176 A), "can never quite pass away; of necessity there must be something somehow antagonistic to good. Yet they have no abode among the gods; that cannot be; but of necessity they haunt mortal nature and this earthly sphere. So we must endeavour to escape hence to yonder with all speed. And our escape is to become like God so far as we can, and to become like him is to become righteous and holy, not without wisdom."

However, to return to the making of the world: though God thought out creatures of air and sea and land, he did not himself make them, but delegated their creation to intermediate gods whom he had made—gods, but neither immortal nor beyond dissolution altogether, yet exempt from dissolution and death because they had in his will a bond mightier and more sovereign. He would not himself create the lower beings, for, if by his hands they were made and from him received their life, they would be equal to gods. So upon the gods, whom he addresses in a strange phrase as "gods of gods," he lays the charge of making the other beings, but he gives them an element of soul that they may interweave mortal with immortal.[32] So came man, with being; and his ultimate Author, according to this myth, is at an infinite distance in the heavens, out of contact with the world of evil.[33]

[32] *Timaeus*, 41 A-D.
[33] Adam, *Religious Teachers of Greece*, p. 372.

These intermediate gods, some of them stars,[34] whatever be the measure of stress that Plato meant to lay upon them, were disastrous in the later development of religion. A later age hardens the suggestions of genius into authority and makes dogma out of the phrase, the playful word, the myth that carries no such weight for the man who made it.

Plato was not a Thomas Aquinas, at the end of an age developing and bringing to full expression conceptions exhausted, and destined soon to be thrown aside. He was a pioneer, a radical, a reformer. With his conception of righteousness as progressive likeness to God he could have nothing but contempt for "the noble Hesiod" [35] and his prudential virtues—the good peasant's faith that piety makes the crop heavier and the fleece thicker. "Still gayer ($\nu\varepsilon\alpha\nu\iota\varkappa\acute{\omega}\tau\varepsilon\rho\alpha$) are the blessings that Musaeus and his son Eumolpus gave the righteous at the hand of the gods; they take them down into the world below, in their story, and make them lie on couches, a banquet of the holy, and picture them garlanded, passing their whole time drunk; their idea seems to be that the fairest reward of virtue is immortal drunkenness. This is the style in which they praise justice." [36] This was not excessive parody, it rested on evidence; and it shows how far removed from common belief was Plato's conception of the real nature of righteousness and its real significance. People praised not "righteousness itself" [37] but the advantages that accrue from an established reputation for righteousness; and one great problem of the *Republic* is to show that righteousness or justice, even if stripped of every advantage and associated with all the penalties of unsuccessful un-

34 Cf. C. C. J. Webb, *Studies*, p. 125.
35 *Rep.*, ii. 363 B; Hesiod, *Works and Days*, p. 230.
36 *Rep.*, ii. 363 C.
37 *Rep.*, ii. 361 C.

righteousness, is none the less worth while. If we define it as likeness to God, and conceive of God and the universe as Plato did, then Hesiod and Musaeus and the moralists of the market-place are talking of what they do not understand and with the irrelevance of fundamental ignorance.

With their notions of divine reward and punishment, Plato swept away as indignantly their conceptions of relation with God. If God is without envy, these teachers, one would presume, would conclude with the modern animist that it is waste of time to conciliate him; a good God does not come into practical politics; it is gods who are envious and evil who hold the central place in every-day religion—so much is evident to the prudent. But the idea that gods can be bought to frustrate justice, can be influenced by entreaties and by gifts, though Homer be quoted in its support, is blasphemous. Mendicant prophets may go to the rich men's doors and persuade them that they have a power committed to them by the gods of making atonement for a man's own sins or his ancestor's sins by sacrifices or charms, and to heal them in a course of pleasures and feasts; they may quote the books of Musaeus and Orpheus; [38] but it is all immoral, irreligious, and a negation of the real truth about God and righteousness. It is not on such lines that access will be found to a good God whose chief concern is to have his creatures good and like himself to the uttermost. Escape from the body (*sôma*), the "tomb" (*sêma*) of the immortal soul, is the real way to God; and Plato leans unmistakably to what later days called asceticism and commended as the one path that can take men out of the sensuous and the material; he too urges "withdrawing from the body so far as the conditions of

38 *Rep.*, ii. 364 B, E.

life allow," "dishonouring," mortifying it, and "making life one long study for death." [39]

If Plato dismisses the whole apparatus, intellectual and mechanical, of sacrifice, he must find some other means of contact or relation between the human soul and God. For, as we have seen, the development of experience had been calling for it, and the strength of the mystery-cults and the less regular initiations lay in their promise of effecting it. Plato finds the secret of this contact with heaven in the very nature of the soul itself. When the great God set the gods of his creation to create in turn the rest of beings, he himself gave them, as we saw, the element of soul that they might interweave immortal with mortal. So Plato puts it in the form of myth; but, whatever suggestion of "non-demonstration" (to use the word of Euripides) recourse to myth may carry, it was the fixed and reasoned belief of Plato that the soul is of divine origin despite its earthly wrappings. Here as elsewhere he comes near the Orphic position, and his language has, or seems to have, echoes of Orphic phrase; but his contempt for Orphic priests and teachers, and his insistence on reason, make it clear that he must have another and very different basis from that of Orphic religion. Had not Socrates suggested that virtue, if it does not understand itself, is no better than vice? A religious conviction must rest on some less sandy foundation than feeling. Right opinion, he says in the *Meno* (98 A), is like the miraculous images of Daedalus, apt to run away unless fastened down; and the fastening is the "consideration of the cause," and this gives it "the nature of knowledge," and with it security. If, for the moment, he is dealing with "recollection" as "the tie of

---

39 Cf. R. W. Livingstone, *Greek Genius*, p. 191; *Phaedo*, 65-7; *Phaedrus*, 250; *Rep.*, 611.

the cause," he means more. Recollection points to something larger and of greater scope; it is a phase of the
soul's activity, which follows from its nature; and the
whole must be understood, if the part is to be intelligible;
the two go together. There must be some fundamental
kinship between the soul and the nature of reality (whatever it prove to be), if there is to be any knowledge that
is more than fancy or guessing.

In the *Meno* (81) Plato quotes certain wise men and
women, priests and priestesses and poets (like Pindar
and other inspired men), for the "true and splendid"
belief that the soul of man is immortal and at one time
has an end, which is termed dying, and at another time
is born again, but is never destroyed. To cite such
authority is playful "irony"; he means to base the belief
on something more, and what immediately follows goes
far beyond priest and priestess, and if it rests on "inspiration," it is on Plato's own inspiration. "The soul,
as being immortal, and having been born many times,
and having seen all things that are, whether in this world
or in the world below, has knowledge of them all; and
it is no wonder that she should be able to call to remem-
brance all that she knows about virtue, for, since all
nature is akin and the soul has learned all things, there
is no difficulty in eliciting, or, as men say, learning, all
out of a single recollection, if a man is strenuous and
does not faint; for all inquiry and all learning is but
recollection."

In the *Phaedrus*,[40] in the famous picture of the
charioteer with the two horses, one noble and one ig-
noble—a symbol of the soul, guided by reason and drawn
by spirit and passion [41]—Plato describes how the immortal soul rises into the ideal world, there to behold

40 Jowett's words, in introduction and translation, are freely used in what
follows.
41 *Phaedrus*, 253, 254.

beauty, wisdom, goodness and the other things of God
by which the soul is nourished, to behold Zeus, lord of
heaven, as he goes forth in his winged chariots and the
array of gods and demi-gods and of human souls in their
train—glorious and blessed sights in the interior of
heaven, and he who will may freely behold them; for
jealousy has no place in that divine chorus.   The gods
can rise still higher, for the horses in their chariots are
all noble, and they behold the world beyond—"of the
heaven which is above the heavens no earthly poet has
sung or ever will sing in a worthy manner."   That is the
sphere of true knowledge.   The divine intelligence, and
that of every other soul rightly nourished, is fed upon
mind and pure knowledge; and it is with that such souls
gaze on Being, that they feed on the sight of Truth, and
behold Justice, Temperance and Knowledge absolute.
So the gods live; but with human souls the sight of that
world beyond is fugitive, the driving of the steeds is
hard; but he who is most like God, and best follows God,
sees most.   The vision passes, but the memory of it
abides; and in this world the sight of beauty recalls that
ideal beauty which the soul has seen on high; this is love.
"Love therefore is the intermediary between God and
man, the desire of the beautiful which is also the good,
an earnest of the divine excellence which resides in
heaven, simple and unalloyed." [42]   Perhaps for an English reader the best rendering of Plato is to be found
in Spenser's *Hymnes in Honour of Love and Beautie,*
and in their sequels upon *Heavenly Love and Heavenly
Beautie.*   So Plato

> Buries us with a glory, young once more,
> Pouring heaven into the shut house of earth.

42 R. W. Livingstone, *Greek Genius,* p. 185; quoting *Phaedrus,* 247-251 on.

The soul that is capable of such vision of God is akin
to God, must be, cannot but be; and it is susceptible of
likeness to God if it keep the eyes open for Truth. That
is the real preparation for the world beyond—the quest
of Truth. For the world beyond is real and earnest;
judgment and righteousness are the foundation of all
existence, and in all existence there is nothing so real
as soul, the gift of God from his own nature. "Every
soul is immortal." [43]

Such, in rough and stammering summary, is the teaching of Plato. Argument and myth are interwoven, as
reason and intuition work together to point the mind to
truth. Reason is not intuition, nor is myth argument, as
Euripides saw; and Plato was no duller-witted than the
great poet himself, but he saw in intuition a promise
which Euripides did not. "We drift upon myths to no
purpose," said the poet.[44] "I dare say," we read in the
Phaedo (85 C), "that you, Socrates, feel as I do, how
very hard or almost impossible is the attainment of any
certainty about questions such as these in the present life.
And yet I should deem him a coward who did not test
what is said about them to the uttermost, or whose heart
failed him before he had examined them on every side.
For he should persevere until he has attained one of two
things: either he should discover and learn the truth
about them; or, if this is impossible, I would have him
take the best and most irrefragable of human words
(λόγοι), and let this be the raft upon which he sails
through life—not without risk, as I admit—if he cannot find some word of God which will more surely and
safely carry him." And in the moral law Plato found
his raft. "Of all that has been said" in the *Gorgias,* the
dialogue concludes (52): "Nothing remains unshaken
but the saying that to do injustice is more to be avoided

---

[43] *Phaedrus,* 245.   [44] *Hippolytus, 197.*

than to suffer injustice, and that the reality and not the appearance of virtue is to be followed above all things . . . for you will never come to any harm in the practice of virtue, if you are a really good and true man." As for the myths, "a man of sense will not insist that these things are exactly as I have described them. But I think he will believe that something of the kind is true of the soul and her habitations."

God, then, and the soul and righteousness are the fixed points in religion, and in all time and all existence they belong together and cannot be thought of apart. This is the great contribution of Plato. Greek thought had been moving tentatively to this conclusion for centuries; Plato gave it an immense lift forward. That he did not solve all the questions, a genius of such glory did not need to be told; his critics have never been his peers. He left gaps and difficulties; his star-gods made trouble; he seemed to fluctuate between God, gods and the vague "divine," perhaps wavering less than the phrase of the moment suggested to duller minds, perhaps still hovering over a difficult question. But he became the teacher of all the thoughtful, of all the religious. They fell far below him; but, till he became a canon and a dogma, Plato was to every age of the Greek world, and to all who have loved that world, though born themselves

Beyond the sea, beyond Atlantic bounds,[45]

an inspiration and a glory. "It is written in its nature that the soul takes wings," said Longinus, "at the very sight of the true sublime, and soars on high with proud uprising, as full of joy and triumph as if she had herself produced what she sees." [46] And that has been the constant effect of Plato's teaching.

45 Euripides, *Hippolytus*, 1053.
46 Longinus, *On the Sublime*, vii. 2.

IX

THE GREEK WORLD AFTER ALEXANDER

THE age of Greece which Homer sums up is far removed
from that which reaches from Heraclitus to Pericles;
but hardly less is the difference in character between
Periclean Athens and the Hellenistic cities of Antioch
and Alexandria. Thought and society react on each
other. An age when social landmarks are swept bodily
away will, as we have seen, show great changes in the
ideas of men; the fundamental preconceptions will be
altered. Even a very short experience of social chaos
will shatter men's best-established intellectual cosmos,
and conversely a new idea will revolutionise society.
France took seriously the idea of equality with liberty,
and her revolution was the precursor of a revolution still
greater, if less vividly dramatic, over the whole world.
The idea of the survival of the fittest, and the philosophy
moulded upon it, have already bad results, but the full
outcome of them we cannot even forecast. The sophistic
movement in Greece is beyond doubt connected with the
Greek expansion over the Mediterranean, and the development of the Greek city, and above all of the Greek
individual. The age produced by such factors could not
be like that pictured by Homer, however strong the
family likeness.

It is a commonplace that, while Aristotle was making
his collection of the constitutions of the Greek cities,
Alexander, as much by his career as by any action in
particular, had relegated the cities and their constitutions
to the dead and irrecoverable past. Even with the Eu-

ropean war fresh in our memories, with the new Europe and its new nations before our eyes, its new politics and principles, the League of Nations and the direct action of labour upon the state, it is hard for us to realise how completely a short span of years may transform the world. Philip of Macedon died in 338 B.C.; it was to be expected that his empire would fall to pieces, that the people he had welded would break up into its original tribes, that Macedon would be again in the welter of civil war with no principle beyond the interest of this pretender and that, that Greece would go on as before, weakening herself as one city claimed and lost leadership of the Greek world after another. "The thing that hath been, it is that which shall be" (Eccles. i. 9). But it was not to be. Fifteen years later Philip's successor died— not in Greece, not in Macedon, but in Babylon. The world he left was as little like the world he found, as the nineteenth-century Europe was like the fifteenth-century Europe.

Alexander had led his conquering Macedonians to lands that lay almost beyond the knowledge of man. Of Indians Greeks had long spoken, but not with much very close knowledge. Herodotus tells us that early morning is the hottest part of the day in India and that the heat grows less towards noon.[1] So the historian had conjectured on the basis of his physical theories scarcely more than a century before, but Alexander's soldiers knew better when to look for the cool of the day in the Panjāb. Common men had ranged outside the map, had seen things and been in places which in the great days of Greece had been almost mythical. The God Dionysus, legend said, had conquered the world, but a later day modelled his adventures on those of Alexander—a fact

1 Herodotus, iii. 104; but see H. G. Rawlinson, *Intercourse between India and the Western World*, pp. 21-24, for the real knowledge of India shown by Herodotus.

that may serve as a sort of symbol for us.[2]   Alexander,
then, had given the world a new Geography, vastly
larger than it had had before, and based on knowledge;
for, beside marching over strange lands himself, he had
sent his admirals to explore the rivers and the Southern
Sea;[3] and he involved the whole ancient world in new
conceptions of godhead.   Dionysus was not the only god
to feel his influence; all of them felt it, as all the human
inhabitants of the world felt it.   Life in every aspect
responded to the new knowledge and the new conditions.

The great new idea of Alexander has been summed
up as "the marriage of Europe and Asia"—an epigram
and an ideal to which he gave symbolic form, in a terribly concrete way, by marrying some thousands of captive Oriental women to his Macedonians.[4]   What befel
the victims of this experiment in idealism, when the lord
of the husbands died at Babylon, we are not told.   A
prosaic mind might have prophesied failure for that
experiment and for the larger experiment of uniting Asia
and Europe in one kingdom under one head.   The kingdom endured for the last two or three years of Alexander's reign, and then it fell to pieces; it too was a
failure.   It is the function of prosaic minds to predict
failure almost automatically.   But it is only the practical
people who fail utterly; if the first crude embodiments
of the great ideas come to nothing, the ideas do not
perish.   The long Persian wars, the long intrigues of the
Persian court with the dominant cities of Greece—were
they the real world, or a hideous perversion of it?   Was
the East East and the West West; were the twain never
to meet?   Or was the world one, and humanity one—
the bright varieties of race and speech and religion all

2 Cf. story quoted but not believed by Arrian, *Anabasis*, vi. 28, about a
triumph celebrated in Carmania by Alexander in the style of Dionysus.   See
W. S. Ferguson, *Hellenistic Athens*, p. 12, n.
3 See Arrian, *Anabasis*, vi. 18, 19, 20.
4 Arrian, *Anabasis*, vii. 4, 4-8.

significant of a higher life yet to be, all contributions to an ideal mankind? Once Greek travellers and thinkers had unconsciously accepted the larger world; Xenophanes had corrected Colophon by North Africa, Herodotus had drawn on Egyptians, Persians, and even Scythians for ideas that would enrich Greece; Xenophon had sketched the ideal ruler in the Persian Cyrus. But the intrigues of peace perhaps had effected what open war had not, or it may be that Greek culture grown self-conscious was alone to blame; Greece had committed herself to the view that the Greek is Nature's aristocrat, the rest of men slaves by Nature's design in many cases, and nowhere much better.[5] It was a shock to this frame of mind to see Macedon rise swiftly in twenty years from being a welter of tribes and cantons to be mistress of the Greek world. But the shock was softened by the reflection that Macedonians were a sort of Greeks—not the best sort, but poor relations, a cadet branch if not a shade illegitimate, intellectually unequal, but Greek enough to save the theory.[6] The Persian nobles with whom Alexander consorted, with whose daughters he and his captains married, were not Greek at all and could never be disguised as anything but what they were—barbarians.

The great Empire broke up, but certain things remained. The world had been one, actually and politically, if only for a few years. That of itself was a revelation, a stimulus to thought, a challenge, a prophecy. The unwieldy unstable kingdoms that succeeded the Empire, and their hideous wars—wars vulgar for the want of any ground higher than mere personal ambitions, and waged by troops with as little principle as the kings to whom they were bound by the cash nexus alone

5 Aristotle, *Politics*, i. 6, p. 1255a.
6 Cf. Herodotus, v. 22, on the claims of the earlier Alexander and his family to be Greek. Demosthenes ranked them as barbarians.

—there seemed to be little of the ideal in these. Yet ideal there was, vulgarised for the moment, but an echo of the great idealist himself, and again a prophecy; the unity of the world underlay all these confusions, and nerved the vulgar hope of each mock Alexander.[7] It was no longer in Nature that East and West should be separate. Our modern belief in the mailed fist, in efficiency and the survival of the fittest, is not after all quite new. Nature, as sophists and soldiers saw her then, "red in tooth and claw," shouted aloud that the world was one and awaited the Conquerer. "To the strongest," murmured the dying Alexander,[8] when his guards asked what should be done with his empire. Nature said the same, and offered the strongest One World for his own. This drastic expression of the unity of all existence was a lesson which humanity could not fail to grasp, however badly the dynasts failed to achieve their purpose.

To pass from kings to commoners, lowlier men but not more vulgar, the new era gave them a world with barriers swept away. When the Roman Empire was at last established after three centuries, men from Plutarch to Claudian remarked with a wonder, which perhaps surprised us in the days before the war with its submarines and peace with its passports, that all the lands and all the seas were open for every man. Alexander was the great opener of the world. Greeks from Antimenidas to Herodotus had travelled the East and the West; but in the track of Alexander's battalions traders and settlers and would-be civil servants followed in swarms to the new centres to which trade was shifting. To be an exile was a tragic thing in the old days, bitterest of experiences; now it was preferable and natural. Then the

---

[7] Compare what Polybius (v. 102): says of Philip V. of Macedon in 217 B.C.: "a family which above all families has somehow a tendency to aim at universal monarchy"; also v. 104.
[8] Arrian, *Anabasis*, vii. 26, 3.

Greek was driven out of his city by violence; now he chose to go and live at Antioch or Babylon, and the little provincial town among the hills could carry on its high politics without him. The vulgar Greek had found out what the kings had learnt, that all the world was one. To trade or to fight or to administer at the foreigner's expense, he left the homeland for ever; he was done with the parish, he chose the world.

The thoughtful element in Greece made the same discovery. When it was suggested to Socrates that he might break prison and live in Thessaly, "What would one want to live in Thessaly for?" [9] he asked, and he might well ask. Isocrates, his younger contemporary, makes it abundantly clear, as do the lives of the philosophers, that educated people preferred one city to all others. Education and culture drew men from their own lands to Athens, as art draws English and Americans to Italy, to live there. Gradually other centres sprang up which had similar attractions. Alexandria was not the least like Athens, as little like it as New York is like Oxford; but, as in our modern parallel, it was not hard to surmise that a man of culture might prefer the larger place and have reason, intelligible enough, for his choice. Or if he did not care for Alexandria, there were Antioch, Rhodes, and Pergamum, and further afield Seleucia on the Euphrates.

The spread of Greeks all over the eastern Mediterranean and into the lands of Seleucus, to Babylonia and to Bactria, produced many by-products. To-day in India the Indian himself will wear European boots and trousers and sun-helmet; he will have a European house in a hill-station; he will send his son to England to be educated; he may remove to England himself; and all this despite barriers of colour and creed that were non-existent in that ancient world. It is not the product of government

9 Cf. Plato, *Crito*, 53, 54.

policy; it is the result of continuity, of intercourse. So in that ancient world, men everywhere learnt Greek, read Greek, talked Greek, and at last thought Greek. The Hellenisation of the world had begun.

The Greek spirit made its way into the strongholds of what we may call the old world; for the Greek spirit is always new, the Greek "ever young, a child in soul," as the old Egyptian in Plato's story said to Solon. Barbarians, as Celsus conceded in his attack on Christianity, are able to discover religious truth—religious ideas, we might translate it, *dogmata* is his word; but to criticise and to establish what the barbarians have discovered, to develop it and bring it to bear on virtue (the Greek *aretê* is hardly translateable in any of our modern barbarian tongues)—the Greeks, he held, are better at that task.[10] To criticise, to compare, to judge—that is the Greek gift; the foreigner shall amass the evidence, the Greek shall sum it up and give the verdict. All was confusion, says the Greek philosopher speaking of the universe, but Mind came and made a cosmos of it. So the Greek was to do in the world of the mind; and men responded, obstinately and slowly, but under the irresistible compulsion and charm of higher thought. The dynasts made the world one; they abolished the old ways of life, city and king and cult; they opened new trade routes to bring the nations together; and the Greek came and made the whole intellectually right, and therefore first tolerable and then natural. The man who thought on Greek lines had, more emphatically than the trader, emerged from the parish; he lived and thought, a citizen of the world. The eyes of mankind were opened and they had a new spiritual justification for the largest life. The dialects recede in speech; Attic becomes the one language of letters, the language of government used by the Macedonian kings,

10 Celsus, quoted by Origen, *adv. Celsum,* i. 2.

modified inevitably;[11] and in the world of thought and
spirit it is the same; the rustic is shed, the local discarded,
and men of all origins become mutually intelligible. This
is no slight thing; it has invariably spiritual consequences
of the most momentous. The international exchange of
writers and thinkers is one of the greatest and most hopeful factors of the modern world. This was one part of
Hellenisation. In the ancient world it took another form.
Men of every race virtually became Greek; they did their
thinking in Greek, and made their contributions in Greek.
The Greek language and literature became a sort of
clearing-house of ideas. Man became "cosmopolitan"—
the word was newly coined by Diogenes[12]—they were
citizens of the world; and it has been shrewdly noted that
the world as a rule was as Greek as the word.[13]

It is never an easy thing to make out the pedigree of
an idea. The collection of literary parallels is a beginner's game; sometimes it tells us a little, but as often
nothing. Macrobius, or anybody else who has scissors,
can show us that Virgil read Homer, or that Milton read
Virgil, or both Euripides. But quite as often, or more
often, the great influences are not to be catalogued in
this simple way. No book perhaps has had more influence on modern thinking than Darwin's *Origin of
Species*; that influence is not to be demonstrated like that
of Homer upon Virgil, but it is not the less real. If Zeno
the Stoic became a Greek, and one of the greatest forces in
Greek thought, his first lessons in thought were given him
by Phoenician mother or nurse; and however effective
a man's conversion or perversion in religion or race may
be, it is never complete; his sub-conscious mind never
loses its earliest acquisitions. The Semite might be Hel-

11 J. H. Moulton, *Grammar of New Testament Greek*, pp. 30 ff., on the rise
of the "Common Greek' as a by-product of Alexander's achievement, in the
great armies, and in the new cities.
12 Cf. *Diog. Laert.*, vi. 63.
13 Beloch, *Gr. Gesch.*, III. i. p. 412.

208 PROGRESS IN RELIGION

lenised and meet the Greek on equal terms, but unconsciously his Greek friends would absorb from him ideas
not primarily Greek—not inconsistent perhaps with their
Greek training and Greek ideas, but not of the original
stock. Intermarriage invariably blends types of minds
as it does types of race; he is a father of strong character
whose children are not more moulded by their mother.
Even foreign servants, as English parents in India know,
can do almost as much; sometimes it might be truer to
say they do more. The Macedonians, says Livy, degen-
erated into Syrians, Parthians, and Egyptians.[14] If men
did not speak then as now of Levantines, none the less
Levantines there were. There were half-castes long before Alexander's experiment in international intermarriage. Antisthenes the Cynic was said to be the son of a
Thracian woman—*i.e.* a foreigner and a slave-woman.
Birth, adoption, migration, reading, and, as ever, talk,
were factors making for a new world. These are forces
ever with us.

But in that world more than these permanent and natural factors were at work. The kings were Greek, or suf-
ficiently Greek to be conscious that they must be quite
Greek, must make good any gaps in their qualifications.
The simplest way was to emphasise Greek culture; to be
missionaries of Hellenism. Ptolemy Soter founded the
Museum in Alexandria, a library, a place of study, a
University—if the word may shed enough of its Latin
origin to suggest studies and students with a minimum of
organisation, learning without examinations and degrees,
but not without disorder and other diversions—

> The due vicissitudes of rest and toil.

The example was, more or less, followed by the Seleucids
at Antioch and by the Attalids at Pergamum—by both

14 Livy, xxxviii. 17.

with very conspicuous results. Schools sprang up or were founded elsewhere; sophists or lecturers travelled everywhere, and taught and lectured as they went. Books were cheaper [15] and were multiplied. Politics there were none, and patriotism was difficult; to what could a man be loyal? The last of the Attalids bequeathed his kingdom to Rome, probably the best thing for the kingdom in such times, a kingdom without race or nationality, without a past, and without self-government. Men who wished to live were driven to thought or to art.

For thought the world was in many ways better equipped than ever before. Men had not indeed the political sense, which only personal experience of politics can give; but the training of the old days was not all lost. To it was added the consciousness of a larger world, of a great expansion of experience, of the value of the contributions of other races and other times. There was Geography, there was natural science, there was the great brotherhood of the human race, never so fully realised, so painfully or so gladly. Above all, everything was reduced at last to a common denominator, if we may so put it; it was possible to compare things at last, which could not before have been brought together. And the man who was to do the thinking had a new standpoint. Athens would have none of Anaxagoras; it gave Socrates the hemlock; that was how the most cultivated and developed community of antiquity stood towards the philosopher's position, how it regarded "the contemplation of all time and all existence." By now all that was gone; the thinker was set free—free as the mercenary soldier to voyage where he would, and battle as he pleased, in the realms of thought; and the religious was as free. It was no matter of choice; the freedom was forced on men by the kings who blotted out the past and made nothing

15 Cheap, and inaccurately transcribed; cf. *Strabo*, xiii. 1, 55.

of frontiers old or new. The very chaos of the world
and of Society made reconstruction easier and more inevitable. The comfortable systems were gone, so far
as they had ever existed. The thinker had to start again,
with a new freedom and a wealth of material that might
be stimulating or might paralyse.

He must start as an individual face to face with the
universe; and there lies the key to most of the thought
of the period. The universe is the most splendid of societies, but compared with Athens or even with Phlius
it is a dull club; it is impossible to know the members,
and there is no blackballing; it is like a university without colleges. The best a man could do was to pick up
with whom he could, as one does on ship-board; and, as
on ship-board, the antipathies are dulled. You sit next
a foreigner, but it is not for long, and by and by the
courtesies of the table open your minds; so in that world
there was no longer any sense in race-feuds, and very
little in any feuds at all. If the ties that bound a man to
his neighbours were all loosed, the barriers that kept him
from his enemies were broken. Theban, Athenian, and
Corinthian, how they had warred in the past![16] Now
they lived in the same king's camp as their grandfathers
had in Xenophon's in perhaps the same regions; they
traded on the same quays in the Nile or the Euphrates;
and among barbarians the old stories grew dim and the
race-hatreds with them. Courtesy, kindness, the good
turn received and repaid—they were nothing, the mere
decencies of ship-board; but, being nothing, they came
to be something—the expression, half conscious, of a
new sense of common humanity. So the solitary thinker
brought to his task of the reconstruction of the universe
an unconsidered equipment of new human feelings, the
more potent for being half-conscious, natural, and not

16 Cf. p. 210.

based on a view of life or a philosophy; and in time they passed into his philosophy and contributed to it more than might have been expected. It was easier for the Stoic to reach and to teach his dogma of our common humanity, when he and we had fallen into the way of recognising it by instinct, without the horrible disturbance that the old hatreds of neighbour cities had once made.

There, then, is the new world, larger, vaster, stranger than the old; traditions broken, the future uncertain; but the human soul as ever gaining something out of loss, finding freedom and friendship in chaos, and bravely setting about a permanent home for itself where all was fugitive. For those whose theme is progress in religion, there could hardly be a more promising field. It is when an old world breaks up past repair, that it is possible for new truth to inspire souls set free to divine a new cosmos and a larger God behind it.

The re-thinking of God in the age after Alexander was, as it always is, conditioned by the dominant thoughts and experiences of the time. The movement of thought, when it does move, has always been towards unity and personality in God, to a heightening of the emphasis on man's personality, to a demand for justice in the relations of God and man, for righteousness in the Universe. Greek thought in the great old days had been more apt to recognise the unity than the personality of God. The Greek had been conscious of law and of mind in the universe, and polytheism was already some generations before Alexander losing its hold upon thinkers; though there were still now and then reminders that Athens had its national gods and counted it important that the education of youth should include them, that people perhaps still believed that those gods made national prosperity depend upon national piety. But Alexander, it would seem, had declared to all men that the local gods of Athens were politically negligible. Not that he said so, or even thought so, any more than Athens perhaps had felt about the gods of Melos eighty years before; but his career gave men new conceptions of the physical world and new knowledge of the ideas of other men, and the result was a decline of interest in the gods of the city state.

Men would seem to have reflected that these gods had never been of much account outside their little frontiers, and the world was very wide indeed, very much larger than one could associate with those gods. If one can imagine how an English villager, who migrated to the New World and became a millionaire, might feel toward the squire and parson of the parish where he grew up, the analogy may help us. There the squire is with his old acres, the parson with his little school, laying down the law and receiving local homage as of old; the returning emigrant may find them absurd or pleasant as may be, but he will certainly feel them to be narrow and trivial in outlook and sympathy, unrelated with the new large world he knows, and unintelligent of his own experience —his inferiors, in short, unless they have special grace. This special grace the old gods of the city state had not. Their statues had it, because a sculptor of note made them—"a sculptor who," the returning soldier of fortune reflected, "will make my statue one of these days," and who probably did it better, finding portraiture more congenial than creation. What made the gods more absurd was the practice that flourished in the third century and onward, of deifying adventurer princes—Demetrius is the great classical example, a god of very present help in trouble, as the famous Athenian hymn [17] said about him, bluntly adding that the other gods were of little

17 Quoted in *Athenaeus*, vi. p. 253.

use; they either did not exist or did not attend to men; Demetrius was not stone nor wood, but real. There are more points of view than one from which these deifications may be considered; there is a philosophic defence of them which we shall have to consider later on; but to any one who knew Demetrius personally the hymn and the consecration made both the Athenians and their gods absurd. None the less, like the squire in the parish, the local gods maintained themselves in their own homes, as is proved by coinage and dedication.

The real gods must in any case be beings more really related to the world men know; a god like the squire of the old village does not fit with the new world that Alexander rules. Alexander is better, or even Demetrius, as the Athenians said. But Demetrius would not do. The real gods must have range of mind, and actual power, beyond even Alexander's. And gods, or more often goddesses, were found, as we shall see, whose sway outran and outlasted the great king's—gods of life and death, goddesses of birth and re-birth, of this world and the world beyond. Simultaneously, another disaster befel the old gods; the deification of army leaders inspired the suggestion that they too like Demetrius had originally been men and women. Euhemerism discredited the old gods; but it did not touch the deities who give life and who rule death, and the sole defence for the old gods became the plea that they are subordinates of these greater gods, or, better still, that perhaps they *are* the greater gods, named or mis-named in each locality. They began gradually to lose their personality as the many Zeus-es of the days before Homer became fused, as we saw, in the Homeric father of gods and men.

The new gods, however gracefully accommodated in the Greek pantheon, were patently of foreign origin. It could never be obscured that Isis belonged to Egypt and

Cybele to Phrygia.   But somehow they had the power, that Greek gods and goddesses lacked, of extending their frontiers with a sweep like Alexander's.   If the gods of the Greeks imposed their names on those of the Romans, it was for literary purposes chiefly; but with Isis and Cybele it was quite different.   They gradually captured the world and held it long.   The barbarians, it would appear, really were better at discovering religious beliefs, at discovering gods.   But the Greeks brought their minds to bear on the gods and goddesses so discovered, and gave a rather different explanation of them.   They became functions of something else, more divine or less divine as one chose to regard it, but probably less personal if more powerful.   But what it was, was a problem not easily solved.

There were two sets of phenomena to explain, even if one did combine them and call the compound, the totality of all experience, the underlying reality, Nature. The word was by now an old one, long used by the Sophists, and to be used again and with more grandeur by the Stoics.   But the explanation men give of gods and laws and experience often needs itself to be explained; and how was one to reconcile the facts of Law and the facts of Lawlessness?   The beautiful cantos of Spenser's incomplete seventh book of the *Faerie Queene* remind us of the difficulty of Mutabilitie in a Universe of Law.   Let us look at what the citizen of the world found.

He found, as his great-grandfather had found, a world ruled by law—generation, growth and death, controlled by laws whose action could be observed, even if their causes were hard to divine.   Summer and winter, seedtime and harvest—all seemed fixed by law.   We know the effect of scientific research and scientific theory in the nineteenth century, and we can appreciate that Reign of Law (I borrow the phrase from the title of a book now

forgotten) which the ancients observed, not indeed over
so wide a sphere as our fathers, but over one wide enough
to stimulate thought and to suggest tempting generalisations.   But what has happened in our own day befel also
in the era of the Macedonian kings.   What Biology has
done of late years, Astronomy did then; it gave a heightening to the idea of Law, and weight to the conception of
the unity of the universe.   Whether the stars, as some
people began to say under Eastern influence, were gods,
or were brute matter controlled by Necessity, that vague
term which served Greece for our Natural Law—was it
not possible in a world, which certainly appeared to be
one, which might, not inconceivably, be a living being itself, that the various parts of that world were members
one of another, that not merely crops and blights, and possibly the tides of those larger seas about the world's outer
edges, were ruled and given their seasons by the heavenly
bodies, but that the lives and destinies of men also were
controlled and shaped by those "bright rulers, gleaming
in aether, bringers of summer and winter to men"? [18]
After all that the philosophers had said of Mind in man,
it was clear there was Mind of some sort beyond him;
was his mind, was he, independent of the greater Mind?
Was that thinkable?   So the steps were taken that led
men to the conception of Fate—*Heimarméne,* that absolute inevitable control of all things by the power that
wheels the stars, we should say and expect them to say,
but many of them said "by the stars" and left it there.
The emphasis on the unity of the universe can hardly
go much further.

But there were other phenomena which it was hard to
reduce to law, hard to make intelligible to reason at all,
hard to find any sense in whatever.   To many the collapse of the old order was a mystery with no solution,

18 Aeschylus, *Agam.* 5, 6.

beyond solution, and it had all turned on the accident of Philip having a son of genius, or (a more desperate thought) on the accident of Alexander having an incredible run of luck. Four hundred years later Greece was still capable of debating whether Alexander owed his greatness to genius (*aretê*) or to luck. In 312 B.C. Seleucus was a beggar at the court of Ptolemy; next year he was King of the East. Thirty years later he defeated Ptolemy Ceraunus in battle, took him prisoner, forgave him for his father's sake, and was murdered by him. "The Queen is dead; how fortune does banter us!" The ejaculation of the English eighteenth century gives the only clue that some could find to the history of Alexander's successors and their sons. Luck made a man king, luck saved a crown, luck established a dynasty; and luck became a candidate for the throne of the Universe. *Tyche* was no new word in Greece, but now it gained new significance; *Tyche* ruled the world, prince and beggar.[19] Men lost faith in order; things happened, whatever a man might plan, however he might work; virtue, vice, wisdom, folly were irrelevant; all was freak and whim, or if that imply some sort of personality behind phenomena, all was pure fluke, like the falling of dice. As Menander said, fluke was God:—

τἀυτόματόν ἐστιν ὡς ἔοικέ που θεός.

If the stars are ruled by Law, and all human affairs by Chance, what can be made of life? The riddle was

19 Cf. Tte story which Polybius (viii. 22) tells of the tears of Antiochus when Archaeus was brought before him in chains and he saw τὸ δυσφύλακτον καὶ παράλογον τῶν ἐκ τῆς τύχης συβαινόντων; cf. Bevan, *House of Helecus*, ii. pp. 5-13. See also the comment of Demetrius of Phalerum (*Polybius*, xxix, 21) on fortune's freaks in fifty years, the fall of the Persians, the rise of the Macedonians, and Fortune still uncertain what to do with them. One may recall the lines quoted, it is said, by Brutus before he killed himself at Philippi (*Dio Cassius*, lxvii. 49):

ὦ τλῆμον ἀρετή, λόγος ἄρ' ἦσθ', ἐγὼ δέ σε
ὡς ἔργον ἤσκουν· σὺ δ' ἄρ' ἐδούλευες τύχῃ.

insoluble, and the only outcome of attempting to solve it was despair. There was a painter, says Sextus Empiricus,[20] who tried again and again to paint the foam on a horse's mouth; he lost his temper at last, and in anger threw his sponge at his picture; the sponge hit the mouth of the horse, and produced the foam that skill could not achieve; so with the thinker—he thought hard, wrestled with the problem in vain, and then he too (as we say) threw up the sponge, and found peace in so doing. So came the Sceptic.

But scepticism is not a working basis of life; a man cannot maintain a family on scepticism. Faith and hope are the foundations of the family, and they are laid by love, unconscious of its great spiritual venture in laying them. Men felt there must be some reality somewhere, or something that would serve for reality; but everything broke down that a man touched; thought failed to solve the problem of man's life and the problem of the universe; righteousness did not achieve reward in comfort or in happiness; trade and business were wrecked at any moment by the meaningless war of some foolish greedy despot; the human mind was reduced to desperation. There were the children; what was to become of them? If the physician could not hit the cure for their ailments, perhaps the quack could; or the old barbarian nurse who loved them might remember something her people far away had practised. If the gods of Greece had collapsed, if the philosophers were reduced to throwing up the sponge—well, in this world, where we are learning that there are other people besides the Greeks, perhaps some of the barbarians know of gods or daemons, something or other effectual, that, if not final, will tide us over the interim. The interim was the urgent problem; the mysteries of the universe and their eventual solution could

20 Sextus Empricus, *adv. Mathematieos.*

wait. Isis and Cybele may be eventually as fugitive as Alexander or Demetrius, things of a longer day, but ephemeral too; well, our day is shorter, and they may avail to help us and our children. Melancholy and depressing as is this all-round despair, there is in it still a heightening of love, a keener sense of individual needs. The state was gone, the race was going; Alexander had swept the state away, the races were being merged in one another, for if he too was gone, his work went on— still the family remained, and the *ego* found a new interest in it, where it could face the venture. There were indeed many who would not take the risk; the philosophers generally did without children, and common people of means began to limit their numbers; and race-suicide did not go unrecognised.[21]   Still, where men dared to live, where the venture of the family was made, some attempt must be made for what Plato called a "raft" to take men over the sea of life. Gods of some sort seemed the obvious solution; and if philosophy will not support us in our new alliances, well, philosophy has nothing to offer us, and facts of a sort, facts however temporary, "rafts" however precarious, are better than instant drowning.

To sum up, the new age found the problem of God immensely hard. All the facts of experience pointed to the unity of the universe; that received more and more emphasis. But Law and Chance disputed the throne, both impersonal in themselves, both enemies of human personality. Once more pain and bereavement were emphasising personality. The world baulked it and mocked it, and men began to look beyond the world for righteousness. There could be no restoration of nerve till mankind was off the waters of uncertainty, free of the quicksands, the rocks, the incalculable tempests. The

21 See p. 263.

problem was certainty. Men craved, as ever, a divine personality; they felt that their own personality was real, or ought to be real; they demanded fair play of the universe. So much emerges from the actions and reactions of thought and religion and scepticism in this strange period. To trace more fully some of these movements as they illustrate our subject of Progress in Religion is the task before us.

X

THE STOICS

IT has been remarked that none of the great Stoics was a native of Greece proper. Zeno was a Semite—"with no Greek charm about him," it has been added, and unable to write Attic Greek.[1] Stoicism, to look Westward, was of all Greek philosophies that which most appealed to the more serious Roman mind. But, whatever its antecedents and whoever its followers, it was intensely Greek. The East, the West, and the influence of Greek— it sums up the new world in which Stoicism grew; and in many other ways Stoicism shows in its very texture the milieu and the date of its origin. It is a curious coincidence, too, that with the coming of the Northern peoples, who were to break up that society of the world in which Stoicism began, the last great Stoic name is written in history. Alexander abolished the nations, the Germans brought them back, and in the interval flourished this great system of Cosmopolitanism, humanitarianism, and pantheism—and, we may add, of rationalism; for no body of teaching, at least before the advent of modern physical science, has perhaps ever had so strong an influence, and made so great an impact on mankind, with so little of the romantic and so little of the religious.

The general teaching of Stoicism is so familiar, it has been handled so often, and so ably by modern English writers, that it will not be necessary for us to survey the

1 Beloch, *Griech. Gesch.*, III. i. 466; ohne alle hellenische Anmuth. Cf. Edwyn Bevan, *Stoics and Sceptics*, 17, on "an Asiatic darkness of skin, a long, straggling, ungainly body," and his gaunt bluntness in speech and life; following Diogenes Laertius, vii. 16.

whole of it. We may pause to remark this modern appeal of Stoicism, for it will do something to explain its rise and its influence in antiquity; and then it will suffice to consider in turn the bearing of Stoic thought upon the four lines along which we have been tracing the progress of religion, and the evidence given by the fortunes of the system to the validity of our deductions.

First, then, a few words on the modern revival of Stoicism. Renan said that Marcus Aurelius is the saint and exemplar of Agnosticism. The very word Agnostic is a nineteenth-century coinage; and, if popular use identifies it with Sceptic, that was not Huxley's intention when he launched the word. Nor, one may add, was it the idea of the ancient inventors of the term Sceptic that it should imply the dogmatism of the closed book, the affair judged, the case dismissed. Agnostic and Sceptic by first intention do mean the same thing, so that for once popular usage is perhaps justified. Stoicism rose in an age of uncertainty and flourished again in the nineteenth century, naturally and properly. Its fixed points appealed to the better minds of the nineteenth century; its great principle of reference to Nature, its instinct, as great and as sound, that duty must be somehow real— these are the cardinal points both for its earlier and for its later *floruit;* and its failure in either period sheds light on the other.

Stoicism was the offspring of Cynicism. The long debate of the Sophists about Nature and Convention, the many battles whose echoes we find in Plato's dialogues, produced their inevitable effect in the fourth century B.C. There can hardly be a more splendid defence of the idea of a state than in the Funeral Speech of Pericles, which Thucydides records, not without traces of his own mind and hand. Fifteen years later Euripides wrote his *Trojan Women,* which won no prize from the Athen-

ian people, which he could not have expected to win a
prize. The will-to-power of Nietzsche was already familiar to thinking Athenians, the survival of the phys-
ically fittest in the horrible Melian dialogue in Thucydides. Euripides showed in his *Trojan Women* that
there is something just as sacred as the so-called state;
that the state may be a lie against humanity; or, if
that is too abstract, that, if a state kills my son and
starves my wife and daughter for an abstract idea like
power, or even equality, or for the squalid ambition of
the merchant to capture another huckster's trade, that
state is a lie, and shall end. The Peloponnesian war
wrote the doom of the particular variety of that type
of state which the ancient world knew; and Alexander
fulfilled it. The sixty-seven miserable years between the
end of the Peloponnesian war and the accession of Alexander showed that the ancient state had ceased to be real;
it lasted on, struggling to seem real; but it was a survival, a simulacrum, an anachronism that warred against
life.[2]

The great philosophers saw clearly that the state needed
a new justification. The ideals of "the man in the street,"
which the Cleons and their modern equivalents grasp so
well and utter with all needed blatancy, do not justify a
state. Plato sketched a state on a new basis, in bitter
revolt against "man-in-the-street" democracy [3]—a state
with a coherent aim, with a central idea. Other philosophers, and some very unlikely ones, wrote their *Re-
publics* too. These were all visionary, but they all point
to one thing: the state as men knew it was an anachronism, impossible and undesirable. It was reserved for the
thinnest and poorest nature of them all, as sometimes
happens, to forecast the actual future, absurd and un-

2 Cf. Polybius' stories of the Spartan, Aetolian and other wars of the century before him.
3 See Plato, *Rep.*, viii. 557-562, on the democratic man.

practical as all sensible men must have realised him to be. Isocrates saw at last that Macedon must be the Prussia to unite Greece and rule the world. Philip achieved this, but achievement is not always justification. The Cynic was as little moved by the success of Philip as by that of Pericles; all he wanted of Alexander, according to the story, was that the Macedonian would stand out of the sunshine. There was the issue nakedly enough; Alexander, empire, Hellenisation, the "marriage of Europe and Asia" on the one hand—Diogenes and the sunshine on the other. It was more crudely put, more adapted for the intelligence of the meanest intellect, the antithesis of the *Trojan Women*; Menelaus, victory, glory, national efficiency and the vengeance which the vulgar call justice—or Hecuba and the natural relations of wife and son. Diogenes for the time impressed men as the *Trojan Women* had not.

Antisthenes, the first of the Cynic school, was, as we saw, the bastard son of a Thracian slave-woman. Well, if he was, he said, many of the great in Greek legend came from abroad; and the Athenians, if they were the children of the soil, shared that origin with the insects. He was human; he had character; and he was a pupil of Socrates, he would define his terms, know what he meant and get back to the real. From one point of view, there is nothing more real than the actual man. Thracian or Greek is a trivial distinction; slave or free is accident, accident in the philosophic sense, accident in the popular sense. So Antisthenes anticipated the Stoic insistence on the common humanity of all men, of all ranks, of both sexes. Diogenes went further. A curious mixture of charlatan, or at least advertiser, and genuine thinker, he had, like a popular preacher of to-day, the gift of getting his idea, generally a simple one, into the intelligence of everybody. The idea might be repugnant to common

notions of decency or of religion; he took pains to say
things about marriage, to do, or to suggest the doing of,
acts in holy precincts that were taboo; and his audacity,
his studied absurdity, suggested the train of thought
which he meant to start. The Stoic was less bizarre; he
was more sober, and a good deal less amusing; his para-
doxes were heavier and more laboured; but Cynic and
Stoic pointed the same way, both emphasised Nature.

The Sophists had raised the question of Nature. Plato
had gone deeply into it; all he says of the soul, of righteousness, of immortality, is based on their ultimate nature. The Stoics set Nature in the very forefront of
every argument; they made Nature not merely their last
court of appeal, but their first, and where they could not
as it were lay their hands on Nature visible and obvious,
they took the next thing to it. The consensus of mankind was not exactly Nature, but it raised a fair presumption that Nature was behind what Nature suggested. So
far as it goes, the presumption is sound. The probability
is that error will be corrected out, if we take a large
enough group of observers; it is still more likely that
we shall escape the errors inherent in our own local and
national traditions, and so far get nearer to the universal. So much for the central principle; all now turned
on the range and sureness of observation, and on the use
made of what was observed.

The Stoic, beginning with Nature, had his principle
of unity at once; and he carried it faithfully through all
his thinking and, as suggested above, he gave it every
emphasis that he could think of. In one picture and another he tried to carry it into every man's business and
bosom. "He of old said, 'Dear city of Cecrops,' " writes
Marcus Aurelius, alluding to Aristophanes and Athens,
"and thou, wilt not thou say, 'dear city of Zeus?' " [4]

4 Marcus Aurelius, iv. 23.

That thought runs through all Stoic teaching; it is no
abstract dogma, it is the foundation of all life and all
thought. The universe is the "great city." Every Greek
knew the meaning of πόλις; the empires had not
abolished that glorious memory. A virtual republic, of
which all are citizens, of which the laws are at once intelligible, just and unalterable, an equality and a fra-
ternity—"the common home or city of gods and men together " [5]—it is a great and an invigorating conception.
The forces of Nature and the details of Nature, man's
mind and the external world, are all delicately adjusted
to one another, in profound and eternal sympathy. We
remember how this idea reappears in Wordsworth, and
what happiness it brings with it; and, in passing, we may
recall and link with this conception the "Ode to Duty"—
exactly the sort of poem a Stoic would have written,
if only he had the poetic feeling and genius; Cleanthes
was very far from having Wordsworth's gifts. The
world was not a mere mass of material, of brute stuff
out of which life was to be carved, a wilderness into
which man might hack his way and slowly, in such corners as he might make his own, induce order; it was
order.

Cosmos is no new word in the Greek vocabulary, but
it gains a new meaning and a new thrill. The wise husband, in Xenophon's pleasant tale, inculcates order, and
bidding his little wife see the boots and shoes in a row,
"for all their different sizes, how *beautiful* it is!" he
cries.[6] The order of the universe was a joyous discovery; the thought that this order is not one of parts, but
of the whole; that it is the order, not of boots on a shelf,
not of a museum, but of an engine, a splendid mechan-

5 Cicero, *N.D.,* ii. 154.
6 Xenophon, *Oeconomicus,* 8, 19. I should like to refer to Mr. J. A. K.
Thomson's lively discussions (in *Greeks and Barbarians*) of the Greek finding
romance in order, not in disorder, in the disciplined society rather than in
Mexican ideals.

ism, better still of an organic body or even being—this was a conception to make the heart beat. What is true of all great discoveries and advances in the realm of spirit and intellect, is true here also. The Stoic conception of the Cosmos and its living beauty has never been lost. They passed it on to all sorts of thinkers, and, in its joy and its wonder, it is a permanent endowment of the race. If others led the way, the gift of the Stoics to mankind is not lessened. Genius perhaps more often shows us the value of what we have than it gives us what we have not.

Stars and seasons and souls of men, a living vital principle animates them, a principle intelligible because it is one in all things and all men, a principle that is intellectual, a *Logos,* and yet the seed and source of life, *Spermaticos.* The kinship within the great *polis* is real to the utmost. If man and star are made of one matter, that is kinship; but if the soul in both is one, the kinship is a deeper and dearer thing; and that this is true is shown by their mutual adaptation, and clinched by the fact that man understands what he sees, that his reason can deduce law and principle, and that Nature verifies what he finds. The whole is the outcome of Providence; if the Stoics did not invent this great word, they gave it connotation and currency. With us Providence almost inevitably involves personality, but, as we shall see, this is only very doubtfully the Stoic view. Law and principle—if we draw our deductions rigidly, and the Stoic did—may reduce freedom to a minimum; and the Stoics sometimes, proceeding from the laws of Nature, contracted the area of human freedom with a speed and a drastic incisiveness only equalled by men of science to-day who start from the same point. The Stoics would have none of the *Tyche* that the vulgar believed to rule the world; all was order, all was law, all was fate. The

course of the universe was ordained; it moved steadily
on, and, when its course was complete, a conflagration
dissolved it; and then, like the phoenix from its ashes,
it emerged again to pursue precisely the same course. In
prose and verse they laid this down—all is Law;

Fata regunt orbem; certa stant omnia lege.[7]

So stiff a determinism inevitably affected the Stoic
conception of God. A uniform doctrine in a philosophic
school is not to be expected; the Stoics were many, and,
as happens in other groups, different teachers emphasised
different points. Stoic teachers fluctuated a good deal
upon God, but on the universe they were generally agreed;
and that was central in their thinking. A universe, where
all is determined by unchangeable law, leaves little room
for a God of much personality, unless we hold that he
leaves that universe very generally to itself or, with some
of the Stoics in certain moments, that God and the universe are an identity. They credited this universe with
some sort of self-consciousness or intelligence, to which
their doctrine of Providence may seem to be attached.
"Constantly picture the universe as one living thing,"
writes Marcus (iv. 40), "with one substance and one
soul; and mark how all things are referred to the single
perfection of this; and how all things act with one impulse, how all are joint causes of all existing; and of
what sort is the contexture and concatenation of the
web." The system is pantheism—the triumph of science
over theology, Julius Beloch calls it.[8] When the Emperor
Tiberius dropped all religious observance, because, as
Suetonius says, "he was addicted to astronomy and full
of the conviction that all things are done by fate,"[9] it

7 Manilius, iv. 14.
8 *Griech, Geschichte,* III. i. 453.
9 Suetonius, *Tiberius,* 69.

was not an illegitimate inference. There was, as Bishop
Lightfoot pointed out, a contradiction between Stoic
dogma and Stoic hymnology. To the latter we may now
turn.

The hymn of Cleanthes is famous, and a few lines
from it in James Adam's translation will give something
of its quality—and land us in fresh perplexities.

> O God most glorious, called by many a name,
> Nature's great King, through endless years the same,
> Omnipotence, who by thy just decree
> Controllest all, hail Zeus, for unto thee
> Behoves thy children in all lands to call.
> We are thy children, we alone of all
> On earth's broad ways that wander to and fro,
> Bearing thy image wheresoe'er we go.
> Wherefore with songs of praise thy power I will forth show.

The philosopher then pictures the universe circling
round the earth, willingly ruled, and controlled by the
thunderbolt—

> Vehicle of the universal Word, that flows
> Through all, and in the light celestial glows.

No deed is done on earth apart from thee, he continues,
neither in the divine aetherial sky nor in the sea, save
such acts as evil men do by their own folly. God knows
how to make the crooked straight, to order the disorderly;
and things unlovely are to him lovely; so has he fitted
all good to evil that there is ever one Reason, or one
account, of all for ever. This, however, evil men fly
from and neglect, pursuing advantage and finding the
opposite. And he ends with a prayer to Zeus to save
men from ignorance, "that honoured we may requite
thee with honour, hymning thy works for ever as befits a mortal; for neither for mortals nor for gods is

there greater gift than justly to hymn the universal law for ever." "What else can I do, a lame old man," asks Epictetus, "but hymn God?" [10]

God is responsible for all, except man's folly; but how that lies outside his responsibility is not explained. Plutarch's attack on the Stoics shows that he, and others, saw the inconsistency; it may even imply that some Stoics definitely credited God with everything done, as genuine pantheism involves. In other words man seems to have as much freedom as God, perhaps more; and man has, as far as we can see, a good deal more personality. What volition the universe has, it is hard to learn. In fact, God is not the main interest of the Stoic. "I put myself in the hands of a Stoic," says Justin Martyr, "and I stayed a long time with him, but when I got no farther in the matter of God—for he did not know himself, and he used to say this knowledge was not necessary—I left him." [11] Law, order, cosmos appeal to the Stoic; on God he is content to be indefinite, at least in public speech. Zeus or Jupiter will serve when he writes poetry or preaches; but Plutarch's school saw how little it meant. The gods of the Stoic, said Plutarch, melt in the general conflagration like wax or tin; they have as little final permanence as man resolved into elements.[12] The Stoic more or less conceded gods to the vulgar; but, when their nature was understood, they were in general less than mankind wanted—temporary expedients, that will carry a man some way, but not all the way, comfortable for the time, if you can shut your eyes to the future.

"The gods," says Seneca, in a letter not without hints of characteristic eloquence, "are not scornful, they are not envious. They welcome us, and, as we ascend, they reach us their hands. Are you surprised that man should

10 Epictetus, D., i. 16; Conflict of Religions, p. 62.
11 Justin, Dial. c. Tryphone, 2 (about 160 A.D.).
12 Plutarch, de comm. not. adv. Stoics, i. 31; and de def. orac., 420 A, c. 19.

go to the gods? God comes to men, nay! nearer still! he comes *into* men. No mind (*mens*) is good without God. Divine seeds are sown in human bodies." [13] And, in another place, Seneca puts the other side: "We understand Jove to be ruler and guardian of the whole, mind and breath of the universe, lord and artificer of this fabric. Every name is his. Would you call him Fate? You will not err. He it is on whom all things depend, the cause of causes. Would you call him Providence? You will speak aright. He it is whose thought provides for the universe that it may move on its course unhurt and do its part. Would you call him Nature? You will not speak amiss. He it is of whom all things are born, by whose breath (or spirit, *spiritu*) we live. Would you call him Universe? You will not be deceived. He himself is this whole that you see, fills his own parts, sustains himself and what is his." [14] That, after all, is the last word of Stoicism on God.

Epictetus, as we saw, purposes like Cleanthes to hymn God; the nightingale does the nightingale's part, man a rational creature ought as he works, digging, ploughing, eating, to sing to God and tell his benefits.[15] But Seneca is as explicit, and a good deal more rhetorical, and perhaps more intelligible in forbidding everything that common people called worship—the lighting of lamps on the Sabbath, the morning salutation, the tender of towel and strigil to Jupiter, or of the mirror to Juno. "The beginning of worship is to believe Gods exist, and then to attribute to them their own majesty and goodness. Would you propitiate the gods? Be good. He has worshipped them enough who has imitated them." [16] So, while the gods resolve themselves into phenomena, allowed a sort of honorary degree of existence, worship becomes virtue

13 Seneca, *Ep.*, 73, 15, 16.
14 Seneca, *Nat. Qu.*, ii. 45.
15 Epictetus, *D.*, i. 16.
16 Seneca, *Ep.*, 95, 47-50.

and sinks sometimes to being mere endurance, submission to Fate in its inevitable sweep.

So far we have bandied quotations to and fro, *pro* and *con*; and they have for us such interest as a scheme of thought will allow, that is on the whole dead or alien. It is interesting to remark the fluctuations between pantheism and popular nomenclature, between hymns of piety and philosophic definitions—to watch the human spirit hovering between personal names for God or gods and a thoroughgoing impersonal conception of a Law. It reveals to us the conflict and the difficulty that filled the religious arena in that day, that are not unknown in our own day. The battle over the personality of God was reaching its second phase. The personal gods had vanquished the dim figures that held the field before them; now they are going down before an interpretation of the universe reached by a larger and truer thought; yet we feel that the conquering new dogma does not cover the whole experience of man. So we reflect in looking back. But how did they feel, for whom it was not a question fetched from the past, who had not the use of nineteen centuries of experience, which, whatever we make of them, do come into the story and do suggest possible alternatives—experience not then so available? What did Stoic teaching mean to "God-intoxicated" souls, to men who wished profoundly to relate themselves and their lives to some sort of real and effective personality, more reliable than the most inspiring of abstract nouns? Stoicism, in its teaching of the universe, made, as we have seen, a very great contribution to human thought— but a contribution, not a complete and exhaustive answer to all our questions; and there were plenty of people at the time who felt they could accept the contribution, provided it was not to be taken as a substitute for what they felt to be more urgent. But before we turn to their crit-

icism, we must see how the Stoic treated human personality, a separate issue indeed, but of first importance
along with the being of God in the story of progress in
religion.

Plato had struck the note of human grandeur; what
the poets had made clear in great story, he put in the
explicit language of the philosopher, in glowing sentences
that could not die, but must quicken the mind of man
for ever. The Stoic, with his conception of the universe
and of God filling it and moving it, seemed able to go
even further. It was a proper conclusion from his premises, that man also is filled and moved by God; and he
did not hesitate to draw it. No teachers of classical antiquity set man so high in the universe. Man is "a little
portion of divine breath," [17] "a holy spirit (or breath)
inhabits within him"; [18] man is a "son of God," [19] "a
fragment of God." [20] The "fiery breath," the Spermatic
or life-giving Reason, that animates all Nature, reaches
consciousness in man. The Stoic sage at last maintains
that he and God are equal [21]—a paradox resting on the
conception of their common nature, but (as Seneca's
confessions show) not to be pushed too far. A being,
who is indeed a part of God and consciously so, must
be at home in a universe which is, in a sense, merely the
rest of himself. Reason in man, in the universe, in God,
is one and the same thing—a genuine bond of kinship.
So says Epictetus, "our souls are bound up and in touch
with God, parts of him and portions of him"; [22] and
Marcus Aurelius emphasises "a kinship, a community of
mind" (xii. 26). Thought and reason are not accident
in man; they are his essential nature. "Slaves and
women, the Stoics felt, should be philosophers," said

[17] Horace, *Sat.*, ii. 2, 79.
[18] Seneca, *Ep.*, 41, 1, 2.
[19] Epictetus, *D.*, i. 9.
[20] Epictetus, *D.*, ii. 8.
[21] Plut., *Adv. Sto.*, 33.
[22] Epictetus, *D.*, i. 14.

Cicero.[23] This was to make us all citizens of the universe, indeed, in far more than phrase.

The Stoic did not leave man with this new consciousness of Divine kinship and membership without a call to use it and to live in a new way. "The things in thine own power" is a recurring note, now of warning, now of encouragement. There are things which are not in a man's power—storms at sea, for instance, and the conduct of other men and women. But there is nothing in these which interferes with or limits a man's power of keeping a balanced mind, unswayed by the forces that overset the vulgar, desire, fear, pleasure, and pain. "Enough," writes Horace, "to pray Jove for what he gives and what he takes away; let him give life, let him give resources; I myself will provide the calm mind." [24] That is in Horace's recurring Stoic vein, which crosses his Epicureanism so often and so charmingly and perhaps more than half seriously. It is writ large in later Roman history; for this strong and glorious Stoic doctrine undoubtedly made men, where the material was available. Thought was fired by the consciousness of the divine element within and the divine without, and their unity; and men reached a level of courage, a tenacity of endurance, and even a height of cheerfulness, which make them signal figures in an age of depression and weakness.

At the same time, while Stoicism emphasises and develops fortitude by its doctrine of the kinship of the universe and of the sympathy of all beings with all other beings, that outcome of kinship and sympathy, which would seem to us most natural and spontaneous, is markedly wanting in the Stoics. It might be put epigrammatically that they have no sympathy, that the outcome of their doctrine of the sympathy of the universe is that

23 Cicero, *N.D.*, iii. 25.
24 Horace, *Ep.*, i. 18, 102.

"savage and hard apathy" which Plutarch denounces in them.[25] The Stoic really failed to use his doctrine to the full; and he failed as a result of at least two causes—first, he was holding the fort in a world very alien to him in spite of his belief in its sympathy; and, secondly, he was wholly dependent on himself, he had nothing in the way of personal touch or fellow-feeling to look for from God, in spite of the hopeful language about the gods and their friendship which he addressed to his acquaintance in the world. The walls of his fortress would be sapped by emotion, by human ties—the beauty of a man's own wife may undo him, and the charm of his child; they will tempt him into desire or fear, they will make him wish in his power what is not in his power. A man cannot be "self-sufficient," as the Stoic felt he must be, if he depends on the smiling caress of his little son; no, he must fortify himself, as Epictetus said, by murmuring as he kisses the child, "To-morrow thou wilt die." [26] Human relations on such terms are intolerable—all pain, all weakness, and little reinforcement. The Stoic, in spite of his great doctrine, did not really believe that the universe, apart from its main current, its drive forward, its major laws, does contribute. Marcus Aurelius wrote in his diary, "Decay is in the material substance of all things—water, dust, bones, stench" (ix. 36). The comparison of Stoicism with Wordsworth's philosophy has often been made; but what a contrast is here to the poet's mind, as for instance shown toward the end of the *Lines written above Tintern Abbey*! The humanity, which the Stoic emphasises, is incomplete in what we feel to be one of its most significant and valuable aspects.

It is indeed a curious thing that with all their im-

---

25 Plutarch, *Consol. ad Apoll.*, 3, 102 C.
26 Cf. Epictetus, *D.*, iii. 24; iv. 1; *M.*, 11, 26.

portant contributions to Psychology, including a new
vocabulary which held its place in the Greek world and
holds it still in translation, the Stoics made so little of
emotion, that they missed its higher significance, and
could suggest little beyond its repression or extermination. This was a defiance of that Nature which the
school deified, a defiance that cost them much. It made
demands of men which they might not have logic to resist
but which instinct made them refuse. It wrecked the
chance of Stoicism achieving more than the discipleship
of a few, however much in eclectic days might be borrowed from the system by other schools. It reacted un-
favourably on the disciple; it made him hard, self-centred
and self-pleased, as well as self-sufficient. Add this spectacle of the isolated sage to the want of motive, the
Apatheia, declining into apathy, which the system involves for most men; and the ultimate failure of Stoicism was inevitable. Again, the Stoic missed development
as the key to man's nature; their cycle of being, that
returned again and again after each periodic conflagration, made progress meaningless as the stone of Sisyphus.
Here as with their gods, the interim is all; everything is
make-shift for the meantime; there is no real achievement. The most striking outcome of this attitude is to
be seen in Marcus Aurelius, working for ever for the
good of his subjects and more than half convinced that,
in spite of all his labour and thought and care, nothing
worth while would ever be effected.

These were heavy deductions to make from personal-
ality, much as the Stoics had done to establish it with
their incessant emphasis on "the things in thine own
power," and their deliberate development of it in their
pupils. The word personality, it has been noted, is lacking in their vocabulary, a gap in the equipment of all
ancient thought. Cut off from emotion, deprived of the

real hope of progress, human personality suffered almost desperate loss at the hands of the Stoics, set adrift
from its own nature. For, if the school forbade emotion,
Nature gave it; as she gave that instinct to act, to stand
for right, to work for the good of mankind, which the
school encouraged indeed by the appeal to duty and discouraged by the withdrawal of hope. These defects in
the system man, subconsciously, tended to make good for
himself—instinct proving too strong for thought, without reason necessarily noticing what was happening. But
there was worse, for Stoicism forbade man's supreme
hope. From days before Plato men had been reflecting
upon Immortality. Plato had held by the faith in it—
"the venture is a glorious one." As the perplexity of
the world deepened and intensified the fear of life, with
every fresh exhibition of the intolerable instability of
things mundane, with every fresh reminder by the kings
and the soldiers to the individual that he was an individual, a mere item and nothing else, man was more and
more driven in upon himself and found in personality,
his own, and the personalities of those whom he loved,
all he could have or hope to have. And now when he
kisses his little son he must say: "To-morrow thou wilt
die."

In the *Dream of Scipio* Cicero sketches a future state
of glory among the stars for those who serve their country. Glory—yes! but Virgil's sixth *Aeneid* shows a ten-
derer realisation of the meaning of that instinct which
makes men "reach forth hands in longing for the further
shore." Beyond the grave are—or ought to be—those
whom we loved in this life, those whom we love still.

> *Venisti tandem tuaque expectata parenti*
> *Vicit iter pietas?*

But the Stoic addressed himself to the individual whom

he had trained to apathy. He must practise resignation; he can begin on a broken cup, a coat, and then a puppy, and so on to children, wife or brothers. While the ship is taking water aboard at a port, you stroll on the beach and pick up a shell or pluck a flower; but when the call comes, you drop it and go aboard; "so in life suppose that, instead of some little shell or plant, you have something in the way of wife or child, very well!" [27] So the deaths of those we love are dismissed; cockleshell or eldest son, something external to self, "not in thine own power." And if a man, faced by prospect of death, lament: "But my family will hunger," what then? Does their hunger lead them to another goal? Will it not come to the same for them and you? [28]

What *is* death? "It pleased me," wrote Seneca, "to inquire of the eternity of souls—nay! to believe in it. I surrendered myself to that great hope." [29] "How natural it is! the human mind will have no bounds set to it unless they are shared by God." [30] Nature is invoked; but reason and dogma have something to say to Nature when she is interpreted by such simple instincts in so popular a way. Seneca wrote a *Consolation* to Marcia for her son, and, after speaking of his future life, he remembers the ultimate conflagration. "Then we also, happy souls who have attained eternity, when God shall see fit to reconstruct the universe, when all things fall, we too, a little element in a great catastrophe, shall be resolved into our ancient elements. Happy is your son who already knows this!" So it is only a temporary immortality, a fugitive eternity, and then like a sleep comes for all the conflagration, with a new start for the universe, and no Marcia and no son and no Seneca for how many myriad years? Elsewhere that dissolution into

27 Epictetus, *Manual*, 7.
28 Epictetus, *D.*, iii. 26.

29 Seneca, *Ep.* 102, 2.
30 Seneca, *Ep.* 102, 21.

primal elements seems even nearer to Seneca—"Why should I be wasted for desire of him who is either happy or non-existent?" [31]

Epictetus is blunter than Seneca; there were fewer ties in his life, and his was a spirit of less range, if more intense and of harder metal. God opens the door and calls man "to nothing terrible, but whence you came, to the dear and kin [both adjectives are neuter] the elements. What in you was fire shall go to fire; earth to earth, air to air, water to water." [32] "Death is a change, not from what now is into what is not, but into what is not now. You will *be,* but you will be something else, of which the cosmos has just now no need. You came into existence, not when *you* wished, but when the cosmos had need." [33] So the great individual personality, sternly repressing the emotions that might waste him, keeping his eyes fixed on God (whatever God is, concrete, abstract, personal, or Destiny), firmly obeying the order of the universe, resolutely concentrated upon the things in his own power, is as unstable and fugitive as a chalk sketch on a blackboard that a schoolboy wipes out when the master's step is heard. It is resolved into atoms of chalk on duster and floor; it has not perished; it is something else. What stuff it all is!

Who would say that a house burnt to the ground with all it contains, furniture, books gathered by one who loved them, pictures of friends and kindred, is the same thing as the ashes to which it is reduced, because there is the same quantity of carbon in the charred heap and in the gases liberated in air? The personality is gone, and men who laid such stress on personality knew it.

Men and women who did not philosophise, but who felt, and now and then thought on the basis of what they

31 *Ad Polyb.,* 9, 3.
32 Epictetus, *D.,* iii. 13.
33 Epictetus, *D.,* iii. 24.

felt, knew also what this teaching of the Stoics meant. For centuries, as we have seen, the individual had been growing in self-consciousness, realising his place in the scheme of things, and now he is told to be for the moment supremely more than ever he was before, with the prospect of being utterly blotted out by death.

Progress in religion, we have seen, is marked by emphasis on the unity of existence, on the personality of God, on righteousness, on the personality of man. The Stoic taught nobly of the unity of the cosmos; of righteousness his discourse was full; here too he made contributions of a great kind, in giving righteousness a purpose and a centre—life "agreeably with Nature." But if there is to be righteousness in the universe, something more is due to the human soul, some fuller recognition of its nature and of its claims. The Stoic magnified personality and blotted it out; and God he left an enigma— an enigma more enigmatic for all the emphasis he laid on the wonder and glory and wisdom of all God's works.

XI

THE JEWS AFTER THE EXILE

THREE great landmarks divide the history of Judaism. The first is so hidden in myth and legend that it is hard to be certain of more than the bare fact, and even sane criticism may hesitate about that. But that Israel was delivered from Egypt, that this deliverance was associated with Moses, and that a new epoch began then in the national and the religious history of the people, is implied, as we have seen, in every retrospect of prophet and psalmist, and is generally conceded by historical critics. What precisely Moses did or was, what was the nature of the "covenant," whether Jehovah was a new or an old god of the people, and how far his religion was what we have learnt to call spiritual, or mere cult, or something of both—these questions are, as we saw, harder to answer, but happily definite answers to them are not essential for our present theme. The other two landmarks involve no historical doubts whatever; Judah was carried captive to Babylonia by Nebuchadnezzar—Jewish graves have been found at Nippur; and Titus destroyed Jerusalem and the Temple in 70 A.D.

The rise and progress of Jewish religion down to Jeremiah, the most modern and the most moving personality of the Old Testament, we have already considered. Slowly Israel had come to recognise the unique and dominant position of Jehovah. Jehovah was no longer a god of a tribe or a land, as at one time good Israelites had supposed;[1] He was Lord of the ends of the earth,

1 Cf. 1 Sam. xxvi. 19.

He had given the nations their lands, He and not Chemosh and Dagon and other abominations. He had not
been defeated and overthrown by Nebuchadnezzar and
his Babylonians; on the contrary, He had caused His
people to be carried captive; it was His design and His
doing, and He knew His thoughts toward them.[2]

The 137th Psalm is a tragic document of the captivity—vivid, personal and passionate beyond any con-
secutive nine verses of the Old Testament. The writer
has seen his city sacked, his home destroyed, and on its
threshold the blood-stained remains of what he loved
best in the world. With the rest of the well-to-do and
noble of the kingdom, he has been marched northward
through Syria, across the desert, down the Euphrates, to
the land of captivity. There his captors, companions of
the long march and now home again, singing their native
songs, ask him for "one of the songs of Zion." They
did not get it. Instead he broke away, and wrote a song
that throbs to-day with the terrible passion from which
it came. His central question sums up the problem of his
people in exile. "How shall we sing the Lord's song in
a strange land?" Long after, the answer was given by
another poet of his race in the 139th Psalm, happily
placed beside his own in the psalter, whether by accident
or by an editor who saw the relevance of the two poems
to each other.

It is a good test of any product of human brain or
spirit to see how far it will bear transplanting. Will
your wit keep its flavour in the next parish, across the
border or the channel? Will your poem attract translators, or will they capture enough of it to make it a
household word in the new tongue, like Homer and
Shakespeare? Aristocracy was never really rooted in
English America; poverty, the forest and the Indians

2 Jer. xxix. 4.

made too hard a soil for it; in French Canada it was
planted, but its life depended on the governors and bish-
ops sent from old France. Buddhism and Islam do not
prosper outside the tropics and the subtropical regions;
the climate is against the ascetic and against Ramadan,
and the Northern peoples believe in activity, in the strenuous life; in their latitudes blood and brain call for it,
it is the condition of survival. Athene, as we have seen,
had little to do in further Asia; Adrastus nothing; Zeus
had to be translated into a dogma. But the uprooting
of Judah and the destruction of the temple were the
making of Judaism.

Judah had listened only casually to the Prophets. "He
is a dreamer; let us leave him; pass!" is the attitude. But,
as commonly happens, the practical man was wrong; the
dreamer, who quarrelled with his people's ideas and common-sense, was right. Jerusalem fell; the policy and
the cunning of its rulers had been silly, and it proved
futile, as the greater prophets had foreseen it must; the
floods had washed away the refuge of lies.[3] If the people
in exile was to survive at all as a distinct entity, only a
religion could save it. India shows how small racial
groups, protected by a religion, become castes and maintain themselves for centuries in extraordinary detachment. The story of the Beni-Israel in the Bombay Presidency is the closest parallel to the Jewish captivity in
Babylon. No one knows how or when the Beni-Israel
came to India; they were discovered there in the Middle
Ages by Jews from Cochin. Their Jewish ancestry and
religion are recognised by themselves and all other Jews,
but inter-marriage with the Jews of Southern India, the
Bagdadis or the Jews of Europe, is not practised. Their
religion has kept them and still keeps them; and there
they are still—a little people of 6000 persons, not rich,

3 Isa. xxviii. 17.

but people of brain, who gave officers to Indian regiments, till caste became the basis of recruiting, and the Beni-Israel could only be officers to one another.   But had those earlier sons of Israel a religion strong enough to keep them?   If it was to be a religion of the high places, of altar and sacrifice and ceremony, then, in the absence of all these things, it must die.   It is true that a curious modern discovery of papyrus about 1907 has revealed a Jewish *Temple* at Yeb or Elephantine in Upper Egypt.[4] This temple, its maintainers say in the surviving document, Cambyses spared and authorised when he conquered Egypt and destroyed Egyptian temples (about 520 B.C.); but, they lament, their heathen neighbours, egged on by the priests of Chnum, the ram-headed god of the island, have destroyed it (about 410 B.C.).   A later Jewish temple at Leontopolis in Egypt is attested as having existed.

In Babylonia, however, the religion, cut off from its old supports, learnt to stand alone; and the loss of its old associations threw its adherents back upon thought; and thought is individual.   The leaders of religious thought had been the Prophets; their writings and records had been preserved, and now they were read and understood.   The national tie was temporarily broken; men thought and began to choose for themselves.   The weaker spirits probably fell away into new attempts to combine the worship of Jehovah with the cults of the land, not unlike those made for centuries in Palestine; and all such syncretisms were inevitably avenged by the merging of those who made them into the communities among which they lived.   Fusion in religion meant fusion in blood and the utter disappearance of the new-comers in the course of a few generations.   Syncretism was no doubt defensible on philosophic grounds as well

4 Cf. Driver, *Schweich Lectures*, pp. 28-30; Charles, *Apocrypha and Pseudonyma*, i. pp. 180, 187, 194.

on the more vulgar grounds of superstition and social and economic gain; it could be described as a larger life, a broader outlook, a recognition of other spiritual values —we know the insidious jargon, shallow with its brag of width, and we can understand how it meant religious and national death.   But if the shallower and the feebler fell away, there was a growth of stronger fibre in the fittest of spirit who survived.   When the prophetic religion became the centre of national existence, the centre of thought, it began to react more and more upon all life; it drew to itself passion, it became, in Seeley's phrase, enthusiastic and was safe.   Monotheism proved then for the first time what it has been triumphantly since then all over the world and in all sorts of races, the most powerful and the most permanently attractive and inspiring type of religion; and further it showed its independence of what till then had been regarded as the essentials of religion.   Jeremiah had prophesied of what we call personal religion; there would be a new covenant with Israel, every man would know Jehovah, none would need to teach his brother, but in every man's heart the laws of Jehovah would be written.[5]   Religion began to become an individual thing, conviction not tradition. Thus in Israel, as in Greece, the breakdown of the national preconceptions, the collapse of state and temple and old belief, worked out in new emphasis on the universal reach and significance of God and a new weight and stress thrown upon the individual.   The spiritual conception of religion had gained a victory, the results of which have never been lost.

Israel, it has been said, went into exile a nation and came back a church; and it is true in more ways than one.   The old tendency to lapse and lapse again into idolatry is gone; Israel is solid for Jehovah and there are

[5] Jer. xxxi. 31; cf. p. 148.

(eventually) no other gods. He overtopped them all, and gradually they fell into utter nonentity; they simply did not exist. The transformation of Israel's belief was the transformation of Israel; the national character took a new development; the Jew became distinct among Semites, definite, pronounced, exclusive. Heine's *Princess Sabbath* reads like a fairy tale and it is history; and the Jew is the only race with such a history, with such a fairy tale. Polytheism for all its legends is a squalid unromantic thing; but Judaism has always had its elements of passion and romance. But when Israel is described as a church, more is indicated than pure spiritual religion. The Israel that returned from exile is not so much the Israel of Jeremiah as of Ezekiel. A church is always associated with organisation, and often overshadowed by it. Side by side with the individualism and the romance of Hebrew religion, there has been an element of legalism—an element that grew progressively in its hold upon all life and its influence upon all thought.

Ezekiel was hereditarily a priest of the Jerusalem temple, a student of the earlier religious and ritual customs, legends and traditions of Israel, a man who read books and who perhaps found the pen a more natural and ready means of expression than the voice. Symbol and art appealed to him, where Nature moved Jeremiah. When Jeremiah is stirred, pictures of nature, of animals of the desert and the farm, rise in his mind. Ezekiel's pictures are of cherubim, of eagles, bulls and lions as they are, not in the desert, but on the monuments.[6] Babylon is written in his mind. The future religion of Israel will be a development of the past; a priest can never forget the past; to maintain and transmit it is his trade and his instinct. Ezekiel begins that fusion of priestly and prophetic religion which makes the later Judaism. He and

6 Cf. J. P. Peters, *Religion of Hebrews*, p. 286.

Ezra are the two great figures of the revival, as significant in their way as Moses.   Indeed, a modern scholar
says that Ezekiel had a profounder influence on Judaism
than any one man.   He is a pastor of souls, the dreamer
who builds a sanctuary, a system and a law, which become the inspiration of the people.   The Temple, Judaism, the Torah—these things are Israel's religion; and
not one of them is of first importance, or perhaps of any
importance at all, to Jeremiah.   Free of the past and yet
devoted to it, the new type of religious Israelite can develop the past and transform it without realising how
revolutionary is his work.   The very distance from Jerusalem made the city more significant and more easy to
remodel.   The law itself is rewritten; the code known as
the Priestly takes shape, and at last—the process and
the dates do not concern us at the moment—the Pentateuch, as history knows it, is evolved.   The anthropomorphisms of the older books are toned down, the sensuous imagery reduced.   God becomes transcendent; He
no longer shapes man of clay, He speaks and it is done;
He breathes no breath into man's nostrils, He plants no
garden, nor is heard walking in one.   When He will
communicate His will to man, it is by intermediaries, by
angels.

The history of the Jews in Palestine from the return
under Cyrus to the invasion of Alexander is obscure.
The policy of the Persian was in general not to interfere
with local religious practices—in spite of what Herodotus was told about Cambyses in Egypt.   If a nation is
happy in having no history, the Jews perhaps were happy
then.   But the story of Nehemiah around the year 444
B.C. shows how small and anxious the Jewish state was.
The mutilation of that attractive autobiography, in order
to its fusion with the poorer matter now combined with
it, is the worst editorial crime committed on the Old Tes-

tament. Nehemiah and Ezra between them achieved
the victory of particularism among the Jews. Worship
was at last concentrated at Jerusalem, if we neglect, as
we may, the heretical offshoot at Gerizim. The High
Priest became, like a Greek patriarch in old days at Con-
stantinople, the head of the nation. In this period the
Pentateuch was not only given its present form, but became the book of the religion, the code of the community.
The national history shared the fate of the national law;
it too was rewritten, adjusted to the law-book; the good
kings were good because they observed the law as re-
written after the exile, the bad were bad because they
did not.

In this period, however, we must date the rise of the
Synagogue alongside of the Temple—a natural simple
development which has outlasted the Temple by many
centuries, and which, in spite of the enormous importance
attached by Jews and by a too imitative Christian Church
to the Pentateuch, has had a greater influence than the
Temple on mankind. The Temple had the fate of temples; its hereditary priesthood became like other priesthoods, worldly-minded, conservative and important. The
High Priests were practically princes, and like the prince-
archbishops of the later Middle Ages they shaped their
conduct by the maxims and policies of the world, secure
that the religion which gave them their place could maintain it without the help of their example. Deuteronomy
enacted three pilgrimages to Jerusalem a year to be made
by every adult male. Of course this was impossible for
Jews living in Babylon or Upper Egypt, as it was impossible, later on, for Jews in Italy and beyond; and if
the religion was to continue effective, some plan must
be devised for keeping Jews together and in touch with
the essence of their religion. The Synagogue managed
this. It became, we can believe, unofficially, a gathering

of Jews on Saturday; and in the casual references of New
Testament writers we can make out the general course of
proceedings. The Pentateuch and the Prophets were
read aloud; [7] the psalms were sung; there was prayer;
persons spoke. To the Gentile the whole thing was queer
and rather absurd. Worship without a proper temple—
without sacrifice and altar (for there could be neither in
the synagogue; both were concentrated at Jerusalem)—
without a priest (for the synagogue ministrants were
technically laymen)—without a god (for there was no
idol or other symbol)—the idea was ludicrous. Call the
Jews however a nation of philosophers,[8] and it might
pass; the synagogue was more like a school than a temple.
As a manifestation of religion it was an innovation and
a daring one; and not only so from the Greek but from
the Jewish point of view.

The Synagogue was a visible expression of some of
those tendencies in religion which we have been studying.
It meant the universality of Jehovah and the unity of
God; or it was meaningless. Its democratic ways recognised practically what the Christian Church later on
called the priesthood of all believers. The reading of the
Prophets and of the Law, remodelled with some of the
prophetic inspiration, kept the great standard of Monotheism before men; more, it kept before their minds the
great conception of the personal God Jehovah; no abstract noun, no dogma, but God Himself was the centre
of this philosophic school. Again, the exposition of Law
and Prophets, not strictly official to begin with, meant
that religion was the real business of every man; he

---

7 Josephus, c. Apion. ii. 18, "to hear the Law and to hear it accurately."
W. Fairweather, Background of Gospels, 25-27; J. P. Peters, Relig. Hebr.,
381-392; 397.
8 Clearchus, the Peripatetic, appears to have written a dialogue, in which
Aristotle says that philosophers among the Indians are called Kalanoi, among
the Syrians Judaioi, and adds that he met in Asia Minor a Jew with a Greek
soul. Josephus, c. Apion. i. 22, p. 454, cited by Eusebius, Praepar. Evang.,
ix. 5, p. 409 C.

must understand what he was doing, the prophets were
not irrelevant to him.   The great principle that Paul
long after laid down, when he said "I will sing with my
understanding; I will pray with my understanding,"
underlay the practice of translation and explanation pursued in the Synagogue; it was an attempt, not designed
perhaps, but the more effectual for being spontaneous,
to fulfil the prophecy of Jeremiah, that every man should
know and understand to keep the law.   Hebrew was becoming an obsolete language, maintained for religious
purposes, while Aramaic was the current speech of Syria
and reached eastward to the Euphrates.[9]   The device of
keeping sacred texts in Hebrew and translating them in
the Synagogue into Aramaic was a characteristic compromise.   Later on the Old Testament was translated into
Greek under the Ptolemies.   Legend [10] gave the translation a fixed date, a royal origin, and the sanction of
miracle; but probably its real source was a higher thing—
the sense that the individual has a right to know the mind
of his God in the language that comes most naturally to
him.   Schürer compared the effect of the Septuagint with
that of Luther's German Bible; it was the very foundation of a religion.

   It may be remarked that, while no competition was felt
or suggested between Synagogue and Temple—indeed
later on we find special Synagogues in Jerusalem itself—
the two centres of religion evolved types markedly different.   The Temple produced, as already said, a hereditary priesthood, more interested in the performance of
ceremony than in the progressive discovery of truth,
conservative in ideas, but for all its orthodoxy, more
amenable to easy Hellenistic ways than those whose religion was more reflective.[11]   It was a real gain to Juda-

9 J. P. Peters, *Rel. of Hebr.*, 397; Neh. xiii. 24, contrast 2 Kings xviii. 26.
10 See R. R. Ottley, *Handbook to the LXX*, pp. 31 ff.
11 Strabo, c. 761, says they were much involved in brigandage.

ism, and to the world, that concentration in Jerusalem kept the priesthood from exercising a preponderant influence on the scattered Jewish people. In the synagogues there rose another sort of man, the Scribe, a layman, a student of books, a teacher, and in real contact with his people, more open to movements in religion, a democrat without knowing it, a pioneer in religious thought in spite of himself, as he read and thought and possessed himself of the problems that bore hard on the ordinary honest people he met.

It was the Scribe who made the new Judaism, and who, himself more responsive to Greek thought than to Greek ways, maintained against heathen influences a religion which meant more and more in time—a religion of men deepened by the battle with doubt, made at once harder and more tender by their experience of life, and ever more deeply rooted in Jehovah. Jesus was probably far from being the only visitor to the temple who was shocked by its naked commercialism, its shallowness and vulgarity, who felt the contrast between the house of prayer and the den of thieves.[12] The Synagogue was a house of prayer; so on a smaller scale was the *Proseucha,* if it was not the same thing; in both religion was for the time real, nursed in freedom of speech, in spiritual traditions free from the mechanical taint of priest and sacrifice, not yet overborne by conservative erudition—the Wonder House of the Princess Sabbath; for the Synagogue transformed the Sabbath too from a day of taboos (though these indeed survive) to a day of worship, of spiritual deepening and spiritual imagination. The Psalter in the main belongs to this period and gives a vivid picture of the religion. The extreme ease with

---

12 Dr. Theodore H. Robinson has suggested that, quite apart from money-changers and traders (who at tourist centres and places of pilgrimage might merit the hard name), the sanctuary at Jerusalem drew to itself a more openly recognisable thief element, as sanctuaries have done elsewhere.

which the Christian Church annexed the Psalter and found in it the word for much of its own richest experience, is evidence enough of the character of the community and the religion from which the Psalter came. In this case the adoption of the book meant neither a false system of interpretation nor a violent return to pre-Christian and indeed pre-prophetic notions.

But even the most alive and progressive religion is exposed to the danger of conservatism. The old man, the old place, the old ways, have an appeal to which all human beings are susceptible, an appeal legitimate but seductive. In the Gospels and in the Talmud we have evidence of how settled and how wooden a living religion may in time become. Prophets emancipate religion and priests re-enslave it. In every man there is some element of prophet and some of priest; and timidity, routine, the lapse of years tend to atrophy the prophet in all of us and to develop the priest. When religion begins to succumb to tradition, and when progress and the broader and higher life which it means begin to be associated with a body of ideas actually or supposedly hostile to religion, we know by now what dangers await the spiritual life of a people; we have seen it again and again in history; we are face to face with those dangers to-day. Judaism was saved from those dangers by a storm of persecution that threatened its existence.

Little is known of any real relations between Alexander the Great and the Jews.[13] Later Jewish historians filled the gap in knowledge with legend. It is curious how uniformly generation by generation the Jews rewrote their history.[14] A certain parallelism may be noted

---

13 Josephus says that Alexander visited Jerusalem; Arrian has no such story nor the other historians of Alexander, and it is not believed. See Niese, *Griech. Gesch.*, i. p. 83, n. 3. who agrees with Ewald that it is an invention of the first century B.C...

14 Cf. Wendland, *hell.-röm Kultur*, 197; Sir George Adam Smith, *Jerusalem*, ii. 407.

with modern Hinduism, and may suggest a common explanation. There is the same writing up of the glories of the past; the same extravagant claim that the foreigner owes all his inventions, his poetry, his philosophy, to borrowed models—the Greek to the Jew in the one case, the Greek and others to the Hindu in the other; there is the same want of criticism, the same indifference to real history, the same absence of seriousness. Side by side with these more outward expressions of national feeling, we may note further the same exclusiveness in life, in marriage and food taboos, and the same rigidity of law, while the sicarii and zealots of Roman Palestine have their parallel in the bomb-throwers and Tilaks of British India. The Jews re-wrote their history, filling it with imaginary glories and false records of persecution gloriously overcome. As a result, little is known of actual history for several periods, which were obviously formative. But with Antiochus Epiphanes we reach real history, and a strong clear light falls upon the people at a critical moment. The story is familiar, and the detail does not concern us at present.

Antiochus,[15] a king with a slight hint of genius, a deal of the charlatan, and something of the madman, came of a family of princes progressively declining from the solid merits of their founder, the sturdy general of Alexander. It was about a hundred years after the death of his ancestor Seleucus that he returned to Syria, to be king. After a childhood in a Seleucid palace, he had lived in Rome for about thirteen years as a hostage. He liked Roman ways, and, as a good successor of Alexander, he believed in his mission to extend Hellenic culture; but he was a sultan by inheritance and by long residence a foreigner. He did not know the vital facts of the situation.

---

15 Polybius, xxvi. 1; Livy, xli. 19; Bevan, *House of Seleucus*, ii. chap. 25; *Jerusalem*, pp. 74 ff.

If the Jerusalem prince-priests, as degenerate as he, were ready to be Hellenised, it did not follow that all the Jews were equally ready. We have seen that Temple and Synagogue represent two distinct types of religion, linked by tradition, by sacred books, and by race, but different in spirit, in ideal, and in life. The Temple was quickly Hellenised by the king—polluted, good Hebrews said. Next a royal mandate prohibited the practice of Jewish religion (1 Macc. i. 44). Then came the real struggle with the people for whom Jehovah was real, and a family of heroes led them. As has happened so often in history, the seed of the future is saved by a happy series of ir- relevant chances.[16]   Properly led and organised, the forces of Persia could have crushed the Greeks, always ready to betray one another. If Antiochus had had his hands free—but that sort of man never has his hands free; the man who acts on imperfect realisation of a sit- uation is always falling over himself, as Thucydides said of Xerxes.[17] The Greek proverb put it that "the dice of Zeus fall aye aright." [18] Providence, in spite of our cyni- cisms about the biggest battalions, manages in spite of them. The forward movements do survive against the probabilities; the irrelevant chances saved Judaism in Palestine. If it had been crushed there, as it was two centuries and a half later by Titus, there were still the synagogues elsewhere. However, not to speculate on what might have happened and did not happen, Judaism survived Antiochus. It gained from the struggle a new dynasty which contributed to it in two ways, giving it heroes and ideals to begin, and, later, oppressors and re- actions; and in both ways the Maccabaeans did service.

16 Tacitus, *Hist.*, v. 8; Antiochus was prevented by a Parthian war from civilising a horrible race.
17 Thucydides, i. 69, 5.
18 Sophocles, *Fr.* 763.

But the spiritual gain from the struggle with Antiochus was independent of any dynasty.

The Maccabaean movement has been well called the watershed of those centuries.[19] Before it the nation showed signs of religious decay. Haggai and Zechariah had had difficulty in getting the Jews to rebuild the Temple. *Ecclesiasticus,* a book which is roughly coeval with Antiochus, gives a picture of Judaism as it then was—none the less telling a picture for the writer being highly satisfied with himself and his outlook. A cultured and liberal[20] and yet genuine Jew—orthodox, moderate and canny—he shows us to what the national religion might come. He is monotheist, of course, and he says the usual and proper good words about God, for whom he has respect without warmth. He emphasises the glory of the Law, and lays stress on the central idea of personified Wisdom. He believes Judaism superior to Hellenism, as a good Jew should; but he is not very nationalist. He is not interested in angels nor very much in a Messiah; he has no great hope of Immortality nor much desire for it. "What pleasure hath God in all that perish in Hades, in place of those who live and give him praise? Thanksgiving perisheth from the dead as from one that is not; he that liveth and is in health praiseth the Lord" (xvii. 27, 28): "Fear not death; it is thy destiny . . . this is the portion of all flesh from God, and how canst thou withstand the decree of the Most High? Be it for a thousand years, for a hundred or for ten, that thou livest, in Sheol there are no reproaches concerning life" (xli. 3, 4).

After the crisis that Antiochus so suddenly brought upon Judaism, everything is altered. As in so many times of crisis, a great call is made on God; God has to

---

19 Fairweather, *Background of Gospels,* p. 128.
20 Cf. Eccles. xxxii. 3-6, music; xxxviii. medicine.

answer many more demands of the human spirit, which
in days of smug prosperity, like those reflected in *Ecclesiasticus,* are deadened. God must be more interested in
Israel than in days of peace; He must take more care
of the individual Israelite. Once more, as in the captivity, emphasis falls on God and on human personality.
The individual reaches a new level of self-consciousness.
The sense of having a real witness to bear for Jehovah
raises the nation to dignity. The misery and anxiety
of the struggle throw thinkers back upon the former
days when the arm of the Lord was revealed, when fire
would not burn His confessors nor lions tear them, when
the Lord intervened and saved His own. Antiochus
first, and later on the degenerate Maccabaeans, and later
still Herod and the Romans, drive men to range into
the next world for truth and comfort and salvation.
Fierce as the antithesis of Judaism became to Hellenism,
the Greek had made some contributions, or had asked
some questions, in the matter of God and the soul. Contribution and question are often the same thing. From
the Maccabaean resistance to Antiochus we may date
the later Judaism, self-conscious, nationalist, and yet
more universal than before in outlook.

Hellenism made its effect at once by charm and by
repulsion, by insidious appeal and by bold challenge.
The Jew could no more escape this influence than any
other thinking people. By way of reminder let us look
again at what Hellenism did and made men do. It drove
them to think of all the world at once; this habit of
mind it might call philosophy, but it is an integral part
of religion as we have seen, a tendency operative
wherever religion is to be deep and real. Where
Hellenism came, men could no longer be provincial.
Local and racial tradition must be re-examined, univer-

salised. The Hebrew might call Jehovah God of the whole earth; but was He? Many a trivial King of kings is known to history who was not King of kings. Our own coinage proclaimed our kings for centuries kings of France when they were nothing of the sort. Was this Hebrew claim for Jehovah the language of Temple-praise, or did it answer to discoverable fact? Was He anything like Plato's "father and maker of all things"? Did He stand actually behind all Creation, in it? Hellenism, again, always emphasised the individual by claim and question. He shall stand up and challenge the universe to be intelligible to his mind, to be endurable to his heart, to explain itself and submit to him. And then he shall ask that self of his, what is it and for how long? Do his powers of mind suggest or promise anything to his soul or to his heart?

We must now deal with the new views of God, which emerge and grow more and more dominant in the five centuries after Cyrus and the return from the captivity. The period is a long one, but our task is not to chronicle; it is to watch for movement, to mark progress. While we try to relate religious thought to the personal and national history of the thinkers, our main interest is in its development, and that is not to be recaptured by an annalistic method, even if for years we substitute decades or sometimes half centuries. Later on we shall have to inquire as to the way in which this developing God is conceived to manage man and his affairs, to intervene in history, and (most Greek idea of all) to plan, to geometrise, to economise, the whole story of our universe and our race.

We have already noticed one feature of the newer conception of God, in the elimination of the anthropomorphisms of older story by the authors of the Priestly Code. There are scholars who find the same desire shown by Septuagint translators;[21] by slight but subtle alterations the adaptation to the Hellenistic standpoint is made, and the path becomes plainer for those who seek to reconcile Hebrew religion with Greek philosophy—the inevitable outcome of the meeting of the races. With this impulse to obliterate the old naive notions of a God visible and audible, as He walks in the garden, and susceptible of feelings very like the emotions of man, there is a tendency to remove God to a higher and higher elevation, which makes relations with man more difficult. There is a loss of some of that tenderness which Hosea portrays in God for Israel.[22] God must be transcendent, they feel. The God of the Levitical cultus is a far-off God, aloof from sinful men, jealous in guarding His holiness;[23] into His holy place only the priests may go, and they with precautions; and men become growingly anxious to avoid using His name. Jehovah is replaced by Adonai.

The distresses of the time brought men face to face with the problem of evil. God had to be separate from evil, and this involved a dualism in religious belief. Slowly there grew up the conception of a war in the spiritual sphere, a war of Satan and his hosts against God—a vivid and even dramatic way of figuring the division of good and evil in the universe; it acquitted God of all responsibility for sin and suffering.

But God could not be left out of touch with the world, and under influences whose origins are looked for Eastward, Judaism began to develop angels and other intermediaries. They are found in Ezekiel; while Daniel shows a much later stage of their growth. Michael is there and other Princes presiding over the nation.[24] At

21 W. Fairweather, *Background of Gospels*, 329.
22 J. P. Peters, *Rel. Hebr.*, 392-3.
23 A. B. Bruce, *Apologetics*, 286.
24 Cf. Deut. LXX iv. 19, b; xxxii. 8, b.

the end of that century, the second B.C., there are more
elaborate groupings of the angels in the *Book of Jubilees,*
including angels set over the Gentiles to lead them astray
from God (xv. 31). In that strange congeries which
forms our present book of Enoch there are whole
hierarchies of angels. But, says the author of *Jubilees*
(xv. 32), there is no ruler set over Israel; God Himself
is Israel's ruler. In *Tobit* [25] we learn that God hears
prayers through angelic mediation—a doctrine which
puts God very far away.

There are noble conceptions of how God communicates
with men. His Glory is all but personalised.[26] His
Name becomes a reality in itself—a notion which reopens
the door to a great deal of primitive magic which religious thinkers had been driving gradually out of the
house of Religion.[27] But above all, the most fertile of
all these attempts at finding an intermediary was that
which chose God's Wisdom for the rôle. Wisdom begins
by being an attribute of God; there follows a poetic
personification; and at last Wisdom becomes a divine
personality subordinate to God, distinct yet not distinct
from God. It receives a large number of striking names
—Providence, supreme Power, Justice, Mercy, and more
significant still, Holy Spirit and Word.[28] Some Greek
influence may be suspected behind the last, so markedly
does it fit in with the Stoic *Logos.* But in the meantime
Wisdom achieved all that the *Logos* need, and it had its
place in the canonical *Proverbs.* Wisdom and *Logos* ran
together, and enabled those who sought reconciliation
between religion and philosophy to find a way. The
identification had a great history; it is the basis of Philo's

---

25 Tobit xii. 12.
26 Tobit xii. 15; xiii. 14.
27 Tobit xiii. 11; viii. 5.
28 Fairweather, *Background of Gospels,* 342; *Wisdom of Solomon,* ix. i,
Word; xviii. 15, Almighty Word; ix. 17, Holy Spirit; see also Drummond,
Philo, i. p. 214 ff.

thought; and in the Fourth Gospel it gained a central place in Christian Theology. Something was lost for the time of the Personality of God; for personality at such a distance and mediated through angels and abstract nouns seems something less than itself. But Jehovah even at a distance is personal. Judaism has kept what Hellenism had never gained, a fundamental conviction of God's personality; it has cleared God of the evil that haunted Greek conceptions of deity; and, even if the device of personifying this Wisdom is clumsy, it has yet managed to keep God in relation with the world.

XII

THE GODS OF THE ORIENT

ALEXANDER, as we saw, made a new world out of an old. He shifted the centre of gravity for all things human and divine, and he gave men new outlooks and new ideals in politics, thought and religion. The old gods of Greece remained as they had been; which, when everything was changed round about them, meant that they stood no longer in the old relation to life; that, remaining the same, they too were changed. The Stoics brought to bear upon human life, minds emancipated from the local and the temporary; strong, clear intellects that rationalised all human relations as well as the divine, and did it with a swiftness and a thoroughness that was ruthless and really unscientific. Everything was submitted to reason, and had to be quick in explaining itself. As a result a good many permanent features of the human mind were brushed away as weaknesses. Perhaps in the contemporary expression of them there was weakness; but even a weakness when it is recurrent, when it is virtually universal, calls for attention and explanation. A system which is built on the strength of the human mind to the neglect of its weakness, is not destined for permanence. A religion that is to endure must recognise the weaknesses of men; it may do so by accepting them as inevitable and not combating them, or it may do so by overcoming them, by bringing a force into play that outweighs them. Stoicism did neither; and the weak, the vulgar and the irrational elements of life militated against it, and not these alone; the natural affections which it trampled down rose up again; they too were Nature, and Stoicism paid the penalty of being insufficiently loyal to its own great principle.

The little states and the loose-hung hegemonies of the Greece best known to literature were, as we have seen, gone for ever.[1] City and region alike were details in one or another great empire, and were ruled by foreigners, the agents of a great king who perhaps never visited them himself. The citizen sank into the subject; he was driven in upon himself, to be more individualist than ever. Whether he preferred the temporal or the eternal, it was his own affair; he must help himself.

If he chose the temporal, the new age offered him new opportunities of enjoyment, unburdened by new ideals to replace the old. The traditions of society were changed; new men, mercenaries and traders, had wealth that made the old families look beggarly; and new cities which the Macedonian princes planted all over the Orient did much to depopulate Greece, and to change what was left of it. The passing of old standards in duty and morals, in wealth and ideals of comfort, in the unrecognised backgrounds of thought, gave the individual a new freedom; the world was all before him where to choose. The most obvious choice was not the highest. One of the inevitable consequences of the break-up of the old society and of the enormous pillage of further Asia was a great development of luxury. Alexander's zest for the style and pomp of the Persian court was aped by his successors in Egypt and Syria; and what in a great nature was perhaps ennobled by imagination and love of symbol became in successors of poorer grain rank vulgarity, however cloaked by culture and etiquette. Palaces full of marbles and

---

1 I do not forget the weary wars that Polybius records, exactly like the wars of the great age of Greece, except that these were formative and the later ones echoes; then the intense nationalism had quickened the Greek mind, now it simply wore it out.

bronzes, of mosaics and pictures, of gold and silver plate;
great gardens; personal adornment, flowered robes and
bleached hair; famous cooks; theatrical pageants, parades
of strange beasts; professional athletes, dancers and
singers, organised in societies with high privilege and
exemption from military service—these meet us in the
new age. Even Sparta succumbed to the taste for
luxury.[2] Women gained a new freedom; and as happens
with people new to freedom, their use of it was not
always wise or helpful to the community. Men of letters
sank to gathering the witty sayings (not very witty) of
the adventuresses and *hetairai* who hung about prince
and parvenu, and telling their stories in the metre of
Sophocles.

Simultaneously a certain exhaustion of the human
mind was widely felt. This is a curious experience
which the race has known from time to time, chiefly
perhaps when social change is swifter than intellectual
adjustment. It is not always true that the human mind
really is declining at such periods; but, for the moment,
missing what is called the "integrity" of its age, and
out of its bearings, it is afraid of its great task of creation, and, beating about to find itself, it turns to criticism.
Thinkers, artists, and poets no longer have, consciously
or unconsciously, with them or in them the sense of the
community, the sense of humanity, the sense of the universe, as the great Greeks had it—Homer, Aeschylus,
and Plato. They are solitary except for the past, the
great dead; and where they do not give themselves to
science, they are antiquaries—a safe and happy trade.
The old is revived, reproduced, interpreted; and attempts
at originality suffer from over-consciousness of the great
triumphs of genius in the past as much as from the sense
of inadequacy to get any effective grasp, to achieve any

2 J. Beloch, *Griech. Gesch.*, III. i. pp. 415-423.

real synthesis, of the present.   Men cannot be themselves
in the presence of the old masterpieces; they are driven
to emulate or to rebel, and neither course leads to great
achievement.   So they take refuge in the pretty, the
sentimental, the small mastery, the art and literature of
revolt or the clique.   Not that the human mind was
not inactive in this period; scholarship, geography,
astronomy and other natural sciences flourished; but
these did not give, they never give, the same sense of
freedom and grandeur that is received from genius more
original; and without it their flourishing was not to be
for long.

The quiet individual, then, revolting from the luxury
and display in which the adventurer spent his new wealth
and gradually extinguished his faculties, and conscious
of sharing the decline that was overtaking the world,
was faced by despair.   The old gods were not what they
had been; philosophy trampled on human nature; right
and wrong were confused; genius was dead; what was
there worth while?   There is world-weariness in this
age, weariness of culture,[3] fear of life, "failure of nerve,"
as Professor Bury puts it.   The Stoics ministered to the
relief of this feeling by teaching the lawfulness and
propriety of suicide.   True, Seneca later on urged that
"you should leave life, not bolt from it," *exire non
fugere*; but the pace is nothing, the exit was permitted.
But a form of surrender as fatal and requiring less resolve, is race-suicide.   "In our time," writes Polybius,[4]
"all Greece was visited by a dearth of children . . . and
a failure of productiveness followed, though there were
no long-continued wars or serious pestilences among us.
If, then, any one had advised our sending to ask the gods
in regard to this, what we were to do or say in order to

3 Wendland, *Die hell-röm Kultur,* p. 40.
4 Polybius, xxxvii. 9.

become more numerous and better fill our cities—would
he not have seemed a futile person, when the cause was
manifest and the cure was in our own power?   For this
evil grew upon us rapidly, and without attracting attention, by our men becoming perverted to a passion for
show and money and the pleasure of an idle life and
accordingly either not marrying at all, or, if they did
marry, refusing to rear the children that were born, or
at most one or two out of a great number, for the sake
of leaving them well off or bringing them up in extravagant luxury." It sounds very modern. Probably another
factor operated—a sense of despair of raising the human
crop in a world of war and anarchy, of the futility of
effort, the feeling that the man travels best who gives
fewest pledges to fortune.   Again, the reaction will take
the form of a heightened sense of solitude and forlorn-
ness; and the solitary and forlorn are apt to be the prey
of emotion, especially when the level of culture is not
very high.

A man must have some anchor, some haven of peace
and security. If domestic happiness gives it, he is not
apt to range much further. But here was a world where
all the higher instincts seemed to be mocked—genius,
love of country, family feeling. One permanent instinct
of man was left which was not denied, which could not
be denied, its satisfaction by any combination of adven-
turers.   There was the unseen world, and to it men
turned with a hunger unexampled in the story of Greece
—a craving for something that they might believe, for
some explanation of the horrors of life, for some hope
that would carry them through this mortal scene, through
the unchartered beyond, for something that would guarantee family love and natural affection, for something
universal. The Stoic might laugh at such desires in
another and suppress them in himself. But natures that

were of softer fibre, less logical, less courageous, owned
to these cravings—and natures, too, that were truer to
the large human instincts.   When philosophy gave so
little help, small wonder men went elsewhere in their
need.

The days were past when the enlightened and the in-
tellectuals dominated the field of thought.   The reaction
was signalised by the hemlock given to Socrates.   The
piety of Xenophon is called pietism by some German
critics; but whichever it be, his attitude to the gods
strikes strangely on a reader of Thucydides who remembers that the later historian tried to finish the work of
the earlier.   But as in the Roman Empire, as in France
after Waterloo, men, who had been shocked by what
atheism could mean, swung back to ancient paths.   The
successors of Alexander might be deified by their own
rescripts or the votes of abject allies; but their godless
lives of luxury, licence and war must have made many
sigh for gods real and effectual, belief in whom would
control life and lift it back to the level of an idealised
past.

So, conscious of his own needs and fears,[5] of his
spiritual solitude in a terrible universe, the individual
man wanted friends whom he might know, who would
care for him, not as an item in a community but as a
personality.   He craved communion, in a new way, with
gods.   Homer's heroes had their contacts and conflicts
with gods, but not as men now sought intercourse with
heaven.   The relation must be more personal and more
conscious.   Reason is one thing, feeling another; feeling
was what they wanted.   They wanted to feel secure, to
feel happy, to be conscious of the touch and protection

---

[5] For the fears, some of them, see Theophrastus, *Characters*, xxvii., The
Superstitious Man; who, however often purified, confines himself to Greek
rites—unless Sabazius is still foreign.   The book probably belongs between
322 and 300 B.C.; cf. Jebb (ed. Sandys), p. 7.

of gods. With the long story of the disastrous effects
of unchecked emotion upon religion open before us, it
is easy to see how this emphasis on feeling opened the
door to all sorts of spiritual and intellectual insincerity.
Men were living under conditions which led them to
despair of reason; the philosophers were so hard and so
abstract, and the practical rationalism of kings like
Philip V of Macedon led to so much cold-blooded horror.
Probably feeling had never monopolised so much of
man's attention in Greek history.

The soul had been drawing to itself the interest of
thinkers more and more since the days when Plato
enunciated that philosophy is preparation or practice of
death.[6] It was an inevitable movement of thought, a
real progress; and it illustrates anew and with force that
tendency to lay stress on human personality which we
have found so powerful in the history of religion. More
and more was asked of the Universe, was asked of God.
By now Immortality was becoming the centre of religious
aspiration, a natural outcome of the emphasis on the
individual enforced by all the features of contemporary
life. Something beyond the grave must make amends
for this world. The conviction grows that personality
is a thing that must outlast death; and every man conscious of it has a progressively imperative instinct that
he at least must not be blotted out. This new self-
consciousness, this new demand for life, for fuller and
richer and more enduring life, distinguishes this period
of Greek life from the classical. Stoic psychological
observation, religious impulse, the cry for life beyond,
all bring the soul into a new significance. The development of the soul is to be the real thing in life; the body
and its fugitive interests may occupy the great and the

---

6 Plato, *Phaedo*, 81 A; cf. *Rep.*, x. 608 ff. See James Adam, *Vitality of
Platonism*, p. 66 f.

trivial, but for the earnest and the thoughtful, men or women, the world beyond is the real. The world beyond and the world within; for they are the same thing. The care of the soul is man's chief task, and it involves questions. In the old days any sense of sin that there might be was concerned with acts; now it attaches itself to the condition of the soul. The soul, then, its sinfulness and its purification, draw to themselves an attention which would have seemed ludicrous to the illuminated in the fifth century at Athens, and to the common man too. That marked shifting of interest from the outward to the inward which the spiritual interpretation of History brings into such prominence,[7] is seen again here. Nor is it accident. The trend of thought and experience has been steady. Orphic teaching, Pythagoras, Plato, the pressure of the world and its problems—everything has been reinforcing the necessity of this transition.

When once Immortality and the sense of sin [8] become master factors in man's thinking, a new seriousness attaches to all religion. It ceases to be conventional. Ritual and tradition do well enough for those who do not think and feel. The really religious spirit must have certainty. The orthodoxy of Aristophanes, local and conservative for all his wit, was flippant and shallow. It was easy to be orthodox about what did not supremely matter; but for men with an intense belief in truth and in God conventional orthodoxy will not serve. Still less will serve the doubts of Protagoras and the sophists. It is a question of where the interest centres, of what matters most. Neither Aristophanes nor Protagoras seems to have been interested in his soul's salvation.

The Epicurean dismissed the whole matter and emphasised the senses and the life of sense. Cicero's mag-

---

7 See Shailer Mathews, *Spiritual Interpretation of History.*
8 It will be remembered here that Sin is not a term with one fixed meaning.

nificent refutation of Epicureanism by citing tragic
figures from the dramas of Ennius touched the real
weakness of the system.[9]

> Now what help,
> On what protection may I call, and win?
> Where now in exile or in flight find aid,
> Who am bereft of citadel and home?
> Whither now turn, to whom address my prayer?
> For lo! where stood my home, my fathers' gods
> And altars all are fallen, broken down;
> Their thrones by flame despoiled; the lofty walls
> Rear fire-marred heads, where crackling pine has flamed. . . .

> O father! O land of my fathers!
> O palace of Priam the king,
> And temple, where gates on high hinges
> No more through the silence shall ring;
> All ruined! and yet I have seen you
> When the host of our army stood nigh
> With ivory wrought and all golden,
> A blaze of glory on high.

Andromache widowed, childless, robbed of city and
home—will pleasures of the moment, a cushion or a
cup of mead, or the memory of former cups and cushions,
take from her the pangs of the soul? Never! So
Epicurean criticism fell on deaf ears. The Epicurean
did not understand the human problem; he knew nothing
of the depths of human nature; and there were those
who hinted that his second-hand natural science was not
very sound and did not go far enough. His easy neglect
of the gods was well enough for men who needed no
gods. But gods were the prime demand of humanity.

How the Stoic failed, we have already seen. He too
missed the real springs of the human spirit in spite of
his psychology; and when he turned the gods into

9 Cicero, *Tusculans*, iii. 19, 44-46; the rendering was made by a pupil of
mine, who fell in the war.

abstract personifications of grain or water or of the processes of growth, when he included his gods among the other items of the cosmos which would periodically be dissolved into atoms, and utterly annihilated, he showed how little he understood the cry of the human heart. He might be loyal to truth and great of spirit, but he had missed something real.

The immortal mind craves objects that endure—

above all, its gods must be real, they must give the soul fixity and certainty; and men turned away in disappointment from the Stoics. Sadness haunts Stoicism. If Epictetus is conscious of no sadness, it marks a defect in him; Seneca has an under-current of melancholy, and in Marcus Aurelius it is the dominant note. "Either gods or atoms," says Marcus Aurelius—a question-mark at the very heart of things.

But was it so certain that real knowledge of the gods was unattainable? Men were, in Plato's telling phrase, "examining life" anew and getting closer, it seemed, to reality. Julius Beloch suggests that the decline of polytheism was itself a symptom of the deepening of religious feeling.[10] Abstracts of larger implication begin to appear in men's speech; τὸ θεῖον, "the divine," rules the world, τὸ δαιμόνιον; or the bold vague masculine singular, ὁ θεός, God, comes naturally to men's minds and lips. Even *Tyche,* chance, has at least a grammatical unity about it, a poor enough principle to which to reduce phenomena, but a single one in a sort of a way; it brought all things under one idea, if a bad one. So much was the outcome of long years of thought, filtering into the regions of the less original and less thoughtful. At the bottom, then, of all phenomena and of all experience

10 Beloch, *Griech. Gesch.,* vol. III. i. 444.

lies—the Divine; and the Divine is one, and so far it is intelligible.

But if the Divine is one, there is not one Divine for the Greek and another for the Phrygian and a third for the Egyptian. No; Egyptian and Greek and Phrygian are handling the same evidence, or very nearly the same evidence, of the same one great underlying reality. If one man says Zeus and another Osiris, the presumption is that they are trying to interpret a similar experience. When the Egyptian king in Herodotus' story found the untaught children crying *bekos,* and learnt that the Phrygians give the name *bekos* to bread, he drew the deduction that Phrygian is the oldest, the primeval, language; bread he took to be a constant, however much the languages of men may vary. So God is a constant; and perhaps, if the older peoples give to God a different name from the Greeks, it may be that they, as the oldest exponents of God, are not wrong but right, nearer the original.[11] What if other nations, dealing with the same Divine, coincide more nearly with the traditional religions of Greece than with Stoic or Epicurean? When Vincent of Lerins enunciated his principle *Quod semper, quod ubique, quod ab omnibus,* it was not quite new, nor is it yet quite obsolete or absurd. The Stoic, as we saw, took the consensus of human belief as a valid index to truth; the modern man of science attaches more weight to a law deduced from observation over a wide field, over the widest field, by the largest number of independent observers. For the different observers cancel one another's errors; and, when they reach one conclusion, there is a strong presumption in favour of our acting upon it as true, until it is disproved, or until it is

[11] Compare the view of Megasthenes in the third book of his *Indica* (cited by Clem. Alex., *Strom.* i. 15; Müller, *F.H.G.,* vol. ii. p. 437, *fr.* 41): "All that was said about nature by the ancients is said also by the philosophers beyond Greece, some of it among the Indians by the Brahmans, some of it in Syria by those called Jews."

merged in some larger and more universal law based on still wider knowledge; and in the latter case it is really confirmed. The gods of Sicyon may not have much currency in Argos, less in Athens, less still in Thessaly, none at all in Persia; that is to say, the names given in Sicyon to divine power may be unknown elsewhere, but that in Sicyon divine power is recognised and is named, is a fact that confirms and encourages other thinkers who elsewhere have recognised it, even if they have given it other names. Conversely, when the man from Sicyon draws this deduction from observations made in his travels in Thessaly and Egypt, even if he thinks less of the name used in the old home town, he is confirmed in believing in the Divine.

When the issue was put so, both Stoic and Epicurean admitted the validity of the reasoning; both conceded gods and the existence of gods. The Epicurean, however, persisted that gods may exist, but that they have not necessarily on that account anything to do with us; Indians also existed, but they did not come into practical politics in the Mediterranean world. The Stoic refused this last limitation of the gods; if gods exist, and the consensus of mankind is fair evidence for presuming that they do, then they are relevant to us, in a universe which is an integer with nothing in it that is, properly considered, irrelevant to anything else in it. If the Stoic, like the Epicurean, persisted in a dogma of his own about the gods, if he grouped them among phenomena of only temporary significance, he had at least conceded —they had both conceded—a principle that was giving important results. The evidence of the foreigner was relevant to Greek theology; how far you were to go in using it, was another point. It might be possible to use the conceded principle to yield further knowledge and bring men to a firmer grasp of reality.

For centuries Greeks had been impressed by the East, and especially by Egypt.[12]   Herodotus had held that behind Greek theology lay Egyptian.   He had been interested in Persian thought, so far as he could get at it through interpreters.[13]   The conquest of Alexander had, as we have seen, brought Greek and Persian and Egyptian together far more closely than ever, and under his successors more deliberate attempts than ever before were made to make the religious ideas of the nations intelligible to the Greeks.   The Ptolemies, the shrewdest and most successful of the world's rulers, saw a political value [14] in bringing Greek and Egyptian together on a religious basis, for at first blush the Greek had an ill-disguised contempt for Egyptian worship.   Herodotus had observed with curious but kindly eyes what moved the mockery of later Greeks.   People who could really worship cats and crocodiles, sing hymns to them alive and mummy them dead, who could worship leeks and onions, were obviously contemptible.[15]   Contempt, freely felt and expressed, rarely consolidates kingdoms.   So stress was laid on another side of Egyptian religion, and the priests were probably content with a wise king, who might modify detail but respected and improved their position.   Serapis became the great Egyptian god for mankind at large.   It was a cult fortified by the rejection or modification of gross or repugnant elements and by new emphasis on its mystical features.   In other words, it was Hellenised; it became "the most civilised of all barbarian religions; it retained enough of the exotic element to arouse the curiosity of the Greeks, but not enough to offend their delicate sense of proportion, and

12 Breasted, *Hist. Anc. Egyptians,* p. 40, says that the Greeks never correctly understood Egyptian civilisation, and greatly over-valued Egypt's intellectual achievement: the Greeks were vastly superior to what they so much venerated.
13 See p. 164.
14 Cf. Mahaffy, *Empire of Ptolemies,* p. 72.
15 Cumont, *Oriental Religions,* p. 78.

its success was remarkable." [16]   The Athenian sculptor Bryaxis gave the new or re-discovered god a form which Cumont [17] calls "one of the last divine creations of Hellenic genius"; it became the standard and the prototype of all portrayals of him.

Political attempts, like this of the first Ptolemy, are significant only when they are based on some real factor of the day; and in this case the real factor was a genuine desire for approximation in religion.   Manetho, a priest of Heliopolis, who is credited with a share in leading Ptolemy to this development of Serapis, [18] took the trouble to compile for Greeks an account of Egyptian religion.   Even if his work, as we are told, was careless and uncritical, [19] and tedious into the bargain, [20] so that the Greeks left it on one side in favour of still less exact and exacting writers, it was a sign of the movement of interest.   The king and the priest had hit the moment; and the Hellenised religion of Serapis was spread through the ramifications of trade all over the world before the century was out. [21]   The god had Greek monks devoted to him as well as Egyptian, and recent finds of papyri tell of the life in his Serapeums.   If much of Egyptian religion remained un-Hellenised, a contact had been established which produced the greatest effects.

In the same way, in this period, the Chaldean priest Berossos, under Antiochus Soter, wrote in Greek a short history of Babylonia on the basis of cuneiform tradition, setting forth in dry enough fashion a list of kings reaching back to 468,000 years before Cyrus, and adding mythological and astrological sections.   If the vast antiquity of the East could guarantee the eternity of the

16 Cumont, *Oriental Religions*, p. 79.
17 *Ib.*, p. 76.
18 Plutarch, *Isis and Osiris.* c. 28.
19 Breasted, *Hist. of Ancient Egyptians*, p. 26; Erman, *Egyptian Religion*, p. 217, calls it "a melancholy piece of bungling."
20 Beloch, *Greich. Gesch.*, III. i. 489.
21 Beloch, *Greich. Gesch.*, III. i. pp. 446-449.

gods of the Orient, surely Berossos had done good service; but it is not surprising to learn that he too was little read.[22]

Asia Minor lay still nearer to the Greek, and it was familiar ground, and for a long time influences had been felt from here. The kings of Pergamum, another very astute dynasty, transferred to their capital the great black stone which either was Cybele or was her dwelling, and so doing they gave and gained a new significance. Athens and Rome at once became more attentive to the goddess.[23] The Seleucids, on the other hand, tried to establish Greek cults and festivals in Syria. What response their efforts met among the Jews, we know; how their other subjects received them, is not so well known. On the other hand, Syria had long ago sent Adonis to Greece and now began to contribute other gods— Atargatis, who became identified in the spirit of the times with Astarte,[24] and Adad or Hadad, who had a bookish celebrity through the similarity of his name with the Syriac word for *one*.[25]

In all this story we have to remember that we are not dealing with monotheists and their fierce temper and exacting Theology, but with polytheists easier of habit altogether. It was not hard to identify one's native god with the foreigner's god; it was just as easy to worship both. Gods were taken over as lightly then as religious ideas are from popular magazines to-day. Indeed the mood of vague catholicity and loose thinking that has made the success of theosophy in India and in America was not strange to that age. It is not to be supposed that the pious and the superstitious, the austere and the prostitute, who worshipped Isis side by side, had any

22 Beloch, *Greich. Gesch.*, p. 489.
23 W. S. Ferguson, *Hellenistic Athens*, p. 229.
24 Cumont, *Ar. Relig.*, p. 104, suggests that the identification is wrong.
25 Macrobius, *Saturnalia*, i. 23, 17; Adad . . . *Ejus nominis interpretatio significat Unus unus.*

exact knowledge of all of the history of the goddess.
The literature of the foreigner remained a sealed book
to the Greek; he did not want to read what barbarians
wrote; he picked up a journalist's knowledge of their
ideas, and filled the gaps in his information with guess-
work.[26]   The philosophers smiled benignly on the result
and treated the religions of the Orient as "philosophies."

For our present inquiry the grounds of appeal of these
barbarian religions are more important than the cults
themselves. We have to consider what the Greeks and
others supposed themselves to find in them; and then to
see how the evidence we gain bears upon our subject.

We have seen that the immense antiquity of these
Eastern religions had always impressed the Greek, and
that a feeling, not at all improper, existed that truth was
to be sought even outside the Greek philosophic schools.
As Celsus said long afterwards—the saying will bear
repetition—"the barbarians are equal to discovering religious truths (*dogmata*) while the Greeks are better at
criticising and establishing them when discovered." [27]
But that was only one line of appeal; for, quite apart
from the quest for truth, there was an appeal to imagination and to emotion in the ancient ceremonial, in the
claim to superior and esoteric knowledge, in the promise
of the communication of new life in the mysteries.
Where religion and magic are not clearly distinguished,
there is an additional appeal in ritual. A later age gave
a "scientific" account of the value of ritual as Mrs.
Besant does in India to-day. There are affinities almost
chemical between spiritual natures and material sub-
stances; [28] the physical nature of matter can be modified
or supercharged by formulae; or, at least, you can believe that some such processes and contacts may be pos-

26 Wendland, *die hell.-röm Kultur*, p. 39; Beloch, *Greich. Gesch.*, III. 488.
27 *Ap.* Origen, *c. Cels.*, i. 2.   Cf. p. 342.
28 Cf. p. 336.

sible; and then what prospects open before the worshipper of rapture, of vision, and, above all, of feeling!   ,

There was in the Eastern religions no great moral
teaching, any more than in the religion of the Greek
temples; *that* was never a feature of ancient paganism;
morals, on the contrary, as we saw, came from the philosophers and the fathers of families. But Egyptian
religion had much to give to the mind—the sensation
of exercise, for instance, and the impression of receiving
truth. Its linen, its tonsures, and its rites of washing—
rites easy, natural, and refreshing in a hot climate with
a great river always near—gave the suggestion of
purity.[29] Its occasional taboos of sexual intercourse, its
daily ministry to the gods [30] (closely resembling Hindu
practice), the unity, precision, and eternity of its ceremony, all suggested a seriousness, which to loose-thinking
minds, careless of the distinction between symbol and
thought, was impressive in the highest. We know to
this day the appeal of "holiness," in spite of wrong or
confused thinking that may go with it. The teaching of
judgment after death and the promise of salvation by
Serapis,[31] the claim to control gods or cosmic powers by
prayer and holy formula,[32] seemed to take the worshipper
into regions beyond common experience, to promise him
what was above all the desire of men in that age of
trouble and uncertainty—assurance and certainty. If
questions were raised about gross traditions and rituals,
about worship of lowly reptiles, recourse was had to
allegory and symbol. If, says Plutarch, a god is content
to be worshipped in an idol, how much happier is it to

29 Cumont, *Or. Relig.*, pp. 91, 92.
30 Cumont, *Or. Relig.*, pp. 95, 97, cites Porphyry, *de Abstin.*, iv. 9; Anrobius,
vii. 32; Apuleius, *Metam.*, xi. 20.
31 Julian, *Oration*, iv. 136 A, B.
32 Cf. the theory advanced by Iamblichus, vi. 6.

THE GODS OF THE ORIENT

symbolise him in a living thing!—*e.g.* a crocodile, which like God has no tongue.[33]

Side by side with Eastern religion came Astrology. Professor Burnet and Cumont alike urge that the much vaunted Astronomy of Babylonia was empirical—"an elaborate record of celestial phenomena made for purposes of divination." [34] This was not the view of the Greeks. Diodorus Siculus (ii. 29, 30) contrasts the flimsy amateurish way in which the Greeks handle the science, "touching the philosophy late, studying it up to a point, distracted by the needs of life . . . making a trade of it for gain," with the serious training of the hereditary Chaldaean astrologers, who are the descendants or heirs of the most ancient Babylonians, who have the most accurate observations of the movements and influences of the stars.[35] The planets they call "interpreters," because they move and foreshow the future and interpret to men the goodwill of the gods, and they name them "as our astrologers do" after the gods Ares, Aphrodite, Hermes, and Zeus, though Cronos (or Saturn) they call Helios. Greek astrologers had not always used these names; the planets had been Pyroeis, Eosphoros, Stilbon, and Phaethon, and Saturn had been Phaenion, until in the fourth century B.C. the divine names replaced the old ones.[36] The planet week came into use in Hellenistic times.[37] The philosophers had started the idea that the stars were gods; Aristophanes had remarked that the Orientals worshipped the Sun and the Moon. With the breakdown of old local gods, the deification of adventurer princes, and the theory of Euhemerus that

[33] Plutarch, *Isis and Osiris,* 75, 381 B. Cf. Strabo, xvii. 38, c. 812, on worship of sacred crocodile.
[34] Burnet, *Greek Philosophy,* Part I. p. 5. Cumont, *Astrology and Religion,* pp. 7, 8.
[35] Cf. Strabo, p. 639 C, on Chaldean astronomers, especially Kidenas, identified now with Ki-din-nu read on a lunar table; Cumont, iv. 63, 64.
[36] Cumont, *Astrol. and Relig.,* pp. 45, 46; Dreyer, *Planetary Systems,* p. 169 n.
[37] Cumont, *Astrol. and Relig.,* p. 165.

all the Greek gods were deified men, a place was open, as
we saw, for gods who were universal and unquestionable, who did not depend on popular votes for their godhead; and Astrology offered them.   It is pointed out
that Astronomy only reached Egypt itself about the sixth
century B.C., from which time its significance increased
rapidly and the Egyptians began to claim the credit of
being the pioneers in the Science.[38] On the Hellenistic
mind, Astrology fell, as Professor Murray puts it, "as a
new disease falls upon some remote island people." [39]

Once the identification of stars and gods was made,
the door was open for much more.   To a certain type
of mind, when it is explained that the gods are the stars
and the stars the gods, a new certainty seems to follow;
religion reaches a new plane of truth and eternity, and all
sorts of riders and deductions follow.[40]   The planets began
to have influences, to be tutelary powers of days, hours,
and centuries, to be "world-lords" ($\varkappa o\sigma\mu o\varkappa\rho\acute{a}\tau o\rho\varepsilon\varsigma$);
to each were attached plants, metals, stones, and colours.
The sun becomes "the heart of the universe."   Lest it
should seem that the creature replaced the creator, the
new theologians devised a god beyond the sun, to whom
the sun was a subordinate power, of whom it was an expression in the world of sense, a *Jupiter summus exsuper-
antissimus*.   Then as life came more under planetary
control, the planets became gates [41] through which the
soul passes in descent to earth and again in ascent to the
world of being, at each of which it picks up or lays down
qualities—*e.g.* from Mars it gets anger, from Venus desire; or, it may be, the soul loses some aspect of real being with each gate through which it passes.[42]   Stoic pantheism fitted in well with all this; and if the stars too

38 Cumont, *Astrol. and Relig.*, p. 75.
39 Murray, *Four Stages*, p. 125.
40 Cumont, *Astrol. and Relig.*, pp. 119-131, 135.
41 Cumont, *Astrol. and Relig.*, p. 198; *Oriental Religions*, p. 269 n.
42 Macrobius, *Comm. Somn. Scip.*, i., xi. 9, xii. 1.

were to pass, as stricter Stoics would urge, they had at least a look of eternity that might encourage the believer to hope that things were not so bad as was said.

Not everybody accepted this new revelation. Aristarchos of Samos taught of a heliocentric system, "upsetting the hearth (*hestia*) of the universe." [43] Seleucus of Seleucia, a rationalist indeed, is credited with utterly rejecting astrology, with holding to the heliocentric idea, and offering an explanation of tides.[44] But such men were a minority; they differed so strongly from current opinion that they could not be right, and they unsettled what was becoming the fixed basis in religion. When we recall how in modern times of unsettlement there has been passionate return to common consent, to tradition, as the sure foundation of religious life, we can understand in measure the attitude of the Hellenistic world. No real reaction was made against Astrology till Christians, orthodox and unorthodox,[45] began to turn their criticism on it; and the fierceness of the struggle then shows what was involved. The certainty of the old religion had in Astrology what we should call a scientific basis; the order of the heavens, the uniformity and intelligibility of the cosmos, were linked by pure assumption to a traditional religion. The weakness of the link escaped notice in the relief of finding certainty, and the certainty itself was not too closely examined. The Greek passion for knowledge was cheaply gratified, and the clinging soul was given a sure support. And the rest followed.

Of the stages by which the various religions conquered the world, or of the detail of teaching and cults, it is not

43 Beloch, *Gr. Gesch.*, III. i. 480; Dreyer, *Planetary Systems*, p. 136 f.; the criticism quoted is Plutarch's and very characteristic, *de facie in orbe lunæ*, 6.
44 Dreyer, *ibid.*, p. 140; Strabo, cc. 6, 739, and especially c. 174.
45 *E.g.* Bardaisan's book on Fate.

necessary now to speak, except as they bear upon our general inquiry.

First of all, the individual is promised a surer recognition by the gods. The meaning of all that ancient wealth of ceremony was again and again a real contact between God and man. Symbol as much of it was, symbol and transaction ran into one another, where (as we saw) magic and religion were insufficiently distinguished, where thought was not alert, and where the quest of truth was not the main object. God and man could meet and know each other; mystically or even to the bodily eye god and goddess would show themselves to the faithful, who, duly purified, performed aright the set course of ritual, and in the appointed way was initiated and prepared. The very difficulty of initiation, the seven grades through which the Mithraist was conducted, the strangeness, all heightened the impression, and where criticism or reflection was impiety, brought conviction to the adept. Of the processes of mind by which certainty was achieved, of deliberate imposture and conjuring by the priests, of suggestion and suggestibility, of the will to believe, of the desperation of the religious temperament in the world we have been surveying, much might be said. But for us the main point is this: in all the mental and moral degradation of these Eastern religions, as they spread over the Mediterranean world, the factor of importance is the conviction that man, as an individual, as a personality, with real needs of soul and nature, must have an effective relation with god, gods, or goddesses, a great reassertion, in a terribly misleading and humiliating way, of the principle which we have found throughout—the growing significance of the individual and the imperative call for his recognition by the Divine.

When we analyse further the objects of these initiations, we get still clearer light on this point. The word "salvation" begins to appear in religion. How alien, how unintelligible, to Homer's Greeks the word would have been, it is hard to imagine. In the age of Pericles and Anaxagoras it would have been strange. But in the period before us, it becomes a keyword in religious thought. A careless assumption puts on one level all ancient religions which speak of salvation; but the word obviously is susceptible of many meanings, which will vary with the outlook of the speaker.

Salvation is not a fixed idea; much turns on what it is from which a man seeks to be saved—whether he fears eternal reincarnation, or death physical or eternal, or the pollution and paralysis of his soul by sin.

In the age under our study men sought salvation from three main fears—from daemons, from fate, and from death. The planet "world-lords" had done more than establish religion; they had brought all life under their iron rule. Fatalism began to paralyse the thoughts of men; a doom, a destiny, was read in the stars, and it was at once inevitable; the very belief in it made it so, and life became a thing of horror and dread. Was it possible to break the bars? India has seen a similar endeavour to escape from the pitiless law of *Karma*, with its menace of eight million rebirths into the world of sense till all consequences of all acts are worked off to the utmost; by *Bhakti*, or union with a god, it is taught, a man may be "carried across the stream of the world." The recrudescence of old superstitions and the invasion of new ones from the East had filled the minds of men and women with heightened fears of daemons. Once the outlook of the day was accepted, the consensus of mankind was in favour of belief in a "world all devils o'er"; and magic and religion gained a new value as means of protection against the terrors of the spirit world. It is not easy to understand, apart from the evidence, the lengths to which terror can carry men and women; but Cicero and Plutarch and even Horace give us material for a judgment, which is supported by testimony painfully similar from the animistic peoples of to-day.

Tempers more strictly religious turned to the gods and to the initiations, which linked men with them, for something higher. The soul they came to think of as a prisoner in the body—an idea borrowed from the Orphics by Plato; and they went to the gods for assurance of immortality. The creature's blind dread of extinction was one factor in this impulse, but surely with the growth of the sense of individuality we may recognise a nobler strain too. All the travail of all the world to produce a creature born to reach strange heights of being—and to be extinguished! No, that must not be; the gods must have other purposes; so to the gods men went for deliverance. Another motive, not wholly disentangled from strange antecedents of taboo, was a consciousness of sin and moral weakness. The forgiveness of sins was not a gospel to appeal at once to a world unconscious of sin. Introspection, self-criticism, was a regular part of the Stoic management of life; but there were men who did not forgive themselves their sins with the resolute phlegm of some of the Stoics. It is clear from our evidence that not all men conceived of sin as spiritual; there were many crude and immature thoughts upon it, and men had much to learn here from Jesus of Nazareth. But the whiter souls, it is fair to hold, were turning to shrine and temple for spiritual help in the mending of life and the cleansing of conscience.

Thus, in one way and another, men were led to think of salvation and to expect it from the gods. The Stoic might tell them to save themselves, might question them as to the use of prayer, might set them a great example

of a self-contained, high-minded life.   But in the breakdown of society, amid the crumbling of ideals and the
failure of the old gods, the human heart was still reaching
out for a religion that made it sure of three things—of
the reality of human personality, of some fundamental
righteousness in the universe as the basis of all transac-
tions, human and eternal, and of God.

Whatever criticism has to be passed upon the developments of religion in the Hellenistic world, and criticism
there must be on many scores—cowardice in the facing of
facts, a defective sense of truth, sentimentalism, shallowness, and so forth—it remains that even this phase of
human history bears witness to great instincts.

XIII

ROMAN RELIGION

In studying Greek and Hebrew religion we have to deal with peoples who did their own thinking. From first to last, whatever foreign elements are added by barbarians "more skilled to discover religious truths (*dogmata*) than to develop them," the Greek world thought on its own lines, even when it fell shortest of its own standards. The Hebrew was influenced by his neighbours, friends or enemies, and found his religious ideas modified in one way and another by the peoples he met, above all by the Greek. But the story of Roman religion is very different. The oldest religious ideas of the Roman people, so far as we can lay hold of them and speak of them, continue to the end—down to the final victory of Christianity, and, it is possible to add, after it. The affair of the Altar of Victory at the end of the fourth century A.D. cannot be called political; to call it religious would need explanation. A group of nobles representing a very ancient past, a past far more ancient than the records of their own families, make it a point of religion to retain an antique ritual, a worship of Victory; but we know from other sources that at the same time what we should call their religious life moved about cults and ideas that were originally not Roman at all. For six hundred years, if we take the date given us by a Roman poet for the arrival of "the Muse with wingèd foot," [1] the same confusion exists in Roman religion; the old persists, maintained by superstition, by sentiment and tra-

1 See p. 290.

dition, but what real or spiritual ideas are attached to it, it is impossible to be certain. Native Roman religion became atrophied, failed to develop, perished in fact; but a Roman would have spoken otherwise, and would have maintained that it continued.

The phenomena is not by now a strange one. In Central Africa the negro becomes Muhammadan and repudiates his old religion, however many ideas he carries over to corrupt the faith of Islam. In the South Seas in island after island the old heathenism has utterly disappeared, as it has among American negroes; what survives is not religion, it is magic now, hardly even superstition. The fact is that primitive religion cannot maintain itself against the thought and faith of races that have progressed. In spite of Miss Harrison's enthusiasm for cosy and delightful gods without personality, mankind has never been able to maintain them against personal gods, except in a vague helpless way, in fear and confusion of mind; they prove unthinkable, and mankind insists on religion being thinkable. Where such old forms of religion meet Monotheism, they perish utterly, either by direct repudiation as in the cases just given, or are transformed as far as possible by philosophy and mysticism, as the religions of the Roman Empire were, or as Hinduism to-day is being slowly driven into non-entity by its apologists. The Roman, in his great career as conqueror, lawyer and ruler, early met the Greek, and, in reality, very quickly saw that in all that bears upon religion and philosophy the Greek was on a higher plane than himself. He moved over to that higher plane, and the problem now was what to make of the traditional religion of his fathers. He maintained many of the old forms. Some family cults lapsed altogether; in others when once the formal procedure was accomplished, no further attention was paid to god or cult. Where god and cult received the compliment of thought, the problem was what meaning or value to attach to them at all.

Jewish reliigon kept festivals which belonged to an earlier stage of civilisation and society, transforming them as best it could. Roman religion had the same problem. Agriculture is not very strictly tied to the calendar, especially when the calendar is inaccurate. But festivals, once given a fixed place in the calendar, keep it. Rome ceased to be pre-eminently an agricultural society; and as the festivals, through the vagaries of calendar-making, were less and less recognisable as agricultural, while the people who kept them were more and more out of touch with their own origins, less and less meaning came to be attachable to the old religious usages. The gods of the country-side hardly fitted into urban life. Even great antiquaries like Varro were often unable to explain what the ceremonies meant. Some of them took on new meanings. Whatever the Saturnalia had been, it came to be a midwinter holiday for townspeople and their slaves.[2]

And what were the old gods? Here is what Aust, translated and endorsed by Dr. Warde Fowler, says of them: "The deities of Rome were deities of the cult only. They had no human form; they had not the human heart with its virtues and vices. They had no intercourse with each other, and no common or permanent residence; they enjoyed no nectar and ambrosia . . . they had no children, no parental relations. They were indeed both male and female, and a male and female deity are often in close relations with each other; but this is not a relation of marriage and rests only on a similarity in the sphere of their operations. . . . These deities never become independent existences; they remain cold, colourless conceptions, *numina* as the Romans called them, that is, supernatural beings whose existence only betrays itself

2 Warde Fowler, *Religious Experience of Roman People*, pp. 102, 103.

in the exercise of certain powers." [3] In the fourth and third centuries B.C. the pontifices drew up lists, known as *indigitamenta,* in which they set out the names of what Augustine calls a "crowd of petty gods." [4] Modern scholars attribute a good deal of their work to their own invention, prompted by a love of formalism which they shared with their people. [5]

Such an achievement went far to neutralise any instinct the Roman people might have had for progress in religion. The people had, like other primitive races, a firm belief in divination; and how tenacious their belief in portents was, is shown in the lists given to us by Livy of menacing absurdities which worried the popular mind during the war with Hannibal. All that was worst in their view of life seems to have been maintained by the influence of Etruscan religion close beside them. Etruscans had from time to time held Rome, and through centuries of Roman history Etruscan priests and soothsayers and quacks generally had a hearing and a position in Rome that we might call extraordinary, if the same attention had not later on in a period of more culture been largely transferred to "Chaldaeans." But in our days we have seen two great Anglo-Saxon peoples invited to believe that their real religion is to be found in Tibet. Mankind has always with it a type of mind for which truth is bound up with the exotic and the unexamined. Roman religion produced no cosmogonic myths, and no poetry worthy of mention gathered about it. [6] It remained more archaic than any which we can trace with much clearness in the Greek world.

It is worth while to pause to ask why Roman religion followed this strange course. It may seem like evading

3 Warde Fowler, *Religious Experience of the Roman People,* p. 157.
4 Augustine, *de Civ. Dei,* iv. 9: *turba minutorum deorum.*
5 Warde Fowler, *Religious Experience of the Roman People,* pp. 158, 286, 287.
6 Gwatkin, *Gifford Lectures,* ii. 129, 131.

the question to speak of the genius of a people, but races
differ, in reality as well as in historical commonplace.
Roman history and Greek show an extraordinary contrast of national types. We might, almost without paradox, say there is no history of Greece; that there never
was a Greece till Rome conquered it, as there was no
India till England gave the unity in one rule, one language, and one culture. One Greek state found it as
hard to co-operate even in the smallest and most obvious
things with another, as one party in either of them did
with rivals it met daily in the little market square. Greek
history swarms with individualities; if a typical name
were sought, it might very well be Alcibiades; there is
more than one phase of truth in Aristotle's unkind quip
that "History is what Alcibiades did." [7] But what would
be a typical name in Roman history? It would probably
be Aemilius or Cornelius, or even Marcus; John Doe
and Richard Roe, or their Latin equivalents, represent
Roman history far better than any individual. Roman
nobles made friends with Varro after he had lost the
battle of Cannae; they did it to save the state. Athens
never really made friends with Alcibiades. Broadly—and
remembering there is always error in a sentence that begins with Broadly—we might say the individual is everything in Greek history and next to nothing in Roman.
Corporate feeling was the most difficult thing to create
or evoke in a Greek city state; in Rome, city, land or
empire, it could be taken for granted. This difference
underlies the greatness and the weakness both of Greek
and Roman. For all that requires co-operation Rome is
transcendent; she can develop law and win loyalty; she
can govern; but she cannot do what the Greeks do. Does
religion in our judgment seem to fall more within the
sphere of Greek or of Roman? Corporate religion the

---

[7] A rather loose and colloquial version of Aristotle, *Poetics* 9, 4, p. 1451 B.

Roman knew and managed and maintained, as he did so many admirable things, largely by his faculty of *not* thinking about them. Where he thought at all, the key-thought was the community; but if he went beyond this, he was lost, as is seen in the rapid collapse of social morality and government and everything else in the second century B.C. Whatever group-thinking and corporate religion may be, if they are anything at all, they do not take a race or an individual very far when the mind and the soul become self-conscious.

Moribus antiquis stat res Romana virisque,[8] said Ennius in a memorable line, and Cicero, looking back, quotes the line with regret; he too feels that the old type of character and the old type of man were indeed the foundation of Rome; but the old character is forgotten and obsolete, lost through "penury of men." In his book *On Laws* Cicero writes that "To maintain the rituals of the family and of the fathers is (since antiquity draws closest to the gods) to uphold religion as it were a gift of the gods."[9] If he was speaking less from the heart here, none the less ancient religion and ancient character seemed in retrospect to belong together. When Ovid congratulated himself on the age of his *floruit,* because "it suits his character so well," what was to be said? Is the Ovidian character the outcome of a development of intelligence past a stage at which the old religion was credible or possible? What had made it possible? Is the inevitable production of Ovid, and his like, sufficient proof that a line of development has been wrong? What was it that changed the type so disastrously?

Rome had welded Italy, broken down Carthage, and made the acquaintance of Greece. Masons and artists

8 Ennius, *Annales,* xv. 5 B; (Müller, *Ennius,* p. 50); rescued from a lost book of Cicero (*de Rep.* v.) by Augustine, *de civ. Dei,* ii. 21.
9 Cicero, *De Legibus,* ii. 11, 27: *Iam ritus familiae patrumque servare id est, quoniam antiquitas proxume accedit ad deos, a dis quasi traditam religionem tueri.*

from the Greek towns in Italy had long frequented the city. But in the second Punic war more forces than the Muse with wingèd foot invaded the fierce and warlike breed of Romulus.[10]   Greek rites were introduced early during the struggle with Hannibal, and before it was over Cybele was brought from Pergamum—new religion in both cases fused with old Roman religion under stress of fear, and a turning-point marked in the religious history of Rome, after which "the old Roman State religion may be said to exist only in the form of dead bones which even Augustus will hardly be able to make live."[11]   The war was hardly over when Philip V of Macedon required attention, and Rome was started upon her career of negotiation and conquest in the Balkan peninsula; and "captured Greece took her fierce conqueror captive and brought the arts into rustic Latium." So Horace wrote long after.[12]

In less figurative and more autobiographic vein Polybius tells how his intimacy with Scipio Aemilianus began.[13]   He was one of the Achaeans detained in Italy, and it was contrived that he should remain in Rome. One day Scipio asked why Polybius directed all his conversation to the elder brother (Fabius) and passed him over; could it be that Polybius counted him far below the true Roman character and ways, because he did not care to plead in the law courts? That had not been in Polybius' mind, and from that day they were as kinsmen. But in Polybius' description of the times, of the outburst of dissolute living and the reasons he gives for it, we see what is coming. "In the first place, it came from the prevalent idea that, owing to the destruction of

10 Cf. the two lines of Porcius Licinus, quoted by Gellius, *Noct. Att.,* xvii. 21, which supply the exact date and the adjectives.
11 Wissowa; cf. Warde Fowler, *Religious Experience of the Roman People,* p. 319.
12 Horace, *Epist.* II., i. 156.
13 Polybius, xxxii. 9, 10.

the Macedonian monarchy, universal dominion was secured to them beyond dispute; and in the second place,
from the immense difference made, both in public and
private wealth and splendour, by the importation of the
riches of Macedonia into Rome." [14]   Mr. Warde Fowler
borrows the phrase of another to say the same; Rome
gained the whole world and lost her own soul.[15]   Side by
side with this Polybius noted "a large number of learned
men from Greece, finding their way into Rome." [16]   Foreign religion, empire, the wealth of a great Macedonian
kingdom, and Greek ideas—everything came at once, to
a people unprepared.

The old religion had not been thought out; the old
gods had represented nothing beyond the vague fears of
primitive man and his conceptions of the powers that
stirred in the life of the fields.   Rome had stood on the
old character; that too had rested on unexamined instinct, or on a sense of the community that was now
giving way.   In the hour of triumph the fear, the hope,
the self-restraint, the ambition that had kept her together had no longer any clear object; all was achieved.
Character and self-discipline may be proof against danger, even against defeat, and yet go to pieces in victory.
Conduct had never been closely related to religion in
Rome, or perhaps in any people in its earlier stages.   By
the second century B.C. the old religion was to the modern thinker fabulous; it was at most an affair of magic
to secure crops or to frustrate portents; but objective
truth, reality, moral teaching, moral sanctions it had
none.   Latin literature really began with Ennius, and
Ennius had translated Euhemerus; and his tragedies,
modelled on those of Euripides, emphasised his view of
the irrelevance of gods to human questions.   Nor had

14 Polybius, xxxii. 11.
15 Warde Fowler, *Religious Experience of the Roman People*, p. 331.
16 Polybius, xxxii. 10.

conduct a base in philosophy, for Rome had no philosophy. There was nothing "to fasten down the images
of Daedalus." [17]   For centuries boys had learnt, and for
another century they continued to learn, the Twelve
Tables by heart—a discipline that explains much of the
greatness and some of the defects of Roman nature.[18]
It made Rome a nation of lawyers, a people who never
thought with ease except in legal terms; it shaped the
most enduring part of the heritage of Rome; but Law
by itself is an insufficient education. No Homer, no
Hesiod even, had "made a theogony" for Rome; what
poetry there had been, seemed rude and primitive, as no
doubt it was; and, when Greek literature was revealed,
Latin song was allowed to die. Without Homer, without Plato, without Israel's discipline of prophecy and
captivity—her gods seemed to have left Rome without
any glimmer of light, to have allowed her to reach a
national maturity and a power, greater and more enduring than any Assyrian or Persian king ever knew, but
without a vestige of that training in thought and feeling
that makes men human. The absence of thought-out
views of morality, of God and the soul, left Rome a prey
to any scattered and unrelated notions that she might
pick up by accident from the conquered peoples. The
wonder is, not that corruption swiftly invaded Roman
character, but that the marvellous structure of Roman
empire held together so long.

It was the Roman view, says Professor Gwatkin,[19]
that truth belonged to philosophy, and had nothing to do
with religion. People in the second century B.C. began
to be clearer about this distinction and to draw inferences
from it. The judgment of Polybius, as he looks at a
stage that is passing and another beginning, is significant:

17 Plato, *Meno*, 98 A; see p. 185.
18 Cicero, *de Legibus*, ii. 23, 59.
19 *Knowledge of God* (Gifford Lectures), ii. 138.

"The most important difference for the better which the Roman commonwealth appears to me to display is in their belief about the gods. For what in other nations is looked upon as a reproach, I mean a scrupulous fear of the gods, seems to me to be the very thing which keeps the Roman commonwealth together. To such an extraordinary degree of tragic effect is this carried among them, so ingrained is it, both in private life and public business, that nothing could exceed it. Many people might think this unaccountable; but in my opinion their object is to use it as a check upon the common people. If it were possible to form a state wholly of philosophers, such a custom would perhaps be unnecessary. But seeing that every multitude is fickle, and full of lawless desires, unreasoning anger and violent passion, the only resource is to keep them in check by mysterious terrors and tragedy of this sort. So, I think, the ancients were not acting without purpose or at random, when they brought in among the vulgar those opinions about the gods and the belief in the punishments in Hades; much rather do I think that men nowadays are acting rashly and foolishly in rejecting them." [20] He goes on to speak of the superior probity of Roman officials to Greek, though elsewhere he speaks of a falling off in honesty.[21]

Polybius, as we have seen, was anticipated in this opinion as to the origin and purpose of religion by Critias.[22] It is not so certain, as these writers suppose, that this association of gods with morality is really primitive at all, or at least that such vague ideas of such an association as early men may have had were very effectual in fact in promoting morality. It would seem to belong to a developed stage of religion when men have re-

---

[20] Polybius, vi. 56. See Juvenal 2, 149-152 on the rejection of belief in Hades.
[21] Polybius, xviii. 35; xxxii. 11.
[22] See p. 174.

flected more comprehensively upon life, and a great deal depends on what they have balanced against the pains of hell. Plato, we saw, rejected as immoral the common belief that punishment for sin could be averted by the trivial sacrifices and initiations that the religious of his day recommended as efficacious. Nor is it quite clear that fear of penalty has actually been an effective deterrent from sin; the fear perhaps more frequently has followed the act, and has been a motive to something else. In any case Polybius and Critias both think hell and gods a useful contrivance to influence the vulgar. Critias was not vulgar, far from it, he was a gentleman, and the "pleasant lie" of the witty inventor did not disturb him; it was useful to him in helping to keep the *demos* in its proper place. Nor, one would imagine, were the honest Romans, who in magistracies and on embassies handled immense sums of money and unlike the Greeks stole none of it, exactly to be classed with the vulgar. Still the passage of Polybius is of value, for it shows us that the influence of the old religion at Rome was declining, that simultaneously common honesty was on the wane, and that shrewd and patriotic observers were beginning to foresee the horrible developments of the century that followed.

Atrophy of the spiritual nature proved indeed a poor preparation for the immense and sudden enrichment of life in material and intellectual resources. Apart from tradition and the example of parents and society, both very strong factors in Rome, there was nothing to stimulate to moral endeavour, there was nothing to prompt to progressive education of conscience. Slavery avenged itself on the slave-owning community by sapping marriage; the plundered wealth induced the temper of conquerors and wastrels; pleasure became the guide and motive in life. The individual became conscious of himself, but in Rome religion neither prompted this new self-consciousness, nor solaced it, nor restrained it. To relate this new individuality to the universe, to find within the universe response either in personality or in law, the Roman had of his own neither religion nor philosophy that availed.

If we have been right in our tentative conclusion that there is in the human mind an instinct that drives for the personality of God and of man and for righteousness as the necessary basis and condition of their relations, we should expect such a position as that in which the Roman found himself to be intolerable. The vacuum must be filled, if not by the thought of Roman pioneers, then by the achieved results of thinkers of other stock. Epicureanism and scepticism were never without their representatives in Roman society; the former was indeed the earliest philosophy to make its appearance at Rome, and in Lucretius it found an expositor of a genius such as it has never known elsewhere.

Yet even Lucretius had in him, as M. Martha pointed out, an anti-Lucretius, and in a famous passage he confesses to an instinct of the heart quite contrary to the reason he works out in his head. "When we look up to the great expanses of heaven, the aether set on high above the glittering stars, and the thought comes into our mind of the sun and the moon and their goings; then indeed in hearts laden with other woes, that doubt too begins to wake and raise its head—Can it be perchance, after all, that we have to do with some vast divine power that wheels those bright stars each in its course?" [23] Our task is to look for the factors of progress, and surely this sudden and unwelcome rebound of mind, which the Epicurean poet feels, this instinct for a power intelligible to the human mind, for a divine mind that can organise

23 Lucretius, v. 1204-1210.

a world of real beauty, is evidence for us of the living power of the ideas which we have traced so far and which we might not have looked to find alive in such a region.

Nor is the transformation of the Roman gods without significance for us. Roman religion had been amazingly colourless; but, when contact was really established with Greece, following a practice they always pursued, the Romans began to identify their dim gods with the bright figures of Greek legend. Venus absorbed, for purposes of art and literature, all the charms and graces of Aphrodite; Proserpina became poetic in the garb of Persephone; Mercury had a Homeric hymn to give him personality and character. How far such identifications really affected the religion (in the strictest sense) of the common people, it is impossible to guess. For the Roman without Greek culture did Venus gain divinity, awe or power from the identification? For the artist, she gained infinitely in colour and movement, but when it came to religion, did he worship her more, or less, or not at all? Did the wall-painters of Pompeii, did Horace, promote religion? Had Praxiteles really helped Greek religion? The case of Jove raises these questions still more urgently, as we shall see. But at least, the Roman deities, by being "Olympianised" gained something of personality, real or conventional.

Cybele was fetched to Rome by the government during the Hannibalic war, to quiet the nerves of the people— a function which our own rulers during our war considered proper to the churches. For four centuries she maintained herself there, and grew to be perhaps the chief power of the Pantheon, till Isis at last gained a place of equal or greater importance. When Lucretius wishes to describe the lavish grandeur and wealth of the pageant of Spring, he draws a parallel picture of the procession of Cybele. Augustine speaks of her priests with whitened faces and mincing gait still anticking about the streets in his day. What they were, Lucian and Apuleius tell us. It is impossible not to feel religion degraded by such a goddess and such priests, yet Cybele herself contributes evidence to our inquiry. What gave her such pre-eminence? How did ritual so foolish, so unbalanced, so magical, so evil, appeal to men and women? The answer is that the native gods of Rome and Italy had no personality, were nothing, and were incapable of becoming anything. Greek art and literature for people of culture might give them a literary and artistic interest, but scarcely a religious value. Cybele was much more personal; she was, or she wielded, universal power, and she recognised personality in her worshippers. Whatever her relations with the State, and I am not sure what these were, her main concern was with the individual; she offered man or woman an endless field of activity, excitement and sentiment, and it was the attraction, and the fatal weakness, of her religion, that its moral claims were not exigent. So far, positively and negatively, she too confirms our deductions as to the progressive factors in religion.

If the government invited Cybele to Rome, other gods did not wait for an invitation. Bacchus came unasked, and the staider elements of Roman society were inexpressibly shocked by what he brought with him.[24] Religious ecstasy did not commend itself to them; there had been Greeks, to whom it was shocking, much more did it shock Romans, especially when it so soon became associated with gross immorality, in fact or in report. Rome for the time believed the worst; and whether Livy's story of the discovery is only "an interesting romance" or more than that, the worst is easily credible of religions

24 Livy, xxxix. 16-18; Warde Fowler, *Religious Experience*, pp. 344 f.; W. E. Heitland, *Roman Republic*, II. s. 655.

where excitement is of the essence of the cult, where
thought and examination rank as something like hostility
or apostasy, where feeling is the supreme criterion, and
where secrecy strengthens the spell of organisation. Of
other cults from the East, it is not needful at this point
to speak further. As with Cybele's religion, so with
these; the empty house invited them; they satisfied for
the unreflective the instinct that seeks personality in God
and the recognition of the individual. With right and
truth they had little concern, and their adherents paid
the inevitable penalty that attends forgetfulness of these
things.

Minds more serious and less amenable to the sway of
emotion turned to Greek philosophy rather than to Asiatic cults. God or truth was to be reached rather by the
most divine thing in man, that part of him which is
noblest and leads to least shame and fewest regrets, his
reason. Sentiment betrayed men into folly and superstition, and all the fear and horrors and shame that superstition involved.[25] Of Greek philosophers, the Stoics
were most akin to the Roman of the best type. Romans
who thought or speculated at all, did so in terms of law,
and they had reached a conception very near to Universal
Law in their *Jus Gentium*. The Stoic Law of Nature
at once appealed to them; it was the Law which they had
been feeling after in the usages common to all the tribes
and communities they knew, the same but higher and
grander and of more universal scope, free from the ac-
cidents of race and place—a law of Righteousness. Like
and different at once, it appealed to the greater Roman
lawyers and led them on to a broadening and humanising
of thought, the reaction of which upon Roman law is
one of the great contributions of Greek philosophy to

25 The writings of Cicero (*de Divinatione,* ii.) and of Plutarch (*de Super-
stitione*) may be recalled here.

human progress.[26]   Greek thought saved the better Romans from the effects of Oriental superstition and gave a new basis for the old Roman character—how sound and true a basis we can read in the series of great Romans of history.   For, however much legend glorified the past, the really great and interesting men of Rome come rather after than before the wars with Pyrrhus and Hannibal. Yet, even so, Stoicism among the Romans is amenable to the same criticism as among Greeks.   Its relentless honesty and its imperfect psychology together led to omissions and negations fatal for religious development.

But as in Greek history our minds turn perhaps too exclusively to the fifth century B.C., in Roman history the first century B.C. occupies us above all others, and the pre-occupation is less open to criticism.   Cicero and Virgil and their contemporaries lived in a time of decline and of rebirth; they were bridge-builders from the old to the new across a gulf of chaos.   However interesting to the anthropologist the earliest ages of Roman religion, if recoverable, may be, for our purposes the peoples of higher culture are more important, and our concern is with the factors that make for progress.   Till Rome fell, and when Rome had fallen, the last years of the Republic and the earliest of the Empire gave its great direction to Roman thought.   Caesar made the framework on which society modelled itself down to 11 November 1918; Cicero far more than Plato—odd as it may seem—shaped the thoughts of Western Europe down to the Renaissance; Virgil and Horace—a strange pair of names, however familiar, with Virgil always in the ascendent—quickened imagination, and, as originality declined, stereotyped the modes of poetry.   Whatever Greece and the Orient contributed to Rome, for thinking people those

---

26 Lecky, *Morals*, i. 294-7, refers to the effect on the Reformation of the renewed study of Roman Law. See also Gwatkin, *Gifford Lectures*, ii. 137.

influences were mediated by these great men. Disregarding a strict chronology, we will turn at once to them and take them in the wrong order.

Whether we deal with the politics, the loves or the religious ideas of Horace, the great thing is not to take them too seriously. He was, he said, an adherent of no school, not even an eclectic—

Nullius addictus jurare in verba magistri—[27]

a Matine bee that covered a good deal of ground and gathered honey from opening flowers of many kinds.[28] Nor must it be forgotten, while he preaches—always on the same theme and with perhaps more iteration than was needed—that he was a man of humour, who would say less than he meant or more, and both without explaining to the reader (like a certain modern tutor) that "of course he was only jocose." Horace then has moods of the most charming piety. Faunus frequents the poet's country farm and protects his goats, while the rocks ring to the poet's rustic pipe; "the gods protect me; to the gods my piety is dear, my Muse is dear." [29] When the accursed tree [30] sent its branch crashing on the poet's head, Faunus was there and turned aside the blow.[31] He sees Bacchus amid distant hills, the nymphs around him; though posterity, bidden to believe, has hesitated.[32] Jupiter thunders from a clear sky, and the poet, a careless and intermittent pietist, as he confesses, retraces his steps and abandons an insane philosophy.[33] If old acquaintance tempt one to linger over these poems, it is not altogether idly. In early life Horace had been frankly

27 *Epp.*, i. 1, 14.
28 *Odes*, iv. 2, 27, *plurimum circa nemus.*
29 *Odes*, i. 17, 11.
30 *Odes*, ii. 17, 27.
31 *Odes*, ii. 17, 28.
32 *Odes*, ii. 19, 1.
33 *Odes*, i. 34, 1.

Epicurean,[34] careless of these matters, and a literary conversion rather implies growth in humour than in grace. Yet it must be clear that Stoic teaching came to interest him. Of course Stoic paradox and eccentricity are as amenable to playful handling as the gods and nymphs of the *Odes,* though less charming. But Horace clearly gave more of his mind to Stoic books. Like Robert Burns, where he is most solemn and impressive, he is least serious. He may picture Augustus recumbent and sipping nectar with purple lips between Pollux and Hercules; [35] he may speculate as to what incarnation Augustus really is,[36] and pray for delay in his return to heaven; but he knew Augustus, and he did not push himself on the Emperor's acquaintance. In all, *Odes* and *Epistles* give us the religion of a charming man of letters in comfortable circumstances, a bachelor in every implication of his being, possessed of culture and humour, and owner of a good library. He has never been *vates Gentilium*; even if, a priest of the Muses, he chanted lordly lays, unheard before, to virgins and to boys, the idea of being a prophet to lighten the Gentiles would have amused him.[37]

Cicero had far more influence. A lost philosophical book of his was the first thing to stir the mind of Augustine. He gave Europe its philosophical terminology; he wrote in his *Dream of Scipio* the best religious apologue of Latin literature; [38] he discussed gods and divination and the purpose of life in books that his countrymen treasured. Yet it is hard to find in him a religious spirit. However religious and spiritual he might have been at heart, it would not have been to Atticus perhaps that he could most comfortably have revealed this side of his

34 Cf. *Satires,* i. 5, 101.
35 *Odes,* iii. 3, 11.
36 *Odes,* i. 2, 41 f.
37 *Odes,* iii. 1. 2,
38 See p. 345.

nature.   To his wife's religion he refers in a notable
letter at the moment of his exile; "The gods whom you
have always sedulously worshipped, have not helped us,
nor men whom I have always cultivated." Yet when
Tullia his daughter died, he craved to think her immortal, to deify her and preserve her memory in a shrine.
But shrine-memorials suggest troubled affection more
than clear thinking. What *did* he think? It is noted
that his books on religion belong to the last two years
of his life, when the world crumbled under his feet and
his Tullia was gone.   But the Cicero, who lived in the
stream of the world, who was alert and alive to politics,
to literature, to all the gleam and interest of life, drew
his philosophy and his religious ideas from books.   He
had not lived in religious thought, and he is critical of
it.   Such a mind will inevitably weigh and criticise idea
or proposition that comes from another, and at last all
that itself produces.   "Perhaps" is its last word in religion—"perhaps" followed by a silence and a sigh.   We
must not miss the self-criticism of that last word and of
the sigh; contemporaries caught them and knew that they
must turn elsewhere for certainty.   Teacher as the Cicero
of the speeches and of the treatises was, charming as his
correspondence is still, he too was no prophet of the
Gentiles.

That name was given to Virgil by a later and a Christian generation.   Who gave it, I do not know, perhaps
it is not known; [39] but the Christian world and Dante
accepted it; and common Christian feeling, reinforced
by genius of such greatness, is no bad guide.   The last
fact and the first about Horace and Cicero for students

[39] Tyrrell, *Latin Poetry*, p. 156. The rubric of Rouen includes a ceremony
for Christmas Day, when the priest says:—
> Maro, Maro, Vates Gentilium
> Da Christo testimonium,
and Virgil replies.

of religion is that they were *not* religious spirits; but
Virgil was, pre-eminently. His transcendence as an artist may hide his religious quality from some readers, but
he is not Sophocles. In his youth he was Epicurean. The
graceful *Scazon* verses, that announce his purpose to
study with Siro and free his life from all care, are genuine enough and quite clear in import. By and by he
is reconciling Silenus with Epicurus; he sets the god
singing in Lucretian tones a cosmogony that drifts toward Pythagoreanism. Reconciliation is his work; perhaps if we take it as a true outcome of interpretation, it
is the work of every poet. But Virgil attempts it not
quite as the Stoics did. The world let Posidonius go; at
the best he effected a compromise that worked for a while
and then was more and more patently wrong.[40] Virgil's
compromise was hopeless from the first. Olympus was
not and could not conceivably be as he drew it; "Jupiter's
chance," says Mr. Warde Fowler in a brilliant sentence,
"was destroyed by the *Aeneid*." [41] Virgil's Jupiter had
traits of the Zeus whose loves are portrayed in the wall-
paintings of Pompeii, traits too of the Stoic Zeus, traits
of the Homeric and of Fate; and at the end of the *Aeneid*
Jupiter has to throw the thing up, he cannot settle Aeneas'
affairs, nor his own, he does not know who he is or where
he is—*fata viam invenient*. The Virgilian compromise
will not serve; Virgil had not been an Epicurean for
nothing. But reconciliation there must be, and he saw it
—or, rather, felt it. His heart clearly leaned to the old
impossible Italian gods, far more native to him than any
Homeric Zeus, however Stoical, with time and popular
teaching, Zeus had become. Virgil felt the need of the
heart for God; his solitary unhappy Aeneas, like Marcus
Aurelius, drags along the path of duty, brave and in-

40 For Posidonius, see p. 343.
41 Warde Fowler, *Roman Ideas of Deity*, p. 141.

domitable, but his goddess-mother never really understands her son. Virgil understood him.

Goethe once said that man's business is not to solve the problem of the universe but to understand it. This latter task Virgil achieved, and, for those who can feel, the great question is set out in his poetry. The human heart is there, conscious of its own needs, and those needs are, as we have seen already, God and righteousness and the assurance of one's own personality. The philosophers were discarding two of them, the pietists in the Oriental cults the other. Virgil keeps the problem open. Whatever the theme or the object of his *Aeneid*, the poet's heart is unveiled in it—the supreme thing in poetry, and it answered to the heart of man. When the Roman world accepted Christianity, it threw over Cybele and Isis and Mithras, as it had thrown over the Stoics long before, but it kept Virgil.

Rome gave up its old religion, and borrowed from Greek and Oriental, and all its borrowings are significant. But as Virgil borrowed from Homer, and what he borrowed ceased to be Homeric and became Virgilian, so the Roman gave something to what he took. To the world's stock of religious ideas he added those of order and law and the sense of the practical.[42] These were not new, but he gave them another significance than they had for Greek and Oriental. His religion had been associated with morality, by instinct rather than by reflection. His emphasis on law and on conduct gave men new views which developed into the concept of sin—an idea closely germane to that tendency to Righteousness which we have so often remarked, a legitimate pendant to it, which has been fruitful in human thinking. He recreated the Law of Nature and made it a more effectual

---

[42] To discuss this at all adequately would take us too far into the history of the Christian Church.

thing. He emphasised the community in religion—a new interpretation of the principle of righteousness. Some of his contributions to the world's stock of religious ideas have been less happy. Roman Stoicism influenced Christian views of God and of society too much. Law and order have again and again been over-emphasised by minds of the Roman cast, and the individual has been lost in the over-orderly community.[43] Thus by what he had not and by what he had, the Roman contributed to progress in religion, as a strong and virile race always will.

43 I believe this to be the most potent reason for the fall of the Roman Empire.

XIV

JUDAISM AFTER ANTIOCHUS

ANTIOCHUS EPIPHANES, as Tacitus [1] put it, was prevented by a Parthian war from civilising a very horrible race. He failed to Hellenise the Jews in his sense of the word; Judaism survived, and with a new consciousness that Hellenism and Judaism were two things. The "peaceful penetration" of Israel's religion by Greek influences was abruptly ended; the two things were alien and represented different histories, different outlooks, principles that definitely clashed and that could not be mistaken, that could not slide into one another. The third stage of international relations was reached. The interaction which began unconsciously or semi-consciously was brought to a new stage by the Seleucid king's violence; the violence that failed. Henceforward such relations as there are between the peoples and the ideals are conscious. Contact or conflict, whichever it be, men have their eyes open and know what they are doing.

For contact and for conflict there were more and more opportunities. The Jew had not to leave the promised land to find Greek cities with all their challenge—the naked athletes, the theatre, the idol's temple, the deified king, the philosopher, the Greek hat, all the accursed things that had been the prelude to the attack of Epiphanes. "Jason" says the writer of *Second Maccabees* (iv. 11), "introduced new customs forbidden by the law; he deliberately established a gymnasium under the citadel itself and made the noblest of the young men wear the

1 Tacitus, *Hist.* v. 8.

petasos. And to such a height did the passion for Greek
fashions rise . . . that the 'priests were no longer interested in the services of the altar, but despising the
sanctuary and neglecting the sacrifices, they hurried to
take part in the unlawful displays held in the palaestra
after the quoit-throwing had been announced." Jerusalem was indeed purified; but the tone of the writer, and
the things that he selects as specially horrible, show how
a patriotic Jew might feel towards customs and practices
that would not strike everybody as particularly depraved.
The Hindu to-day has a somewhat similar feeling for
many things that Europeans do without any consciousness that they are unclean or offensive; and to this day
the hat is a symbol—there are some sixty varieties in
Bombay, all with significance, the Parsi horse-shoe hat
being that which is most easily recognised by a newcomer.

But the Jew did not confine himself to the land God
gave to his fathers; he was settled as a permanency in
Babylon, as we have seen, and in Egypt. A quarter of
a century after Antiochus, a Roman magistrate, achieved
glory and a name by ordering in 139 B.C. the expulsion
from Rome of all Jews and other Orientals with them.[2]
Of course they returned, and, as the New Testament
and Tacitus [3] tell us, they were expelled again, to return
again. The Jew was making the world his own, but
travelling as a self-conscious foreigner. Herodotus,
Greek as he was, essentially Greek, travelled and observed with much less detachment. But, however much
one may make detachment a practice or a principle, the
milieu always tells. One's sympathies with persecuted
co-religionists may be immense, but one does not necessarily wish them in the railway carriage; they may be
more alien than their reprobate persecutor. The *milieu*

2 Valerius Maximus, i. 3. 3; the man was Hispalus.
3 Tacitus, *Annals*, ii. 85, *vile damnum.*

tells; the chance remark, the attitude, the written page of the Greek, his quick, bright ways, his shrewd tongue, penetrate the defences. The Jew remains a loyal Hebrew, he resents the criticism, but he cannot ignore it; to meet it he must do a lot of rethinking; is that contact or conflict, or both? But the contact was far more deliberate.

With all that Greeks now and then talked about the religions and the philosophies of barbarians, they seem to have given little attention to their languages and literatures. Berossos, Manetho, and Megasthenes are names that stand out;[4] but when one recalls that Plutarch[5] only once refers to a poetic literature, so near and so obvious as the Latin, and that only to confirm some historical fact from a passage of Horace, it is not surprising that Greek knowledge of things Egyptian or Assyrian was very slight, of things Indian next to negligible. But the Jew is not amenable to this reproach. To mingle in the world at all, he had to know Greek, and the evidences of his interest in Greek literature are abundant. Long before Josephus Jews were writing their history in Greek; they composed tragedies on Greek models about the Exodus from Egypt[6] and so forth, they compiled sibylline oracles in Greek hexameters, and, more significant than all, they read deeply in Greek philosophy. The "Dispersion," of course, had most points of contact; Alexandrian Judaism would necessarily meet Hellenism and be influenced by it more readily than Palestinian; and Galilee would be more susceptible to foreign ways than Jerusalem. In the period now before us we find in Jewish thinking a heightened Nationalism, clearly resulting from the persecution of Epiphanes and perhaps other similar

---

4 See p. 78.
5 Trench, *Plutarch*, p. 9; Plutarch, *Lucullus*, 39.
6 Considerable extracts from Ezekiel, the tragic poet, are given by Eusebius, *Praep. Evang.*, ix. 28, 29, pp. 436-447.

movements, but also a developed Internationalism, cosmopolitan, but Jewish still. A short notice of two characteristic books may serve as well as generalisation.

The book of *Tobit* may be "certainly pre-Maccabean" [7] or it may have been written about 150 B.C. It was certainly not a contemporary story of the man whose name it bears, even if he be historical. It shows easy habits of travel, a wide acquaintance with foreign lands and a free adoption of legends and folk-lore from sources outside Judaism. The writer has liberal sympathies, and lacks that hatred of the heathen which animates much of later Jewish literature. The contact with the strange story of Ahikar, which, we recently learned, existed in Aramaic in the fifth century B.C., is a point of interest; and scholars note the absence of references to later Jewish ideas, such as the personified Wisdom of God, the Messiah, and the belief in resurrection or immortality. Even the dog in the story becomes an indication of an attitude not very Jewish. Whose dog was it? critics have asked, the author's or a interpolator's? And yet this book of many affinities is the story of a good Jewish family. It has always been popular; it was translated to and fro in the languages of antiquity; it has given subjects to art. "Is it history?" wrote Luther. "Then it is holy history. Is it fiction? Then is it a truly beautiful, wholesome, and profitable fiction, the performance of a gifted poet." In any case it gives us a picture of Israel among the nations, not yet antagonised.

The book of *Wisdom* is variously dated between 130 and 100 B.C., after 50 B.C. and under the Roman Empire. The writer reveals himself to us in every page as a reader of Jewish and Gentile literature, a stylist, a thinker. If he is over rhetorical at times, he learnt that from the

---

7 D. C. Simpson in *Apocr. and Pseudepigr.*, i. 183; Sir G. Adam Smith, *Jerusalem*, ii. p. 395.

Greek schools of his day, but the judgment is a sound one that calls his book the highwater mark of Jewish thought between the Old and New Testaments. The author's mind, of course, runs upon morals, like the author or authors of those Jewish writings with which his book is allied. But he thinks of God in a central way, and he has conceptions of God which are not of the Hebrew type. That God is the creator of the world and of all things in it, the Hebrew Psalmists tell us in language of beauty which is a sign of their delight in Nature.[8] This writer has the same thought, but he gives a different turn to it. Men, he says, by not giving heed to the works miss the Artificer; they have deified fire, wind, the swift air, the circling stars; but "if, through delight in their beauty, they took them to be gods, let them know how much better than these is their Sovereign Lord; for the first author of beauty created them" (xiii. 1-4, ὁ τοῦ κάλλους γενεσιάρχης). The Hebrew God created the world out of nothing; this man's Creator made it "of formless matter" (xi. 17, ἐξ ἀμόρφου ὕλης). To find in this expression evidence for his belief in the eternity of matter, is perhaps to make him too severe a Platonist; but he platonises clearly. This reference to matter is followed by a variant on "God always geometrising"—"By measure and number and weight thou didst order all things" (xi. 20). He reasserts "eternal Providence" again and again (xvii. 2):—"Thy providence, O Father, steers the ship on the sea" (xiv. 3); God "thinks ahead, is provident, for all" (vi. 8); "The spirit of the Lord fills the world" (i. 7); God can be known and understood by the righteous and thoughtful. But the most striking expression of God's nature and character is this:—"Thou lovest all things that are, and abhorrest none of the things which thou didst make; for never

8 Cf. especially Psalm civ.

wouldst thou have formed anything if thou didst hate
it. And how would anything have endured, except thou
hadst willed it? Or that which was not called by thee,
how would it have been preserved? But thou sparest
all things because they are thine, O Sovereign Lord,
thou Lover of souls" (xi. 23-26). Is it Plato or a
Hebrew inspiration here? For we have reached a thinker
whose conception of God is a very signal one. He has
a strong Hebrew feeling for the personality of God, he
does not decline like a Greek upon abstracts, though he
can use them; and he emphasises the most personal thing
in personality—love, and makes it the motive of the creation and preservation of that universe to which he gives
its great Greek name of *cosmos*. In virtue of the terms
and spirit of its creation, he can say of it: "The universe
is a champion of the righteous" (xvi. 17). The Hebrew
Psalmist had said "the angel of the Lord"; but this in
its way is a greater saying. The Stoic could have said
this of the universe—did, in fact, say it in one phrase
and another—and fell into pantheism, said it because he
was a pantheist; but the writer of *Wisdom,* as we have
seen, escapes pantheism altogether.

As St. Paul did later on, the writer of *Wisdom* traces
to idolatry a great deal of the evil of the world—"the
devising of idols was the beginning of fornication, and
the invention of them the corruption of life" (xiv. 12).
The origin of idolatry he explains in a Greek way, following Euhemerus, as Christian writers did after him.
The image of the dead child or of the distant king became a god (xiv. 15-17) and Art helped the delusion
(xiv. 19). The consequences, and here he is strictly
historical, were "slaughtering of children in solemn rites,
celebrating secret mysteries, holding frantic revels of
strange ordinances," followed by every sort of moral
disorder; and "that multitude of evils they call peace"

(xiv. 22). Idolatry God judges, and its consequences, but not vindictively. Even to the Canaanites He gave opportunity for repentance (xii. 10), but they would not take it; they were (perhaps he forgets another belief of his here, in a moment of eloquence) "a seed accursed from the beginning" (xiv. 11); and they were destroyed "that the land which in thy sight is most precious of all lands might receive a worthy colony of God's servants" (xiv. 7). Thus Israel's possession of the land with the extermination of its older inhabitants is justified; for he is a Jew, however much Greek thought influences him. But he hints at Nemesis, which is Greek, while he exults as a Jew over the Egyptians in their plagues—"The doom they deserved was dragging them into this end" (xix. 4). Similarly, when he deals with conduct and righteousness, he blends the Jewish and the Greek; he has the four cardinal virtues which the Stoics took from Plato; but he makes the centre of life, as a good Hebrew would, to seek God, to trust God, to be faithful to Him and to love Him (iii. 9)—and then must needs give it a Greek turn again, for it is "to *think* of the Lord with a good mind" (i. 1), since "crooked thoughts separate from God" (i. 3), and "the holy spirit of discipline will flee deceit" (i. 5).

It is, as Dr. Drummond wrote, hazardous to fix on him any defined eschatology; it more and more becomes clear that no eschatology will stand definition. *Aut videt aut vidisse putat* is the most that can be said of any eschatologist; and of another school of Jews Dr. Schechter assures us that "whatever the faults of the rabbis were, consistency was not one of them." Our writer, however, strikes a great keynote (however he is to adjust the rest of his music to it) in saying at the start: "God made not death, neither delighteth He when the living perish: for He created all things that they might have being . . . nor hath Hades royal dominion on earth" (i. 13-14). "God created man for incorruption, and made him an image of His own proper being; but by envy of the devil death entered into the world, and they that belong to his realm experience it. But the souls of the righteous are in the hand of God. . . . Their hope is full of immortality" (ii. 23; iii. 4). He seems to imply the pre-existence of souls, Greek again here. "I was a child good by nature and a good soul fell to my lot; nay, rather, being good I came into a body undefiled" (viii. 19, 20); and in distant reminiscence of Plato he adds: "A corruptible body weigheth down the soul" (ix. 15). But of a bodily resurrection he says nothing. Still, when we link his doctrine of God's love for all He has made, and the thought that the souls of the righteous are in His hand, we see that this brilliant writer is moving somewhat ahead of his ancient people and is teaching what accentuates and emphasises personality.

A man's doctrine of God gives us his centre; this man's treatment of the Wisdom of God is significant, and it heralds further developments. The Stoics taught a divine interpenetration of all phenomena, a world-soul; it was the heart of their pantheism. This writer felt the attraction of their language, and again and again he emphasises how the Spirit of the Lord fills the universe (i. 6, 7). Upon this Spirit, sometimes called Wisdom and sometimes the Spirit of Wisdom, he heaps one beautiful phrase after another (vii. 24 ff.) :—

There is in her a spirit of understanding, holy,
Alone in kind, manifold, subtil, freely moving,
Clear in utterance, unpolluted, distinct, that cannot be
    harmed,
Loving what is good, keen, unhindered,
Beneficent, loving toward man,

Steadfast, sure, free from care,
All powerful, all surveying,
And penetrating through all spirits that are quick of under-
     standing, pure, subtil;
For Wisdom is more mobile than any motion;
Yea, she pervadeth and penetrateth all things by reason of
     her pureness.
For she is a breath of the power of God,
And a clear effluence of the glory of the Almighty;
Therefore can nothing defiled find entrance into her.
For she is an effulgence from everlasting light,
And an unspotted mirror of the working of God,
And an image of His goodness.
And she, though but one, hath power to do all things,
And remaining in herself reneweth all things;
And from generation to generation passing into holy souls
She maketh them friends of God and prophets. . . .
Being compared with light she is found to be before it. . . .
She reacheth from one end of the world to the other with
     full strength,
And ordereth all things well.

No one, I suppose, could fail to miss the influence of
Greek thought in this fine passage. Word and idea
betray it; and, as with Greek thought generally, word
and idea are fruitful and inspire the writers and thinkers
who come after. But no one, on the other hand, could
mistake the passage for one of purely Greek origin; the
writer is a Hebrew, nursed in Hebrew religion and full
of the Hebrew's passion for God. Greek and Hebrew
at once, he speaks of the future of the world's thinking;
he typifies Alexander's Marriage of Europe and Asia;
and when the universal religion came, its adherents found
in him phrase and conception ready to express their own
central ideas of God.

The Jewish world was not all of one texture—far
from it. A race so alive must show great divisions of
mind, much party warfare. Four main groups are outstanding—all interesting, at once in their initial ideas

and in the development to which the reaction of these ideas and of the circumstances and influences of the day brought them. There are the priestly party, the Pharisees, the Apocalyptic writers and the great mass of the "Dispersion," influenced variously by all three of them, and conscious of problems of its own, suggested by its Hellenistic environment.

After the exile Jerusalem, as we saw, became the great centre of worship. Here stood the restored Temple; here alone might sacrifice be performed; here the priesthood was massed. Here, if anywhere, orthodox Judaism should have been found. But living faiths are never very orthodox, or orthodoxy must change its meaning. The Mosaic Law, as written, re-written, revised and combined, triumphed, and for Jerusalem the last word in religion was said. Consequently at Jerusalem the religion loses vitality. Nationalism is not always a pure and unmixed exaltation of the human spirit; and it did not cover the sins of the Jerusalem party. They held by the old ways, and made profit out of them. The new, the progressive, the spiritual conception of religion did not appeal to them. They compromised with Hellenism on its secular side, and missed the inspiration which Greek thought gave to the more spiritually-minded. We need not linger with them; progress in religion is not here.

The decline of the Maccabaean patriot clan into tyranny and the secularism of Jerusalem provoked what we may call a Puritan reaction. The *Hasidim* first (the beloved, the pious, or the saints) and the Pharisees later (the separated) stood for a higher type of religion. They maintained the same Law of God, but they approached it from a different angle. They were more zealous for God, less careful of their own prerogative. The Law was not to be for them a *Magna Charta* of

privilege as for the priestly party; it was the revelation
of God in the form of a call to righteousness and piety.
We have noticed more than once the invincible tendency
in religion, apart from the cults, to emphasise righteousness; and this is the explanation of the Pharisee movement, and it carries with it the two other great tendencies
which we have remarked.   For the Pharisees righteousness had its centre and its motive in a personal God who
required it of the human individual and who thereby
recognised and emphasised human personality.   They
are the successors in part of the prophets, inheritors of
everything the prophets had, their first-hand inspiration
excepted and their authentic vision of God.   It was in
the Synagogue rather than in the Temple that Pharisaism
had its birthplace and its home; where the Prophets as
well as the Law were read, where the psalms were sung,
where religion was not obscured by sacrifice and ritual.
They represented in measure the party of suffering, the
thinkers for whom the world offers problems that must
be solved, men who live for something not visible.
Where religion lives, where thought is still trusted, law
is less dangerous than elsewhere, and for long it is clear
that Pharisaism helped to develop the moral sense of
the Jewish race, to quicken their thinking.   How far the
Law and the Prophets had thought pre-eminently of
Israel as a people, and how far they had recognised the
individual and his life, is a difficult problem.   One great
part of the work of the Pharisees was to individualise
the interpretation of both, so to make relevant to the
individual what the Prophets had taught of God in relation to the people, as to develop Judaism into one of
the most supremely individualist of the world's religions,
a religion where God and man come close together as
personalities, intelligible to each other.   The Pharisees

were, it has been said, "simply Jews in the superlative" [9] as the Wahabis are the true Moslems.

The weak spot of Pharisaism was the closed canon, the holy book from the past, the document susceptible of interpretation but not of addition. The holy book naturally fell into the hands of commentators, and originality is not the badge of that tribe. It is the way of the commentator to make claims for the work of genius, that genius would not make. The Law was less, far less, the work of genius than were the prophetic writings; and it was on the Law that the Scribe chiefly occupied himself. Rabbi and Scribe vied in paradox to exalt the Law, to magnify its claim upon the good Jew, till common sense reacted. For paradox is no substitute for genius, and it rarely means insight of the type which greatly helps understanding forward. The reaction of common sense against paradox is as little apt to quicken the human spirit as paradox or accumulative learning. What genius Judaism still had for origination in religion found vent elsewhere, and was rejected at last—not unintelligibly; and Judaism settled down to common-sense orthodoxy, to nationalism, to the completed book and the closed gates.

Mr. Claude G. Montefiore, in his very interesting book entitled *Judaism and St. Paul,* sketches what, from available Jewish evidence of a rather later date than the Christian era, he conceives to have been the Judaism of Palestine in the days of Paul. If he should prove not to have been warranted in this thesis, his picture will stand as faithful to a later stage; and whatever the date, it serves our purpose as representing the outcome of this development of Hebrew religion. There are curious traits in the picture; but Mr. Montefiore's very evident

9 Quoted by W. Fairweather, *Background,* p. 138.

sympathy with the type of mind which he portrays is a
guarantee that it is free from conscious parody. God
was the creator and ruler of the world, and at the same
time the Father of Israel and of every Israelite (p. 25);
great and awful, but merciful and loving (p. 26). He
did not delegate His relations with Israel to any angel
or subordinate; no human priest obtruded on this simple
and immediate relation of God and every Israelite (p.
26). Israel's belief in angels was highly undogmatic
(p. 27) and may be disregarded. The Law was given
to Israel "as a means by which happiness and goodness
may be secured"—a means by which God also manifests
His own Kingship and glory (p. 28). "It was the grace
of God which was made visible in the Law" (p. 31).
"To the Rabbinic Jew, who conformed to average and
type, the observance of the Law was in no wise a burden.
How should it be so? . . . He has told you to fulfil
certain moral and ceremonial laws to the best of your
ability (p. 31) . . . these laws are His laws, and in the
observance of them you will find satisfaction and joy,
the highest life on earth and the most blissful life here-
after. . . . The laws were not a burden but a delight"
(p. 32). "They were indeed taught to believe that the
average and decent-living Israelite would inherit the
world to come, would be 'saved,' to use other and more
familiar phraseology. But they were not taught to believe that this result would follow as the guerdon of
their own merits; it would rather befall them as the effect
of God's love and God's grace" (pp. 35-6). "God's love
for Israel, His love of the repentant sinner, His invet-
erate tendency to forgiveness, together with the merits
of the patriarchs, would amply make up for their own
individual deficiencies. Their religion was, therefore,
happy and hopeful" (p. 36). "The Rabbinic Jew did
not worry himself much about the theory that the whole

Law (with all its enactments) has to be obeyed. He took a practical view of the situation. . . . There is no commandment which he cannot fulfil more or less" (pp. 41-2). "But is not God angry at man's violation of the Law? Yes, He is very angry. . . . Let a man repent but a very little and God will forgive very much. . . . The Day of Atonement is the day on which both man and God are, so to speak, engaged in doing nothing else than repentance and forgiveness" (pp. 42, 43). "Salvation was the privilege of every Israelite who, believing in God and in His Law, tried to do his best, and was sorry for his failures and his lapses" (p. 77).

Mr. Montefiore rather enjoys explaining that these Rabbinic Jews were "not theorists and had little philosophy" (p. 79). It was "a joyous, simple religion: yet also an intellectual and rational religion in its own special way . . . but not a religion which passed constantly and rapidly into mysticism, a religion more usually (to use the now familiar words of William James) of the 'healthy-minded' and of the 'once-born' . . . without sacraments and without mysteries. It knew of no rapid change from bad to good by any secret initiation or any second and higher birth" (pp. 48-50). The Jew gave up the search for proselytes; "but what I am most keen to emphasise is that this indifference, dislike, contempt, particularism—this ready and not unwilling consignment of the non-believer and the non-Jew to perdition and gloom—was quite consistent with the most passionate religious faith and with the most exquisite and delicate charity" (p. 56). This remarkable sentence is a sort of Rosetta stone that gives us a clue to Mr. Montefiore's language. The Judaism of the Dispersion he believes to have been inferior to the Rabbinic type, "more anxious and pessimistic, more sombre and perplexed" (p. 114). "Hellenistic Judaism . . . had to

look outwards rather than inwards, and began to invent
theories and justifications of its religion instead of accepting it as a delightful matter of course. . . . Some
of them may have begun to worry about their salvation
and the 'state of their soul' " (pp. 96-7) ; they were "dis-
posed to take a gloomy view of the universal domination
of sin" (p. 98).   They would not take their religion for
granted; and there, Mr. Montefiore holds, lay their error.
"Directly you have to justify a thing, it becomes a little
external; you hold it at arm's length and examine it
curiously.   If you live with it, and grow with it, and
accept it as a matter of course, you love it without asking
why, and it becomes a part of your own very self.   You
do not compare it with anything else.   It is just your
own, a sheer privilege and delight.   Perhaps the
Hellenistic Jew was too much surrounded by other people
to feel like that about the Law" (p. 99).   And the God
of the Rabbinic Jew was very like him—"very personal
and childlike; He did not care for system and theories;
but at all events He was always there when wanted, and
He managed His own affairs Himself.   He loved and
was loved. The grandiose conceptions of the Apocalyptic
seers, and the influence of Greek philosophy made Him
more august and majestic, but less gentle and kindly"
(p. 95).   Paul's universalism "probably needed the
stimulus of external and non-Jewish influences" (p 82).
"The author of the 4th book of Ezra gives up the whole
question of the heathen as an impossibly hopeless puzzle.
'Touching man in general, Thou knowest best, but touching Thy people I will speak!' " (p. 110).

It is a curious story. Rabbinic Judaism was heir to
the Law and the Prophets; it inherited other gains of
seer and thinker; but it rested on the fact achieved, it
refused Hellenism—provoked, no doubt, by persecutions
and by war, and it refused progress. On Mr. Monte-

fiore's own showing, it escaped the harassment of
thought, it would not wrestle with problems; it was con-
tented with an easy-natured parochial God, and it dismissed the great world to damnation, while Israel and
his God moved about on the surfaces of things, content
to compromise on an easy-going morality.

But, dismissing criticism, we cannot help noting that
Rabbinic Judaism did not historically do much to influence the world's thinking. Like modern Parsi-ism, it
was the religion of a small community, racially and re-
ligiously closed. Israel's religious ideas as expressed by
Prophet and Psalmist have had an incalculably great
effect; they still exert an influence beyond computing.
The successors of Prophet and Psalmist include indeed
the Scribes and those who gave its grandeur to synagogue religion, and made, as we have seen, a great contribution to mankind; but more interesting to scholars
for the moment are the writers of Apocalyptic books.
It is more than possible that the significance of Apocalyptic is being exaggerated; Professor A. B. Bruce indeed
held that "the great heart of humanity has only one duty
to perform towards it, and that is to consign it to ob-
livion." [10] Whatever attention we pay to it, we have to
remember that it was the Jews of the Restoration and
their successors in the synagogues who established the
first real Monotheism, who claimed all for spiritual religion, who set worship free from the external and the
obsolete, and concentrated the mind of the worshipper
on God and the human soul and righteousness. All that
the Apocalyptist did was to develop this—not in the
lettered and scholarly way of the Scribe, but more as a
poet would—a poet of broken wing.

Once again, we have to look at the environment—at
the unhappy land of Palestine, the thoroughfare of rival

10 A. B. Bruce, *Apologetics*, p. 293.

kings of Egypt and Syria as of old, at the growing chaos and meaninglessness of the world in the last two centuries before Christ, at the helpless posture of true religion between Seleucids, Herods, and Romans without and false friends within, liberators turned tyrants, and priests proved secular-hearted. Once again there was much to endure, much to explain; and, as in such times, questions were asked; religion needed "theories and justifications" if it was to go on; Antiochus was too serious a problem to leave religion "a delightful matter of course"; the thinker had once more to justify the ways of God to men, and it was no easy task.

The questions were the old ones that have haunted Greek and Hindu thinkers, that perplex us still. Why does God forsake His people and cease to be gracious? Is the fault in God? Is His arm shortened? Has He grown obsolete and inefficient among the mailed fists and the cultured dynasties of a later day? Is the religion, in plain fact, an absurdity, a falsity? Or is the fault elsewhere? is it in Israel? Has Israel as a nation failed in the loyalty to Jehovah that would merit or control His support? Was the nation itself a hopeless dream; and, if so, what was left for the individual? What explained his private pain, the failure of his hopes, the vanity of his life, his intolerable solitude in a world where Prophet and Psalmist had promised the presence of God? Death swept heedlessly over the land; good and evil fell unreckoned; and Gentiles were talking more and more of Chance ruling all; were they right? All this meant, as we have seen before, a fresh emphasis on individual personality; and every such fresh emphasis is apt to mean real progress in Religion.

The first and most obvious feature about all this Apocalyptic literature is that none of it was written by

the men whose names it bears.[11]   The authors were not
Enoch and Ezra, to name those to whom more books
were attributed than to any others.   The canon of the
Old Testament was closed, and men mistrusted fresh
revelations; neither they nor their contemporaries, they
felt, were the sort of mouth-pieces that God would use.
Consequently, when a man had a message, he gave it to
the world, not like the old Prophets, as what the Lord
had spoken to him, but as a revelation made long since
in the days of miracle and prophecy to one of those
great figures of Jewish history like Moses or Ezra, or of
world-history like Enoch, to whom it was more credible
that God would show His mind.   The books had been
mislaid, or (better) had been preserved as mysterious
and secret literature, and now came to light with prophetic teaching wonderfully opposite to the present posture of affairs.   As literature Apocalyptic is trivial; its
permanent contribution to thought is slight—facts proved
by the wholesale neglect which overtook its products.
Judaism by and by would have none of it; indeed Professor F. C. Burkitt goes so far as to say that Judaism
succeeded in surviving because the Jews dropped the conviction that had produced the Apocalypses.[12]   No one
who had ever enjoyed a Greek book could find any
pleasure (let us say) in *Enoch* as literature.   *Enoch* is
not a book; it is a medley of bits of books; or, if it is
not, it has lost its one apology.   It is iterative, inconsecu-
tive, absurd, tasteless, and trivial, but it has its interest
as a magazine of what mankind has been content to
forget, a curiosity shop of folklore, fancy, history interpreted, forecast and allegory.[13]   But *Enoch,* as some of

11 Cf. the curious episode of the discovery of the Books of Numa, Livy, xl.
29; Warde Fowler, *R.E.R.P.*, p. 349.
12 Burkitt, *Schweich Lectures*, 1913, p. 15.
13 "A logical Apocalypse," as Prof. Burkitt says, "would most likely be a
dull Apocalypse" (*Schweich Lectures*, 1913, p. 49).   They are dull enough
without logic.

the minor writers of the *New Testament* remind us, offered more than the shadow of a borrowed name; it purported to reveal God's purposes, and something in its story appealed to men's sense of the fitness of things. Thus Apocalyptic, too, will serve us as a guide to the movements of thought. The personality of God, the claims of man's personality, the fundamental righteousness of the universe—the beliefs to which we have seen men moving with steady intensity, these are still the magnets which group the workings of man's mind.

The great problem was God. Apocalyptic was an attempt to get that problem cleared. The very fact that God cared enough for men to communicate to Enoch a sort of philosophy of history was evidence of God— of His existence, of the quality of His mind, of His providence. Tiresome as we, the pupils of Greece, find all, or nearly all, this literature—for the *Book of the Secrets of Enoch,* if it is Jewish at all,[14] must be excepted —it presupposes God as a thinking, planning, provident being; God "geometrises" again, as Plato said. The universe is not a rather meaningless cycle of cause and effect, wheeled into chaos and out of it by a force that is as nearly non-moral and non-intelligent as so great a power could be. God, not Necessity, is at the head of it, at the heart of it; and He is interested enough in His creatures—the sentient, thinking, suffering children of Israel—to explain to them through His saints and His chosen something of the mystery of a universe of tears and death.

One constant feature in Apocalyptic is its emphasis on history. Fanciful as the Apocalyptist may be—and wild exuberant fancy plays too large a part in his work—he is apt to base himself upon the recorded experience of man and of Israel. Using or seeming to use the future

14 It is said to be of Slavonic origin and mediæval in date.

tense he tells over and over again the story of the Jewish race,

immense
With witnessings of Providence.

Jewish writers, from the Chronicler downwards, had retold their national history, they had recast it, to bring out its moral value, and the Apocalyptists did it once more. God is justified in all the story which the reader identifies as behind him, and a presumption is created that, in the remainder of the story, to be unfolded in the future, God will again be justified. The troubles of Israel in the past were largely of his own making, the outcome of his unfaithfulness; but not always, for God had purposes of testing and discipline, a design to prove who are indeed His faithful and to develop them. Hence, and the deduction follows naturally in a tale of one texture and one tense, it may be taken that the troubles of the present, so faithfully foreseen thousands of years ago by the great antediluvian or the national hero or the great regenerator, have the same value; they are not accident nor evidence of the failure of God.

The Wisdom literature affords an interesting parallel here. *Proverbs, Job, Ecclesiastes, Ecclesiasticus,* show minds wrestling with the problem of individual suffering. There is the simple assertion that there is no problem; all is straightforward (Prov. xii. 21; xiii. 21); and there is as direct an assertion that there is no solution (Eccles.). Do the sinners' children suffer, and they righteous? (Eccles. xi. 28; Job v. 4; xxi. 19; xxvii. 14). Would that be just? It is the question of the prophets, who had to deal with the popular proverb of the parents eating sour grapes and the children's teeth set on edge (Jer. xxxi. 29; Ezek. xviii. 2). But is punishment disciplinary, if the sinner escape and the innocent children suffer? Another theory was that the wicked had his

punishment on the day of his death (Eccles. xi. 26)—
a desperate solution, without evidence or likelihood, and
affording loopholes, but a proof of the seriousness of
the interest in the question. The writer of *Job* takes
refuge in God, author of the world and of its beauty,
and implies, if not exactly a future life, yet an assurance
of something after death to verify the reality of religion.[15]

To all this discussion the Apocalyptists were heirs, and
they offered a series of new propositions, which are
rather difficult to fit into any system, and some of which
show ideas marked by an advance on anything in the
Old Testament. The Greek doctrine of the immortality
of the soul is adopted, and gradually it is discovered to
be the very crux and centre of the discussion. Clearness
was no ambition of the Apocalyptic school, but it is an
intellectual necessity which we have inherited from the
Greeks. So that, without going minutely into detail, or
considering various writers in particular, we may look
first at the work of the school on the future of Israel and
then at its thoughts upon the individual and his destiny.

First, as to the Nation. God, to be faithful, must
fulfil His promises to the chosen race. He had always
kept faith in the past; He had called His son from
Egypt, He had redeemed him from Babylon. Then it is
clear that the Lord will have mercy on Zion yet and will
restore the kingdom to Israel; David will perhaps return.[16] The triumph of the early Maccabaeans tended
to bring the kingdom well into sight, as a possibility in
the land of Palestine itself, but the character of later
Maccabaean rule relegated the kingdom to heaven, or to
some strange age and condition, and made it the future
work of another Anointed one, no Maccabaean, but a

15 See W. Fairweather, *Background of Gospels*, pp. 82, 90.
16 J. P. Peters, *Religion of the Hebrews*, p. 428.

greater altogether. Nearer or further away, a fluctuating hope, the dream is a register of the moods of Israel, a register too of progress in religious ideas. The Messiah's kingdom will be an earthly Paradise, to which the dead return with bodies given them to fit them for its mundane joys. But that again will not serve; it is spiritualised, and dead and living alike will receive spiritual bodies, whatever they are. Then the kingdom is transferred to heaven; quick and dead are to be absent from the body; but how are you to reconcile this with the other solutions?[17] David and the Messiah, the kingdom on earth, the kingdom in Heaven, resurrection, immortality —the ideas are disparate enough, and the Jewish ideas among them begin to be overborne by the Greek; and all are crossed with the problem of justice, the sin of the individual, his righteousness and the claims which it gives him on God; and perhaps after all the kingdom will not be a mere national affair, nor can be, but must be universal. Then is it a kingdom any more? or is the idea wanted? Will not immortality serve?

The Messiah, too, is a problem—David or not David, or not even Davidic? Some Apocalyptic writers have no place for him; the writers of the *Assumption of Moses,* of *Wisdom,* of *Fourth Maccabees, Fourth Esdras* and *Second Baruch* ignore him. The *Book of Jubilees* recognises him, but not as of primary import, while the *Similitudes of Enoch* give him high significance. The writer of these, whose work is incorporated in *Enoch* (chapters xxxvii.-lxxi.), and who lived perhaps between 94 and 64 B.C., gives us the high-water mark of Apocalyptic teaching on the Messiah. He is described as the Righteous One (xxxviii. 2; liii. 6); the Elect (xl. 5; xlv. 3, 4); and the Son of Man (lxii. 14)—all titles that reappear in the New Testament. He possesses Right-

17 J. H. Leckie, *World to Come,* p. 30.

eousness and it dwells with Him (xlvi. 3); he has seven-
fold gifts (xlix. 3; lxii. 2); Wisdom is in him (xlii.),
the Spirit of Him who gives knowledge (xlix. 3) and
the Spirit of power (xlix. 3). He is the revealer of all
things, He will recall to life the dead who are in Sheol
and hell (li. 1; lxi. 5); he will be Judge (lxix. 7; li. 2;
lv. 4; lxi. 8; lxii. 2, 3); he slays sinners and unrighteous
with the word of his mouth (lxii. 2).[18]

That the idea of the Messiah rooted itself in popular
imagination was in measure due to thinkers and writers
who conceived of the Messiah so nobly. That it did, is
evident from the Gospels and from the history of those
two unhappy centuries of relations with Rome which
end with Bar-Cochba (c. 117 A.D.). But it is conceivable
that, if Jesus had not adopted or accepted the title, and
given it a wholly new value derived from his own personality, the very idea might have perished. For, despite
the glowing language quoted from *Enoch,* it was hard
for thinkers to explain to themselves that a Messiah was
really needed for the tasks assigned to him by Apocalyptic writers and by popular enthusiasm. Certainly
political Messiahs were long since a conspicuous mistake,
disastrous to the nation and indeed a negation of its
true spiritual life. Even after the rescue of the idea by
Jesus, it was transformed by its fusion with the Greek
idea of the *Logos,* to which Philo had given a Jewish
tinge without obscuring its Greek origin and meaning;
and it is a question whether *Logos* or Messiah has been
the more fruitful name for Jesus of Nazareth. In any
case he only distantly resembled the popular conception
of the Messiah. Once again the Greek doctrine of Immortality cut across the national imagination. If all men
are immortal, if justice is in any case done to all men

18 See R. H. Charles (to whom I owe the collection of these references), *Book of Enoch,* Intr. p. cix.; and index, *s.v.* Messiah; and also his *Eschatology,* pp. 260-264.

in some world beyond, what place and function is there
for a Messiah? That Jesus found worth in the idea is
a hint to us, as it was to his followers, to re-think it;
but, as so often in his teaching, the borrowed idea receives so many new values, that it is hard to dissociate
it from them and to realise how much more was done
for it by the borrower than by the originators.

Immortality—that is the conception to which all these
national hopes and dreams, and visions of God, had to
be adjusted. It becomes the touchstone of men's ideas
of God. There is very little about it in the Old Testament; the nation, not the individual, was the main problem of those writers, though Jeremiah (as we have seen)
has grasped that the real crux is the individual. But the
idea gains ground, and we watch it make its way in
Jewish thought, adjusted as best may be to Jewish
views, but slowly transforming them. All Israelites are
to rise (1 Enoch li. 1 f.)—or rather the Just alone
(1 Enoch lxxxiii.-xc.; xii. *Testaments*)—or, better, all
mankind (4 Esdras, 2 Baruch). Then it is transcenden-
talised; the body and its resurrection recede in interest,
and the emphasis falls on the soul. It swings clear of
Messiahs and Messianic Kingdoms, yes, and of Jewish
nationality. Sheol is progressively moralised; Righteousness invades the grave and brings it also into order.
Reward and Punishment do not turn on race, just as
Right and Wrong are not local or racial but universal.
"If I make my bed in Sheol, behold, thou art there"
(Ps. cxxxix. 8).

Thus once more the Individual claims his own in religion; he must have Immortality for himself or for his
child, and the proper consequences of his acts, his life
and character. Righteousness has asserted itself against
nationalism; the new aeon will not be a mere reign of
Israel, it will be a triumph of God, and it will be shared

by every man and woman who has been loyal to God.
The writer of *Ecclesiastes* might sneer all this away, but
mankind was against him; and the harassing experience
of Israel reasserted and proved again the force of the
impulse that drives men to emphasise human individuality and Righteousness, and God the author and the
guarantee of both.

XV

THE VICTORY OF THE ORIENT

In a famous passage Milton pictures the delights of reading the philosophy of the ancients:—

> Or let my Lamp at midnight hour
> Be seen in some high lonely tower,
> Where I may oft out-watch the *Bear,*
> With thrice great *Hermes,* or unsphear
> The spirit of *Plato* to unfold
> What Worlds, or what vast Regions hold
> The immortal mind that hath forsook
> Her mansion in this fleshly nook:
> And of those Daemons that are found
> In fire, air, flood, or under ground,
> Whose power hath a true consent
> With Planet or with Element.

The linking of Plato with Hermes Trismegistus strikes the modern reader oddly, but for a long time after the Renaissance (as *The Faerie Queene* shows) Plato was read with the eyes of the Neo-Platonists; and our passage sums up a great deal of the thinking of the early centuries of our era. The immortality of the soul, daemons of air and underground, planets and elements, and their "consent" with human affairs, are features of religion, some of which seem to have little affinity either with Plato or with each other. Hermes Trismegistus, too, with people who preferred dogma and the dimness of fancy to clear thought, perhaps even outweighed Plato. Fancy, ritual, mysticism, unsound science, are triumphant for the time, and are united in a tremendous

331

campaign against truth and sense. The Victory of
the Orient over Western thinkers is the subject before us—a dismal chapter in the history of religious
thought.

Centuries of war in the Eastern Mediterranean worked
for what Otto Seeck has called the "extermination of
the best." The very factor which, it is said, has retarded
the development of the negro over millenniums, brought
about the degradation of the Greek and his neighbours.
Independent political thinking in a Greek city, any sense
of individual responsibility, ambition, capacity, marked
a man down. In war or civic tumult such a man was
liable to be cut off, and his influence and spirit were
lost, while the humdrum and the cautious survived. It
was a bad effect of Alexander's conquest of the world,
and of the great empires of his successors, that government and civil service usurped more and more of the
proper activities of mankind. Authority is very well in
its place, but it is never content with its place, and it
becomes as dangerous to human development as Anarchy.
"True Art's a Republic's," says Browning in a poem of
desperate rhymes. We have already seen how decline
overtakes Art, Thought, Poetry, everything that needs
independence of mind, as the successors of Alexander
and the Romans in turn tighten their grip on mankind.
The world went through a long period of imitation and
dictionary-making; collection of extracts and universal
histories compiled without criticism were favourite forms
of literature. In crafts and manufactures the same
holds. Slavery was more naked and undisguised there,
and it is noted that for centuries there was no improve-
ment in tools—a sure sign that progress generally will
be slight. Why should a slave improve his tools?
Slavery, in one form or another, *e.g.* the colonate and

serfdom, strengthened its hold on society.[1] Why should a man think, when thinking makes him suspect with the government, and when there is no Switzerland or Holland to which he can go? Constant pressure from above deadened the mind, and men slipped to lower levels of intelligence.

We have already seen how Sextus Empiricus compares the Greek painter, who in disgust threw his sponge at his picture, and by despair achieved what he could not by art, with the Sceptic, who, failing to find peace in thought, abandoned thought in disgust, and suddenly was surprised to find that he was at peace. That is not the mood of the early Sophists; there was a gaiety, a truculence of youth, about their procedure; their doubt took the form of challenge and emancipation. This later scepticism is sheer fatigue; but fatigue does not eliminate fear, and it is a fertile field for superstition. Fatigue invades every branch of thought in that Graeco-Roman world. The science of Eratosthenes ebbs away in the note-books of Seneca, Pliny and Plutarch; quotation and guess-work replace observation and thought. Authority triumphs in religion, because, like the throwing of the sponge, it seems to achieve what intellectual effort cannot. Meanwhile the steady resolve of the governments that men shall have no outlet for energy in this world perhaps contributed to turn their minds to another world —but minds tired and timid, no longer qualified nor wishful to handle evidence for what they dealt in, anxious for safety, and ready to find it in eclecticism, the subtlest form of scepticism.

The great characteristic feature of Oriental religion as it sweeps over the Roman Empire is, as we saw, its

1 Cf. W. E. Heitland, *Agricola*, p. 425, on the steps to serfdom; p. 436, "step by step they sink under the loss of effective freedom, though nominally free, bound down by economic and social forces; influences that operate with the slow certainty of fate until their triumph is finally registered by imperial law."

vagueness. The Greek had never had as close a knowledge of Egyptian, Persian or Phrygian religion as he
supposed; still less the Roman. "When the eclectic
Plutarch," says Cumont,[2] "speaks of the character of
the Egyptian gods, he finds it agrees surprisingly with
his own philosophy"; and we may interpose that Plutarch's philosophy was a pious impressionism, as little
thought out as it was emotional and respectable; and
Iamblichus found the same freedom. "The hazy ideas
of the Oriental priests enabled every one to see in them
the phantoms he was pursuing," is Cumont's summary.
"The individual imagination was given ample scope, and
the dilettantic men of letters rejoiced in moulding those
malleable doctrines at will. . . . The gods were everything and nothing; they got lost in a *sfumato*." Fog is
religion's vital breath in this period. Modern Hinduism,
in very much the same mood of fear and reaction, ex-
hibits at once the advantages and disadvantages of a
religion, which is anything you like to make it except
monotheism, or even monotheism in a sense that makes
it meaningless, while it is never anything that you can
either grasp or criticise. Whatever feature strikes the
Western observer as objectionable or of doubtful value,
is sure *not* to be Hinduism; even caste, you will be told,
is not Hinduism; what actually *is* Hinduism, you are
less likely to learn, unless it is virtue and spiritual sensitiveness beyond European standards. Oriental religion,
as Greek and Roman knew it, was just as odd and
heterogeneous and indefinite.

The mind of the Graeco-Roman world in general had
reached a stage in which it was unequal to the task of
really examining an idea. The unexamined life, if we
may pervert the phrase of Socrates, was the only one
liveable for a real human being; in this age the Socratic

2 Cumont, *Oriental Religions*, pp. 87, 88.

passion for definition and for exact ideas was lost. Men re-acted to suggestion and to sentiment, now to this, now to that; coherent thinking was beyond them. Even Stoicism, in spite of its central principles, had, as we saw, its unexamined elements, doctrines insufficiently explored and too loosely related to the facts of Nature. The intellectual effort (such as it was) of Scepticism was beyond most men; and, except when disguised in bodily and social comfort, Scepticism would seem never to have appealed to women. Fear overcame what power of thought was left, and fear ruled once more in religion.

No doubt, qualifications have to be made in all this; every universal statement is liable to need them. But as one surveys the literature of the Roman World, when once Cicero and Virgil are gone, one cannot help noticing how very second-rate the best of it is, Greek, Jewish, and Latin; and the literature of an age is apt to reflect pretty accurately its thinking power. Tacitus,[3] perhaps the most powerful mind among them, balances the opinions of the ancients and their modern disciples as to whether fate or chance rules all mortal things; and, without de- ciding that point, he concludes by observing that the mass of mankind cannot get rid of the idea that "there is a lot in Astrology," but that astrological forecasts mis- carry through the ignorance or trickery of those who make them. Pausanias, about A.D. 180, travelled over Greece, and was initiated here and there where oppor- tunity offered; he was frankly a believer in the religion of the day and as frankly third-rate. Lucian's *Lover of Lies* is a witty parody of what educated people could talk and believe in the way of marvels. It reminds one of to-day, though with a suggestion of extravagance in invention; but as one reads in the literature of that period, it grows clear that the parodist is a good deal

3 *Annals*, vi. 22.

closer to what he is mocking than one supposed, that it
is far from being mere travesty.   Celsus, in his *True
Word,* written against the Christians in A.D. 178, assumes
the reality of the theophanies and miracles of the pagan
shrines.   Aristides believes in the healings of Asclepios
at Epidaurus as surely as the most ignorant French
peasant believes in those of Lourdes, and with as little
idea of the real explanation of them.

Stoic teaching of the *sympathy* of Nature, of the cor-
respondences between everything in the world and everything else, gave a philosophic basis to the belief in what
we must call Magic.   Even to this day certain types of
mind cannot distinguish between proof that a thing may
happen and proof that it has happened, and as little between evidence that something has happened and evidence
that the explanation tendered for it has any relation to
the matter under discussion.   To assimilate more or less
the idea of chemical action being possible between all or
most elements in Nature, is enough to warrant some
people in concluding that all thought and all religion are
chemical products.   The ancients had more excuse.
Their terminology betrayed them.   *Pneuma* meant per
haps "breath" or "wind" to start with; it came to mean
"spirit" in something approaching our sense of the
word; and in speaking of Delphi Plutarch uses it much
in the sense of the modern "gas," but he does not realise
that "spirit" and "gas" really mean two distinct things.
It is easy for him to believe that the "gas" coming (or
supposed to come) from the crack in the ground at
Delphi affects the "spirit" of the priestess or *is* the
prophetic "spirit" in which she speaks, or in less modern
phrase, is the "spirit" that enters into her and speaks
through her lips.[4]   The poem entitled *Lithica* teaches
that, with the proper stone in hand and the proper

4 Plutarch, *de defectu oraculorum,* 432 D-435 A; 437 C.

prayer-formula, a man may influence or control the god whose affinity is with that stone or who is amenable to that formula.[5] Perhaps; but it was never demonstrated that the god or any other god really was attached to that stone, gem or other, or that the belief that it was "in sympathy" with him (in "true consent," to use Milton's words), was anything more than the very loosest assumption.   Still, for the quick thinkers, given *sympathy*, there was the system of gem and formula justified, access to gods established, and even control of gods assured— "proved," as loose-thinking moderns of the same type say—"by Science."

But, even apart from philosophic or scientific theory, the religious ideas of the period rested on experience, though the evidence of experience was handled as loosely as this doctrine of sympathy.   Mysticisim is, as Dean Inge has reminded us, one of the most carelessly used of words, more indefinite even than Socialism.   So-called mystical experiences may be induced in a number of ways, notably by hunger and by certain drugs; and when they have such origins, it is hard to believe that they can really contribute to a man's religious knowledge. When instead of hunger we say "fasting," and when the man is one with religious interests or preconceptions, a different problem occurs.   It seems likely that no one sees, feels or hears anything in the mystical state which he had not already laid up in conscious or sub-conscious memory; but it is commonly said that what comes in the mystical state comes with a new emphasis, a new value and meaning.   I incline to think that new emphasis is more near the truth than new meaning; and I believe that some part of the new attention given to the idea

5 Cf. *Lithica* (Eugen Abel), 226-7; and 330-3 (the magnet bends the gods). On this book, see W. Von Christ's *Gesch. Gr. Lit.* (5th ed.), vol. ii. p. 376; he says it is a poetic rendering of a prose book of the second century A.D., attributed to Damigeron the magician, a work which a mediæval bishop eventually got into Latin verse and which in that form had a wide influence.

so emphasised is due to the strangeness of the phe-
nomenon and to the theory that it is of directly divine
origin—divine in a way that respiration and digestion
are not so reckoned. A man once told me how in a
trance a certain text was given to his father, "which he
had never heard before." It is notorious that memory
does not advertise all her methods, and that words are
frequently found to have been stored of which no notice
was taken at the time; but the two men had only one
theory—the text came by special divine communication.

From our records of religious experience in the period
of Graeco-Roman culture with which we are dealing, it
is plain that much attention was given to phenomena of
this kind, and that, as in the case just mentioned, there
was only one explanation available. Men believed the
evidence of their senses; they had seen, they had heard,
and there was an end of it. And behind their experience
stood that of others, and a theory that fully explained
everything. Then, by a swift deduction, all was true
that the Oriental priests taught of religion. Science in
the form of Astrology, Philosophy and Experience all
combined to rivet the chain of superstition.

Certain common features are to be found in these cults
of the East. We know little of any ways in which they
recruited or trained their priests. Our records, which
are generally satirical, suggest very great looseness of
organisation in some of the religions. But the priest is
a constant factor, an inevitable adjunct of worship, a
celebrant in a daily ritual, an interpreter and a mediator
between gods and men. The sacrament is his business,
and without sacrament and priest there could be no communion with heaven. The mystical trance was prepared
for systematically. Even if it came of itself, it was the
business of the priest to lead the worshipper from stage
to stage. The classical document on this is the last book

of Apuleius' *Golden Ass.* Apuleius describes one stage after another, all associated with deep emotion, some blest with actual vision of the gods in person, and all more or less expensive. Abstinence from food and other things for the purpose of immediate religious action, penances for specific acts, and asceticism on a larger scale, went together.[6] A feeling, still not uncommon, that the body and its concerns are on a lower plane than the soul and its preoccupations, was reinforced by a theory, more general and of high antiquity and authority, that matter was inferior every way to spirit, a negation, somehow, in the long run, of God. This theory the philosophers accepted; and a conception of holiness arose which made it largely an external and negative thing.

The power of these Oriental religions and of the beliefs they carried with them may be recognised by their effect in two distinct regions. The Roman government, as we have seen, was at first far from friendly to the cults that brought their exotic appeal to bear so strongly on Roman men and Romen women. From time to time the cults were driven out of Rome, but they returned, and "in proportion as Caesarism became more and more transformed into absolute monarchy, it tended more and more to lean for support on the Oriental clergy."[7] This movement reached its height under the dynasty that succeeded the son of Marcus Aurelius—a curious illustration of time's revenges. How far the Christian Church stood from the ideas of the Oriental cults is written in every page of the Gospels; and as one learns more of what the cults taught, and of the ideas and preconceptions on which they worked, and which became more and more the background of religious thinking in the Graeco-Roman world, the bright independence of Jesus

6 Juvenal, vi. 522 f.
7 Cumont, *Astrology and Religion*, p. 96.

of Nazareth grows in significance. Even Ignatius can
write to the Ephesians: "What ye do even after the
flesh, is spiritual; for ye do all in Jesus Christ." [8]   Yet
Ignatius has a rather magical view of the sacraments,
for he writes, in the same letter, of the Ephesians
"breaking one bread, which is the medicine of immortality and the antidote that we should not die but live
for ever in Jesus Christ." [9]

The common background of all religious thinking outside Judaism was made by the mystery religions. Their
conceptions gave men what they would have called in
our speech their "natural" ways of thought; but the
word "natural" is one of those epithets which, the
logicians say, beg questions. The Christian vocabulary
shows many parallels with the language of the mysteries,
or, more strictly, many terms occur in both, and these
terms of great significance. The Christian and the
adherent of the mysteries may describe central points of
their religions in the same language; but this does not
imply that they meant the same things, or that they
started from the same premises or looked to the same
goal. The same term may be used, but it is the mark
of a beginner to suppose that words can have the same
value when used by genius and by common people.
Spiritual insight differs; and however alike the language
of two thinkers may be, it is the measure of their
spiritual insight that gives meaning to their words. Wit,
for example, is in ordinary life an idea that divides
people; fortunately we have not all the same conception
of it. In religion the great terms habitually divide men
who think deeply about them.

But that the language of these mystery religions found
its way into the Christian Church—and very often the

8 Ignatius, *Eph.*, 8, 2.
9 Ignatius, *Eph.*, 20.

ideas behind the language came with it—as the practice of them imposed itself on the state, is for our purpose very significant. The early Christian owed a great debt to Plato and to the Stoics, which again and again he was glad and proud to acknowledge, though at times he explained it by a previous indebtedness of Greek philosophy to Moses; Plato was "Moses talking Attic." [10] His relations with the mystery cults were different; they were of the devil, and any parallels that could be drawn between them and Christianity were, as Justin and Tertullian said,[11] due to the devil's having stolen the ideas of God, and of course depraved them, as the devil naturally would. But the explanation is interesting in another way; it seems to imply that, behind the parallel of usage and borrowed speech, there lies for those who care to look a more real parallel in religious consciousness. The heathen in these borrowed and debased forms is seeking to meet the same needs that the Christian feels and meets in a nobler way. He is asking for a personal god, who shall be susceptible of relations with men, for the recognition of all that is implied in human nature and for immortality.

The whole story of heresy in the Christian Church, in the early church, is of struggles to adjust the new impulse from Palestine with the religious inheritance of the Orient generally, modified by the influence of Greek philosophy. In one heresy philosophy plays a larger part, in another Oriental cult. This ferment of ideas is characteristic of the Roman Empire. With all the weakness and indolence of thought which we have noted—perhaps in some degree the very consciousness of weakness was part-cause—men were seeking ultimate truth in the pooling of ideas. The barbarians, in that phrase of

10 Clem. Alex., *Strom.*, i. 150, 4, quotes this.
11 See p. 110.

Celsus which I have quoted so often in these pages, discovered the dogmata somehow, and the Greek tried to
give them, or to educe from them, that intellectual coherence whieh should make their value plain, to relate
them to "all time and all existence." For six centuries,
for two before and four after the Christian era, we may
say that this was the chief task which thinkers had
before them. It was handled in many ways.

Plutarch for instance—Sir J. P. Mahaffy held there
was "no more signal instance of this stagnation than the
sayings and counsels of Plutarch on politics and religion" and art.[12]   Then Plutarch is a representative
man. He shows how common minds were occupied with
this business of reconciliation. A patriotic Greek could
have no doubts about the wisdom of his people—
Epicurus excepted and Herodotus. Greek philosophy
was a mine of truth, and if one looked at its teachings
in a certain way they were not really so inconsistent
with Oriental religion. Or perhaps it was that by some
unconscious selective instinct he chose in Oriental religion what, by virtue of its inherent vagueness and his
own gift of confusion, he could suppose to harmonise
with Plato. How little it did harmonise with Plato is
seen in his treatment of obscene myth and statue. "Myth
is a rainbow to the sun of truth," he said;[13] and if the
image of Osiris seemed obscene, triply obscene, it was
an allegory in the round, a symbol of the divine origin
of all existence. There is nothing that Plutarch cannot
talk himself into believing to be right—though, to be
fair, he stopped at human sacrifice and some obscene
rituals which he attributed to evil daemons. For the
rest, allegory did wonders. But, said Plato long before,
we are not at liberty to tell lies about God, whether they

12 *Silver Age of Greece*, p. 371.
13 Plutarch, *Isis and Osiris*, 20, 358 F.

are allegories or whether they are not allegories;[14] and
the study of Plutarch and his contemporaries[15] confirms
one in the conviction that Plato's instinct in this was
sound.   Plutarch did not mean Truth, his aim was
apology; he was afraid.   His father, as he tells us, deprecated inquiry of a certain sort; it unsettled faith, it weakened or destroyed the very foundation of all religion;
and Plutarch's whole attitude to life is the same, though
less explicit.   The religious usages of his day ministered
to his peace of soul; the "dear Apollo" was the friend
of man; the religion of Isis and Osiris was not inconsistent with the dignity of Greek thought.   He too is a
witness to the demand of the human soul for three of
the things in religion which we have traced so far; but
the other, the life-nerve of all, he does not recognise so
clearly, the demand for Truth, the insistence on fundamental Righteousness.   His religion satifies every desire
of the human heart except that; and on that failure it
was ultimately wrecked, and mankind ceased at last to
take any interest in it whatever.

A figure of more interest with scholars to-day than
Plutarch is the earlier scholar Posidonius.[16]   It is partly
that his works are lost in the Greek and that he offers
accordingly a richer field for conjecture—*omne ignotum
pro magnifico;* partly that he led the way for that reconciliation of religion and philosophy which pervades the
ancient world in the period under our review; partly that
he appears to have been a philosopher, and not a blunder-
ing, if amiable, moralist.   It is ungrateful to speak so of
Plutarch, who had obviously claims to survive which
Posidonius had not.   Posidonius was born at Apamea
on the Orontes about 135 B.C., but it is not known

---

14 Plato, *Rep.,* ii. 378 D; cf. p. 186.
15 Plutarch's dates are (rather roughly) A.D. 50-120.
16 Cf. E. Bevan, *Stoics and Sceptics,* 85 ff.; Cumont, *Astrology and Religion,*
pp. 56, 69, 84 f., 93, 101; J. B. Mayor's Cicero, *de N.D.,* ii., Intro., pp. xvi-
xxii; Dreyer, *Planetary Systems,* p. 176.

whether he was of Syrian or of Greek extraction. He
served as ambassador from Rhodes to Rome in 86 B.C.,
and Cicero attended his lectures in Rhodes in 78 B.C.   It
is held that large parts of Cicero's philosophical works,
e.g. his criticism of Epicureanism and his account of
divination, are translated from his teacher, or at least
closely modelled on him.   He was primarily a Stoic, but
he discarded the rigidity of the school and modified its
doctrines to meet the teaching of Plato and Aristotle.
He was the first thinker to establish the true theory of
tides [17]—a matter that earlier Stoics would have considered trifling.   The same intellectual energy, with perhaps
some inherited interest, turned him to Asiatic astrology [18]
with less fortunate results, to daemonology, too.   The
influence of Posidonius is felt in the *Astronomica* of
Manilius, a work which reveals a mind of rare purity
and signal in its detachment from superstition.   But the
system of the world conceived by Posidonius was dis-
figured with a credulity about forecasts derived from the
stars which we have learnt—as Augustine [19] had to learn
—to call childish.   His style, which Strabo rather un-
kindly calls "his congenial rhetoric, his enthusiasm in
hyperbole," [20] appealed to his day, and so did the great
range of his outlook.

    [17] Strabo, iii. 3, c. 229.   Cf. Rice Holmes, *Ancient Britain*, p. 219, n. 4.
Mr. Rice Holmes (p. 499) says peremptorily that "there is absolutely no evidence that he ever crossed the Channel" in spite of an allusion to British tin
trade (Diodorus, v. 38, 5) attributed to him." Mr. H. F. Tozer in his attractive book, *History of Ancient Geography*, p. 191, is as definite that Posidonius
did visit the interior of Britain and study tribe life.   But this belongs perhaps
more to the history of Britain than of Religion, though the discussion may
help us to realise the man.
    [18] Augustine, *de Civitate Dei*, v. 2, Posidonius vel quilibet fatalium siderum
assertor; v. 5, Posidonius magnus astrologus idemque philosophus (cf. Warde
Fowler, *Roman Ideas of Deity*, p. 142, "the philosophical wizard of Posidonius"); a discussion of astrology as it bears on the careers of twins.   See
Garrod, Manilius, *Astron.*, bk. ii., pp. lxv. f., for a discussion of astrology at
Rome; and p. xcix, "Thinking men in Rome necessarily, in the period in
which Manilius lived, breathed an atmosphere of Posidonius, very much as
thinking men to-day may be said to breathe an atmosphere of Darwin."
Manilius did not exactly write with a copy of Posidonius open before him.
    [19] Augustine, *Confessions*, vii. 6, 8.
    [20] Strabo, iii. c. 147.

Here, then, was a teacher of genius who really did "survey all time and all existence," tides and stars, Plato, Zeno, and the learning of the East, and he wove all into one fabric in a reasonable or at least presentable way, and pronounced that man's task was not only to survey but to interpret—οὐ μόνον θεατὴν ἀλλὰ καὶ ἐξηγητήν.[21] He recognised a greater power in the passions than orthodox Stoicism allowed; there is an irrational element in man's nature—the source of evil which is not an external thing. He gave a place to mysticism in religion, which stricter Stoics denied.[22] He is thought to have believed in the spiritual aid of daemons and to have given a great stimulus to Sun-worship at Rome.[23] His aim, in Mr. Edwyn Bevan's happy phrase, was "to make men at home in the Universe";[24] and if, as is supposed, Cicero's splendid and stimulating *Dream of Scipio* is inspired by his teacher,[25] it is easy to understand the appeal of Posidonius. Here the world's best Astronomy is related to the strong sterling instinct of the Roman to serve the state and to the belief in the immortality of the soul. Nor was the idea that souls that do well ascend to the stars, confined to books; Cumont appeals to an "unlimited choice of examples" of it among inscriptions. "The venture is a glorious one," as Plato says in the *Phaedo;* Cicero's picture stimulates and stirs; but the subtler needs and aspirations of the soul are not there. With Cicero these would be lacking where he deals with religion; and we only know Posidonius through his pupils. They were many and their influence was widespread; but the world let Posidonius go at last. It is suggested by Mr. Warde Fowler that he was not really

21 Cumont, *Astrology and Religion*, p. 101.
22 Wendland, *hell.-röm. Kultur*, p. 134.
23 Warde Fowler, *Roman Ideas of Deity*, p. 58.
24 Bevan, *Sceptics and Stoics*, pp. 112, 98.
25 Cumont, *Astrology and Religion*, p. 178; Warde Fowler, *Religious Experience of the Roman People*, p. 383.

in touch with the utmost reality of what he spoke about; and Mr. Bevan's judgment coincides.[26]

Great reconcilers are rarely the world's real leaders; they sum up the past, and however much they may be hailed at the time, however necessary their work may be, it is temporary, both work and fame. Even rhetoric does not save them. For us it is of import to remark that Posidonius owed his influence to his acknowledgment of those instincts in religion which the stricter Stoics ignored. So far he was right and contributed; but in spite of his brilliant discovery about the tides, his science was defective, and he rested too much on tradition. His scheme was perhaps too facile; and it lacked the power that would carry it past the breakdown of the traditions it embodied. As we have agreed already, it is the factor that makes the future that is significant. The religion of Posidonius re-made the present—a long present it was; but it lacked the life that a competitive religion was soon to show, and the power that goes with life of outgrowing and discarding error.

The Stoic, as we saw, taught the individuality of man, but urged that it was a temporary and fugitive thing, which at death broke up into the various elements. Posidonius recognised personality as something of more moment; and he, or those whom he influenced, leant to the view that divine or half-divine beings come in touch with human personality, and that it survives death. Once again we note the discovery of the reality of the human soul by the philosophers. The religious had held to it all along, but on grounds that remained suspect. But now philosophy is driven into accepting the belief; only, as we have seen, it accepted it insufficiently rationalised, and with too much of the hastily drawn consequences of the religious of the time. The central thing

26 Bevan, *Sceptics and Stoics*, p. 94.

is of moment, and everything in religion depends upon it. Ancient religion gave way because that central truth was not disentangled from the temporary, the trivial and the false. When challenged, it had only authority to plead and that false reverence (not yet extinct) which pretends the "holy" to be exempt from examination. "When religion," said Kant, "seeks to shelter itself behind its sanctity, it justly awakens suspicion against itself, and loses its claim to the sincere respect which reason yields only to that which has been able to bear the test of its free and open scrutiny." But reason, as we have seen, had in those days grown very nervous.

So far we have traced the progress of religion from the days of Homer or before. We have seen how man's experience reacted again and again on his judgment of the universe, on his religion; how he came to ask more of the universe for himself and his own; how he insisted upon God too being personal and on righteousness as the base of all relations between man and man, between man and God, the foundation of all existence. This way and that opinion swayed, as men laid stress on one or another phase of the problem of God and the soul. Overemphasis on sheer reason to the neglect of emotion provoked reaction against philosophy. Men and women felt that, in spite of childless theorists, there was something real in their feelings for one another and for their children, that there was in fact nothing else at all so real, that love was not a fugitive and irrational sentiment linking for the time two aggregations of senseless atoms, but the necessary and reasonable expression of personality. The philosophers had discounted what mattered most, and the priests emphasised it. World-weariness, failure of nerve, decline of the race—call it what one may, religion and thought were not working together. If the Stoic preached the righteousness of the universe, as he did fervently, it was a righteousness that ignored personality in God and still more in man. But religion, as we find it in that Graeco-Roman world, is also astray. It has recognised personality indeed, based itself upon its recognition, even pandered to it, and missed the other things.

The reconciliation of religion and philosophy would not do, for neither was building on really thought-out principles. The philosophy was doctrinaire, the religion traditional—both were in the hands of pupils who did not understand their masters. The philosophers belonged to schools, except where they escaped into the false freedom of Eclecticism; "all eclectics," said Novalis, "are sceptics; the more eclectic, the more sceptical." The religious were, not quite unconsciously, following guides of lower powers than their own, savage ancestors and Oriental charlatans, much as men turn to the mediæval to-day—happy in an atmosphere that was fatal to mind, to independence, at last to manhood. None of them were fundamentally concerned with truth as an organising vital principle; they pieced it together as a puzzle at best. Their data were doubtful, and they had lost the instinct for examination. A structure, however ingenious, however cleverly wrought of old and new, modern fancy blended with archaeology, can never be very secure when the foundation is unsound; and here it was unsound.

There was no finality about this Graeco-Roman synthesis of creed and cult and dogma, because truth and ethics were made of less account than emotion and sensation. The religion was beneath the best men; moral sense revolted at much of its teaching and practice, and men tried to deceive themselves with words, as Plutarch did, into thinking they had a right to accept what they knew to be unclean and untrue. Secure of the help of their gods—gods borrowed from the peoples of lower culture and of retarded growth—gods conspicuously obsolete for men taught by Plato to think deeply of right and wrong—they might live on the lower level, if they had by sacrament and ritual made things right with their gods. Asceticism and libertinism went together.[27] They were sure of personal immortality and of all they wanted for themselves, and there was not the perpetual challenge of a clear view of progressive righteousness. They were carried away by an excessive individualism, developed by natural reaction under a government that discouraged individuality, action, and any broad or deep concern for the good of mankind.

The religion was doomed to fail, because it reverted to a conception of God that was not the highest. The motives for this reversion were mean ones—a sure sign that the thought would be wrong somewhere. The gods were personal, it is true, in a certain sense, but they were not righteous; every tradition cried aloud of outgrown morality; the worshippers were above their gods in development; but, choosing the lower, they declined to it. Above all, with all their juggles about deity, they had in practice refused the Monotheism which philosophy had begun to conceive and now in reality abandoned. That Monotheism had been itself defective in the personal, so that even in its abandonment there is a hint of right instinct.

It is a picture of a world astray. All the right instincts are there, but they are scattered and working against one another. Those who believed in divine personality gave up divine righteousness; those who believed in right and in the unity of God, undervalued personality in God and man. Neither way could there be progress. That could only begin again when the scattered elements were re-united, and what belonged together came together

<hr>

27 Wendland, *hell.-röm. Kultur*, p. 168.

again. The future was for a religion that should set the highest value on personality in God and in man and make righteousness, ever more deeply conceived of and understood, supreme. Meanwhile, the world was in a pitiful welter of half-truths—manifestly wrong at every turn; and yet, as Robert Burns says,

> And yet the light that led astray
> Was light from heaven.

www.ingramcontent.com/pod-product-compliance
Lightning Source LLC
Chambersburg PA
CBHW021215090426
42740CB00006B/233